ARTEMUS WARD

BOOKS BY DON C. SEITZ

ARTEMUS WARD
WHISTLER STORIES
THE BUCCANEERS
FARM VOICES
DISCOVERIES IN
  EVERYDAY EUROPE
ELBA AND ELSEWHERE
IN PRAISE OF WAR

HARPER & BROTHERS *Publishers*
ESTABLISHED 1817

Artemus Ward

(CHARLES FARRAR BROWNE)

A Biography and Bibliography

BY

DON C. SEITZ

AUTHOR OF
"WHISTLER STORIES" "FARM VOICES"
"THE BUCCANEERS" ETC.

*With Illustrations
and Facsimiles*

HARPER & BROTHERS PUBLISHERS
NEW YORK AND LONDON

TO

FRANK I. COBB

CONTENTS

ILLUSTRATIONS

FOREWORD

WRITING of Artemus Ward, in *Scribner's Monthly Magazine* for November, 1880, E. S. Nadal, the essayist, expressed the wish that some one would visit the humorist's birthplace at Waterford, Maine, and look into his beginnings, to account for him by a study of the surroundings and his ancestry. I was a boy in the printing-office at Norway, a town adjoining Waterford, and caught the idea. In company with my father, Rev. J. A. Seitz, I drove through a tremendous snow-storm to Waterford, ten miles away, and rediscovered the Browns, to wit: Caroline E. Farrar Brown, his mother; Thaddeus Brown, his uncle; Waldo T. and Daniel Brown, cousins, sons of Thaddeus. Between us, my father and I prepared an article, he doing most of the work, but appending my name to the result, and sent it to *Scribner's*. Two rival writers had also grasped the suggestion—C. A. Stephens, a friend and neighbor in Norway, long distinguished as an author of cheerful juvenilia, and another, whose name escapes me. Dr. J. G. Holland, then editor of *Scribner's* (this was before it became *The Century*) bought these items and forwarded them as "material" to incorporate with our gleanings. We went at it again and the paper appeared as "Artemus Ward: His Home and Family" in *Scribner's* for May, 1881.

Our printing-office was the lineal descendant of that *Norway Advertiser* shop in which Charles F. Browne had worked under his brother Cyrus, thirty years

before. Traditions still lingered. Cyrus enjoyed the
neighborhood reputation of being the "smarter" of the
two. There were local memories of strange pranks
played by intemperate printers in the grave little town,
when stirred by the robust influence of New England
rum. Plenty of people were around who recalled the
tallow-haired, sallow-cheeked boy, and his reckless
elder brother.

This distant relationship had its effect in continuing
my interest in A. W., which was further enhanced by
the knowledge that when he drifted west from Boston,
as a wandering printer, Artemus had sojourned for a
time in Tiffin, Ohio. Tiffin was the city of my dreams,
being the seat of Seneca County, Ohio, of which my
great-grandfather, John Seitz, was a pioneer and one of
the organizers. I used to visit it with my father when
a very little boy in the late 'sixties. He was pastor
of the Universalist Church at Attica, one of the Seneca
County towns, and had been born in Melmore, another. The first printing-office I ever smelled was that
of the Tiffin *Tribune*, owned by Locke & Brother.
They were brothers of David Ross Locke, "Petroleum
V. Nasby," of humorous fame, and had also been
neighbors of my father in his youth, when the senior
Locke owned a farm near that tilled by his own people.
The print-shop into which Artemus had fallen was that
of the Seneca *Advertiser*, still existing. Furthermore,
the Cleveland *Plain Dealer*, in whose office the wanderer first found fame, was a household word in our
part of Ohio. It seems strange that 'way down in
Maine it should have been my fortune to bring together
these incidental contacts.

FOREWORD

The plan of writing a life of the genial showman had long been in mind. The delay in getting it under way was due to the hope of securing several hundred letters, written to Charles A. Shaw, of Boston, who told me they contained much that was funnier than anything ever printed from the pen of A. W. He said he had given them to Mrs. Shaw, who cherished the idea of making a book out of the material, and he would have to await her pleasure. He died in 1908. Mrs. Shaw survived until 1916, but after her death, though most diligently sought, no trace of the letters could be found.

I write, therefore, belatedly and to a new generation, more for the purpose of adding to the annals of American literature than of reaching a wide circle, and of giving to present-day readers some record of the life and personality of the gentle jester at whose outpourings their fathers and grandfathers laughed so uproariously.

Grateful acknowledgment is made for valuable assistance to Charles H. Taylor, Jr., of the Boston *Globe;* E. H. Baker and Miss Georgia L. Andrews, of the Cleveland *Plain Dealer;* Viscount Northcliffe, of the London *Times;* Dr. John W. Cummin, of Boston, Massachusetts; R. B. Wall, of New London, Connecticut; Mrs. Florence Brown Rounds, of Waterford, Maine, and Miss Alice Flynn, my painstaking secretary.

D. C. S.

Cos Cob, *June 2, 1919.*

ARTEMUS WARD

I

CHARLES FARRAR BROWNE, better known to
the world as "Artemus Ward," was born in
Waterford, Oxford County, Maine, April 26, 1834.
His father, Levi Brown, was the son of a settler,
Thaddeus Brown, who came to the town from Har-
vard, Massachusetts, in 1786, and Mary Pollard, his
wife. Levi Brown married Caroline Eliza Farrar,
daughter of Calvin Farrar and Bathsheba Bates. The
Farrars migrated to Waterford from Guildhall, Ver-
mont. Both Levi Brown and his wife were natives of
Waterford, and their lineage was of the clearest New
England line. Levi Brown was born October 10, 1796;
Caroline Eliza Farrar, October 3, 1806. He died in
Waterford, December 23, 1847. She survived until
July 12, 1884.

The families of the Waterford pioneers were all
large, but the crop was not repeated in the later genera-
tions. Levi Brown had eight brothers and sisters—
Daniel, Malbory, Jabez, Susan, Thaddeus, Mary,
Mercy, and Sarah. There were six Farrars, besides
Caroline, all younger—Nancy, Maria, Luther, Calvin,
Mercy, and David. Many collateral Browns and
Farrars are living, but the two sons of Levi, Cyrus W.,

2   [1]

born March 6, 1827, and Charles F., never married. Two other children, both daughters, Maria A. and Ellen F., died young, the first named on February 24, 1833, aged four years and four months; the last, March 4, 1833, aged one year and seven months. The Farrars were persons of distinction in the town and state. Luther and the younger Calvin, were both colonels of militia, and the latter established a water-cure in Waterford that thrived long after his day under the guidance of an eminent physician, Dr. William P. Shattuck. Levi Brown's brother, Malbory, was a captain of militia, and Levi himself became a lieutenant and major in the state service, during the thirties, when the "training days" called every able-bodied citizen to the colors. Waterford teemed with memories of war. Levi's grandfather, Jabez Brown, had been a lieutenant in the French and Indian war and an adjutant in the Revolution, in which his father, Thaddeus Brown, also served, as had most of the other pioneers. A Waterford company formed part of the garrison at Portland in the second clash with Great Britain. Caleb Strong, the Governor of Massachusetts, of which Maine was then a part, would not permit the militia to serve outside its borders, so there was small chance for fame. The company received the rather doubtful commendation from the commanding officer at Portland, where it was stationed, that its members "stole less" than any of the others!

Levi Brown appears to have been a trusted citizen of the town. He was, in his younger days, town constable, when it befell him to arrest some members of a newly formed Universalist church, who refused to pay a state tax in support of Congregationalism. He escorted them to the jail at Paris Hill, the shire town of the county, where, on the advice of counsel, they settled, but later sued the selectmen and enforced a return of the money. This separation of Church and state occurred in 1822. The minister whom these village Hampdens refused to aid was the Rev. John A. Douglas, who had the distinguished record of holding his single pastorate in Waterford from 1821 to 1878. The salary to which they declined to contribute was $400 per year! Further than this, Mr. Brown served as town clerk, selectman, and as a member of the state legislature. By profession he was a civil engineer, and, besides surveying, "kept store" and "farmed."

It would be interesting to compile a gazeteer of the great and so note the amazing contributions of eminence made by obscure hamlets, far off the trail on which life runs rapidly. Waterford gave freely. Hannibal Hamlin, Vice-President with Lincoln, missed it as a birthplace, but was named after his Waterford uncle, high sheriff of the county, father of Dr. Cyrus Hamlin, the founder of Roberts College, in Constantinople, who was born in the town; so was Elbridge Gerry, Congressman and eminent attorney of Portland. The Warrens sent out some able sons, as did the Waterford Hales, Cilleys, Athertons, Chaplins, Houghtons, Coolidges, Davenports, and Haskins. The latter were kinsfolk of Ralph Waldo Emerson, who often visited their seat at Elm Vale Farm, in South Waterford, across the way from the cemetery of that name where Artemus Ward lies buried.

[3]

ARTEMUS WARD

But of all the fine company, the subject of this memoir reached farthest into fame. The house known as Artemus Ward's home still stands in Waterford, facing the village green, of which he wrote so lovingly in after years, the property of Mrs. Louis J. Higginson, of Boston, who inherited it from her mother, Mrs. C. J. F. Eastman. Mrs. Eastman was Mercy Farrar, the last survivor of Mrs. Brown's family. She was born in 1816, ten years later than Mrs. Brown, and lived until 1896. Artemus was not born here, but on a farm at the edge of the village, owned by his father. This, however, was disposed of soon after his birth and the family removed to the Farrar mansion, built by Calvin Farrar in 1805, where Mrs. Brown was born. The original Brown homestead was burned in 1870.

The Farrar mansion is an excellent example of early nineteenth-century New England architecture, beautifully situated on the main street. Before it the steep cliff of Mt. Tir'em rises abruptly, and behind spread the shining waters of Tom Pond, named for Thomas Chamberlain, the Leather-stocking of the east, who killed Chief Paugus in Lovewell's famous fight. The road by which it lies was once the Scoggin or Pequawket trail, over which the red warriors made their way between the Saco intervales and the St. Lawrence, avoiding the shorter route through Crawford's Notch, to the westward, for fear of demons lodged in its rocky walls. The mountain gained its name from the grunting Sokokis. "Tir'em Injun" was the phrase that stuck to it and became its geographical designation.

The town is bountifully watered by many ponds and streams. The Waterford Kezars at the base of the

[4]

THE ARTEMUS WARD HOMESTEAD, WATERFORD, MAINE

BEGINNINGS

Bear Mountain range link up with Long Lake at Harrison, which affords a water route to Sebago through the sinuous Songo, and in the thirties and forties—and, indeed, until the building of the Portland & Ogdensburg Railroad in 1870—connected by canal from Sebago to the sea.

Stages on the route *via* Albany, Bethel, and Gorham between Portland, Quebec, and Montreal rattled daily through the single street, loaded with travelers. It was a pleasant place for a lad, even though not more than two hundred people lived in or near it. Waterford included about fifty square miles of territory, mainly lake and hill, with here and there fertile slopes on which good crops were grown. Timber was the chief asset and numbers of sawmills were in constant operation, cutting up the primeval growths. There were four centers of life in its limits, North, South, East Waterford, and the "Flat," as Waterford proper is known. The "town house" was and remains at the Flat. There were other neighborhoods, like Sodom, over on the Crooked River, inhabited by poor whites, where respectable folks did not go, and McWain Hill, looking across the lakes, where a grim old pioneer, David McWain, had swung the first ax in 1775. He had an eight-hundred-acre Colonist allotment, bought for forty dollars, and lived a bachelor's life in baronial style for fifty years. The Indians were his friends in the early days, but stole his loose change; not needing money, he bored a hole in a tree trunk and plugged some fifty dollars in silver into the orifice. Nearly half a century later a woodman felled the tree and the saw at Pride's Mill struck the hoard. McWain was sent for and sat a long time jingling the coins in his hands until his memory reached back to the incident and the establishment of this strange bank. He raised fine cattle and disliked women and neighbors. The sight of the smoke from a settler's cabin in Paris, twelve miles away, drew from him a cross remark about getting crowded.

So purely New England was the community that it bred plentiful whimsies, many of which cropped out in the writings of the humorist, and to a degree account for him. Old inhabitants recall small escapades, such as can be told about mischievous boys in most country villages, for example:

Cyrus, his elder brother, was an orator of no small ability and frequently participated in political meetings, taking the Democratic side in the discussions of the day. Returning from a meeting one night, he locked his brother, who had been on a lark to South Waterford, out of the house. It was bitter cold. A rattle of pebbles on the window, accompanied by calls of, "Ho, Cy!" brought his shivering figure into the open. His brother below dazed him with this cheerful query: "Say, Cy, do you think it is right to keep slaves?"

He led in getting up shows after the traveling circus had passed and spoke pieces in the red school-house, outdoing the sniffling, bashful lads of his class. The red school-house was not a popular place with the boys, least of all with the small Charley. Wanting a day off, with the help of his fellows he collected all the hens in the village on a Sunday night and locked them in the building. It took two days to restore cleanliness— two days of respite and delight for the scamps.

BEGINNINGS

It would but dull the chronicle to relate much of the idle memories of his early days, of which there are a considerable store, although his life in the town was very brief. When but thirteen years old his father's death made a change in the family fortunes. There was little left but the homestead, and it became necessary for the boy to make a start out into the world where his brother Cyrus had already gone. They began young then. Cyrus had taken up the printers' art and Charles's ambitions led in the same direction.

The stage-line passing his mother's door ran to Lancaster, in Coos County, New Hampshire, and the lad, with a reputation for prankishness already well established, was shipped by coach to that town, where he engaged with John M. Rix, publisher of the *Weekly Democrat*, to learn the trade. Stephen J. Seavey, driver of the stage, was a bit of a joker himself and, knowing the boy well, prepared him for his reception in Lancaster by advising that Mr. Rix was very pious and that his best passport to success lay in knowing his catechism. Unhappily, this phase of his education had been neglected. His father was a liberal-minded Congregationalist; his mother much of a free-thinker. He reached Lancaster late at night and found the journeyman and two apprentices, Edward Cross and a brother, at the office, primed for his examination in religious ethics. He was made to read a chapter out of the Bible, then severely examined in catechism, at which he lamentably failed, and given lugubriously to understand that his chances on earth as well as in heaven were poor. He went to work in the morning with much misgiving. At noon the performance

[7]

was repeated, and the rest of the day seemed saturated with gloom. Coming to the office the next morning fully resolved to run away at the end of the week, he found his pious fellow-workers sleeping the sleep of the inebriated under the back stairs. It appears that the printing-office was located over a store-room filled with barrels of rum, stacked to the ceiling. Some time before, the force had drilled through the floor into one of the barrels with an auger and induced the local tinsmith, Perry Pollard, who shared the spoil, to make a long, thin tube through which the rum could be elevated by suction to the lips of the partaker. This was the source of their intoxication. Disillusioned, the boy wrote a letter to the stage-driver, threatening dire vengeance, which was never carried out. He lived with Mr. Rix, and the family influence was of some value in keeping him level. His gawky appearance made him rather unwelcome at the home; his thinness suggested an insatiable appetite. Margaret Moylan, the cook, remarked, "I guess we've got a queer kind of critter this time, but I bet he can eat." She had seen numerous 'prentices come and go and was skeptical of all of the breed. Eliza Rix, the fifteen-year-old daughter of the house, asked Margaret how she intended feeding the new arrival. "We'll fill him up with green apples," was the tart response.

The boy was sent about the country in a yellow two-wheeled chaise to collect dues from the farmers, taking cash and produce, as came handy. Eliza often went along to see that he showed diligence, a quality always lacking in his make-up. "He would rather talk to the people and tell stories," she said in after-years, "than

[8]

ask them for money." The two Cross brothers were pretty wild and the tube into the rum-barrel bred a deal of mischief. In time the escapades of the boys became too much for the patience of Mr. Rix. They grew so unruly that a cleaning out had to take place, preceded by a last day of disorder, in which forms were "pied" and the shop made useless for a week. Charles had been in Lancaster nearly a year when the break-up occurred. He went home under a cloud, to the dismay of his mother. She wrote an anxious letter to Mr. Rix, inquiring into the moral status of her son, who had returned with a tale that he needed more education to succeed as a printer and wanted to go to school. Mr. Rix, though provoked with the boy, bade him a kindly farewell, gave him a dollar to speed him on his way, and shielded him from the just parental wrath.

Yet the ne'er-do-wells did not turn out so badly, after all. Edward Cross became a very gallant colonel of the First New Hampshire Regiment in the Civil War, and poor Perry Pollard, the tinsmith, gave up his life at Gettysburg.

It chanced that an opportunity for more schooling with work at the trade was ready at hand. Norway, the next town to the east from Waterford, rejoiced in the possession of a neat little six-column, four-page newspaper, the *Norway Advertiser*, which had been founded in 1844 by Ira Berry and Francis Blake, Jr., names long and well known in Maine. After a year the partners disposed of the sheet to Albert B. Plummer, who in turn sold it to Thomas Witt. He made it pay, but late in 1849 transferred the property to Francis H. Whitman, a native of Norway and a cousin

[9]

of the Browns, who had a lively fancy and much enterprise. He acted for Cyrus W. Brown and Albert
Bradley Davis, who made a place for the lad.

Norway was a vigorous village when this change
occurred. The new Atlantic & St. Lawrence Railroad,
now the Grand Trunk, built to connect Portland and
Montreal, reached South Paris, a mile away, January
1, 1850, and put Norway in touch with the world.
The town was the metropolis for the back districts of
Waterford, Albany, and Stoneham, and numbers of
industries flourished, including a paper-mill. There
was a good school, the Norway Liberal Institute, quite
worthy of its somewhat ponderous name, at which
Charles planned to extend his scanty education under
easier working conditions than were possible at Lancaster. He lodged in a shabby room back of the
printing-office, where a rickety bedstead, with a torn
straw mattress, a table, and a three-legged cook-stove
with a brick in place of the missing fourth, were the
chief furnishings. There was another room inhabited
by the stray printers who drifted in one by one to
take a turn as journeyman in the shop and whose
worldly experience went far to sophisticate the boy.
He does not seem to have worked much in the classes,
but took active part in school affairs, including the
lyceum debates, a great source of delight at the institute,
contributed to the manuscript paper read at the
meetings, somewhat loftily named the "Carpathian
Rill," and played amateur drama as a member of the
Thespian Society. He usually occupied one of the
three splint-bottom chairs on the platform reserved
for the president of the lyceum, the principal, or im-

portant visitors, and was the only non-grown-up to enjoy this high estate, probably because of his journalistic connections. He would tilt the chair back against the wall, cross his legs, with his boots much in evidence, and loll in this attitude until his turn came in the discussion, when he easily took the lead in skill and wit as a debater. The drawl that gave charm to his speech was already there, and his cleverness drew large audiences to the school hall, the town always turning out when it knew that "Charley" was to talk.

He was abnormally tall for his age and mature in mind, though weak in body, as the result of too rapid growth, which made him languid. Time went pleasantly with him in the office. He set type, loafed a good deal, wrote items, and led the general mixed life of the devil in a country printery.

The paper had a nominal circulation of one thousand, but Brown and Davis were not good managers and both were unduly convivial, with the result that by the summer of 1850 the paper was on its last legs. The firm dissolved and left the property and its liabilities to Mr. Whitman. Brown had something of a career, editing the New Bedford *Standard* from 1850 to 1856, and later the Fall River *News*. Davis wandered South and, reversing his name, as Davis Bradley, became a theatrical manager of note in New Orleans.

The principal of the Liberal Institute, Mark H. Dunnell, had political ambitions. He had been a Whig candidate for the legislature, opposed by the Democratic *Advertiser*, wherein the future humorist had burlesqued his first speech given at Denison Hall. To him Mr. Whitman turned as a likely salvor for the derelict. In after-years Mr. Dunnell confessed that he could never fully understand how he had been beguiled into taking it over. But take it he did, and with it the idle apprentice. A dress of type, the first folly of all new editors, was procured and the name of the paper changed to the *Pine State News*. A very ornate head-line proclaimed this title, and the new dress made a handsome paper. But the shift in its political color was too great, coming on top of previous troubles, to permit success. Mr. Whitman, who in time became my own guide, philosopher, and friend, once said that people lacking reverence in their compositions called it the "Pitch-Knot." Mr. Dunnell's own account of its coming into and departure from this life, written for the Norway *Advertiser* of fifty years after, follows:

"It was not long before I discovered that it took some money to run a newspaper. That had hardly occurred to me before the purchase. The paper, the ink, and the help had to be paid for each week. It was but a very short time before I discovered that I had an elephant on my hands, and a very costly elephant. . . . In November I brought my young wife to town; we went to housekeeping and in a few days took our first boarder in the person of Charles F. Browne, who became the famous Artemus Ward. He was the younger brother of the late editor, Cyrus Brown. Charles was the encumbrance of the office when bought. He had to be retained. He was what your editors call the devil. Matters still grew worse. In December we took into our home a Mr. and Mrs. Elias Thomas, of Portland, as type-setters. They proved in the end, and very soon, the straw that broke the camel's back,

THE VILLAGE GREEN, WATERFORD, MAINE

for one night—late at night—Thomas was brought home very drunk. I have always thought that young Browne managed for the outcome. He was in high glee when the end came."

The next morning, "in supreme disgust and most unseemly rage," Mr. Dunnell drove the employees out of the office, locked the doors, and turned the keys over to his creditors. His venture had lasted seventeen lively weeks. Mr. Whitman said the verdict was, "Died drunk."

Mr. Dunnell continued to figure in Maine affairs and at the outbreak of the war became colonel of the Fifth Maine Regiment. Military command was not to his taste. After an exciting experience at Bull Run he resigned and, removing to Minnesota, became a member of Congress, representing the First District from 1871 to 1883. After some years of retirement he re-entered politics and served in the Fifty-first Congress from 1889 to 1891. He flashed into fame briefly during the excitement of the "back-pay" grab in Congress by telegraphing his foreman to resume hauling sand for the construction of a residence which had been suspended, pending the success of the bill. President Grant vetoed the measure and there was much laughing at the Congressman both in Minnesota and among the ribald Norwegians in Maine. He died at Owatonna, Minnesota, August 9, 1904.

The end of the *Pine State News* led to the seeking of other employment by the "devil." He went first to Augusta, then, as now, a printing-center, and thence on to Skowhegan, where he found work in the office of the *Skowhegan Clarion*, published by Moses Littlefield.

This place soon proved little to his liking. After a brief bondage he escaped with the help of a bed-cord from the upper window of his lodging and made for home, down the Kennebec to Gardiner, where he raised change enough to reach Waterford and astonish his mother by turning up unannounced.

Skowhegan always lived ironically in his mind. Dr. E. P. Hingston, in his *Reminiscences of the Genial Showman*, recalls his asking an acquaintance if he was familiar with American newspapers. He replied that he was. Artemus wistfully asked if the *Skowhegan Clarion* was among the number. On getting a negative answer he upspake, pityingly: "I am sorry for you if you do not read the *Skowhegan Clarion*. It is your duty to read it. There is no paper like it in the States—nor anywhere else."

The *Clarion* was founded in 1841, and existed as such until April 10, 1868, when its name was changed to the *Somerset Reporter*, now the Skowhegan *Independent Reporter*, which likes to remember that A. W. worked in the shop of its parent. He slapped Skowhegan often, once amusingly in a skit, giving the dialogue of a group of well-dressed men around an Oregon bar, in a state of strong drink, boasting of the states of their nativity:

"I," said one, "was born in Mississippi, where the sun ever shines and the magnolias bloom all the happy year round."

"And I," said another, "was born in Kentucky—Kentucky, the home of impassioned oratory; the home of Clay; the state of splendid women, of gallant men!"

"And I," said another, "was born in Virginia, the

home of Washington; the birthplace of statesmen; the state of chivalrous deeds and noble hospitality."

"And I," said a yellow-haired and sallow-faced man, who was not of the party at all, and who had been quietly smoking a short black pipe by the fire during their magnificent conversation—"and I was born in the garden spot of America."

"Where is that?" they said.

"Skowhegan, Maine," he replied. "Kin I sell you a razor-strop!"

He was now man-size, seventeen, and a citizen of the world, who could not afford to remain idle. Re-employment was sought on the *Democrat* at Lancaster. There was no vacancy, but Mr. Rix gave him a letter to Messrs. George H. Snow and Samuel W. Wilder in Boston, publishers of the *Pathfinder*, who maintained a large printing-establishment, issuing for one item the *Carpet Bag*, a medium through which Benjamin Penhallow Shillaber conveyed "Mrs. Partington's" sayings to the public. It happened opportunely that his uncle, Calvin Farrar, desiring to publish a booklet advertising his water-cure at Waterford, accompanied the boy to Boston, and took his copy and his nephew to the printing-office. The job procured one for "Charley," as he became known in the shop, and here he remained three years, setting rhymes written by John Godfrey Saxe, Charles Graham Halpine, and other wits of the day. Their copy stirred him. He then wrote his first real contribution to a publication of standing, an account of a Fourth-of-July celebration at Waterford long before, which survived in village tradition. This he slipped anonymously into Shillaber's mail. It was printed. He celebrated its publication by going to the theater on the evening of the day it appeared. "Had a good time of it," he said afterward, "and thought I was the greatest man in Boston." The contribution appears in *His Book* as "The Surrender of Cornwallis."

John Townsend Trowbridge, once a member of the *Carpet Bag* staff, in *My Own Story* recalls him as "a sandy-haired, thin-featured youth, with a long nose and pale complexion," and dates his appearance in the office as in 1851, when he had passed his seventeenth birthday, and, according to Trowbridge, "before he was much older began to write mildly funny things for the paper over the signature 'Lieutenant Chubb.' He probably chose the pseudonym 'Chubb' for the reason that he himself was lank. . . . His serious countenance veiled a spirit of original and audacious waggery; and he was even then known to be capable of the same conscientious painstaking in the accomplishment of a solemn act of drollery as when, a few years after, while on a lecturing tour in midwinter, occupying with a friend a room of arctic temperature, he got out of bed in the middle of the night to hang before a windshaken sash a 'skeleton' hoopskirt he had found in a closet, remarking, shiveringly, 'It will keep out the c-o-oarsest of the c-o-old'!"

Mr. Trowbridge thought the *Skowhegan Clarion* was a jesting creation of the young printer's, and asserts incorrectly that he followed his trade in the office of a paper "less grotesquely named."

The printer became friendly with Shillaber, and when the latter, after the death of the *Carpet Bag*, edited the old Boston *Saturday Evening Gazette*, Artemus sent him from Cleveland one of his choicest bits of writing, "Affairs Round the Village Green." It is to be found in *His Travels*. He had no copy and visited the office of the *Gazette* in 1865 for the purpose of getting a transcript. Charles Barron, the actor, kept him company when the call was made. He was offered the loan of the file, but replied, "Nay, nay, Pauline—too much work," and engaged an office-boy to do the copying, remarking, when the job was done, that it was not copperplate, but, like Mercutio's wound, 'twould serve.

3

II

THE printers of the middle 'fifties were an adventurous race, with a contempt for employment and employers that was almost magnificent. This led to the easy throwing-up of "sits" and much wandering. The West was calling loudly and, after his three years with Snow & Wilder, the youngster, then a full-fledged "jour.," yielded to the wanderlust and headed from Boston for the Ohio country. He started blithely on his journey into the wider world, with such belongings as an old-fashioned carpet-bag would hold and a composing-stick, confident that the latter would always enable him to satisfy his slender wants—which it did. He had no special point of landing in view. "I didn't know," he said afterward, "but what I might get as far as China and set up a newspaper one day in the tea-chest tongue."

He reached Cincinnati by a zigzag route across the Middle States, tramping much of the way from town to town, after the manner of his kind. Here he "subbed" a few days in the newspaper-offices, then, led by an advertisement of "School-teacher Wanted" in a Kentucky village, applied for the position and got it. Frail in physique, he soon perceived that he was no match for the big boys who always tested out the pedagogue's muscle; he concluded at the end of the week that teaching was not his forte and, without

ARTEMUS WARD AT TWENTY

waiting for his pay, shouldered his carpet-bag and returned on Saturday to Cincinnati and his trade. He next worked along the Cincinnati, Hamilton & Dayton line, pausing briefly at Dayton and Springfield, finally bringing up in Sandusky. Here he learned that a man was needed in Tiffin, the county-seat of Seneca County, on the Sandusky River, thirty-four miles up-stream. He tramped the distance, arrayed in a linen duster and a chip hat, toting the carpet-bag, and secured the place, that of a sick man, in the office of the Seneca *Advertiser*. It was Democratic in politics, owned and published by W. W. Armstrong, a youth of twenty-three, who found the new-comer, then but twenty, an agreeable addition to his force. "I think," said Mr. Armstrong, to whom the adventurer presented himself, dusty, shabby, and forlorn, seeking the much-needed job, "he was the gawkiest, greenest-looking young fellow I ever set eyes on." He was tall, awkward of build, and loose-jointed in his walk. His clothes did not fit, and his tallow-colored hair, pallid features, and big nose certainly combined to make his personality unprepossessing. However, he soon became a well-known and popular personage in the community, welcoming the stranger and the showmen when they strayed in, and writing pleasant paragraphs about the home folks. The *Advertiser* is credited with paying him four dollars per week, but this was probably in addition to board and lodging. These usually were provided by the rural print-shops, the hotel bill being paid in job-work and advertising. Board and lodging were then worth about four dollars a week more.

Tiffin was the center of a prosperous farming region,

with mills and good stores, rather better built than most Ohio towns of that day or this. It still stands as an exceptional municipality. It had its local limitations, and the printer's longing to progress asserted itself after something less than a pleasant year had passed. He found employment as a compositor on the Toledo *Commercial*, and soon took the complete plunge from "case" to "copy" by going on the staff as local editor. Here his talent at once began to blossom in lively paragraphs and brisk encounters with the rival sheet. Journalism was then very largely a personal affair and editors spent much time and wasted a deal of space in their controversies with one another, news taking a back seat most of the time. His skill in persiflage soon spread his fame through the sanctums of northern Ohio, so that in the fall of 1857, when the city editor of the *Plain Dealer*, in Cleveland, James D. Cleveland, resigned to take the place of assistant clerk in the United States District Court, to subsequently become a judge, Joseph W. Gray, a former New Hampshire school-teacher, turned lawyer, founder and publisher of the paper, offered him the place at a salary of ten dollars per week. He accepted and began his new employment on October 29, 1857. He had successfully passed the easy stage from printer to journalist. The Cleveland *Herald* of October 30th noted his arrival with this paragraph:

"Mr. Brown, formerly 'local' of the Toledo *Commercial*, has taken that position on the *P. D.*"

His intimate friend, James F. Ryder, long a famous photographer in Cleveland, thus described his appearance in the office:

"On going into the *Plain Dealer* editorial-rooms one morning I saw a new man and was introduced to him by head bookkeeper Charles E. Wilson as Mr. Browne. He was young, cheerful in manner, tall and slender, not quite up to date in style of dress, yet by no means shabby. His hair was flaxen and very straight; his nose, the prominent feature of his face, was Roman-esque—quite violently so, with a leaning to the left. His eyes were blue-gray, with a twinkle in them; his mouth seemed so given to a merry laugh, so much in motion, that it was difficult to describe, so we let it pass. It seemed as though bubbling in him was a lot of happiness which he made no effort to conceal or hold back. When we were introduced he was sitting at his table writing; he gave his leg a smart slap, arose and shook hands with me, and said he was glad to meet me. I believed him, for he looked glad all the time. You couldn't look at him but that he would laugh. He laughed as he sat at his table writing, and when he had written a thing which pleased him he would slap his leg and laugh. I noticed that George Hoyt and James Brokenshire, who were sitting at their tables, were pleased with his merriment, and were in-dulging in broad smiles. As I bade him, with the others, 'good morning,' he said, 'Come again, me liege.' I thanked him, said I would, and went my way thinking what a funny fellow he was."

The Cleveland of 1857 was just beginning to feel itself grow. In 1850 the census gave it 17,034 souls. By 1860 the total had reached 43,638. Iron had al-ready become a potentate. Mark Hanna was a hustling youngster about town, and John D. Rockefeller was soon to climb up on a stool in a down-street warehouse to keep a set of books, with oil undreamed of as a base for the greatest fortune in the world. The pollution of the beautiful Cuyahoga, now perfected, had been well begun. The *Plain Dealer* office was in an unkempt and unwholesome building at the corner of Vineyard and Superior streets, dingy, dirty, and uncomfortable. The editorial-room was a shabby loft, furnished with rickety pine tables and half-dismembered chairs. In short, it was a "hole" such as the old-style printing-office was wont to be. The new man worked with the crowd at a table in the corner that joggled as he wrote, amid the scratchings of other pens and the constant howls for "copy" from the composing-room aloft. "Here is where they called me a fool" (for thinking he could lecture successfully), he said to Hingston, his manager, in exhibiting the old shop on their return from the West.

There was plenty of newspaper life in the city when the new Local arrived. The *Plain Dealer*, then an afternoon publication, was Democratic in policy, but supported Stephen A. Douglas. The friends of James Buchanan's administration had recently established the *National Democrat* to defend the President. The *Democrat* had a Local also, who was a humorist, in a way, A. Minor Griswold, who gained much repute as "The Fat Contributor" and lived to edit *Texas Siftings*, thirty years after. The *Press* and *Plain Dealer* alone are now alive. The *Leader*, recently deceased (1917), had been founded in 1848 to uphold the new-fangled doctrines that finally became Republican, by Joseph Medill, Edwin and Eugene Cowles, the first two of whom had departed in 1855 to make the mighty *Chicago Tribune*. The Cowles control of the *Leader*, however, lasted for half a century, as a great Republican force in Ohio. The *Herald*, also Republican, was owned by A. W. Fairbanks, with J. H. A. Bone as the Local. It survived into the 'nineties, a fief of Mark Hanna's, at last being absorbed by the *Leader*. The *Leader's* Local kept clear of the scrapping in which the others indulged freely, with honors usually on the side of the *Plain Dealer* genius, who was a Democrat, while the *Plain Dealer* had a pro-slavery tone, echoed rather loudly in its local columns. The boys were on good terms with one another and the show of ill-feeling was confined to print.

The pages of the *Plain Dealer* soon began to reflect the appearance of the new-comer. It had been a very staid publication, full of the hot politics of the period, and printing little that could be called news. Indeed, Cleveland in that day did not furnish much of the elusive commodity. Its columns twinkled with quips and quirks. The lively junior professional men of the town fell in love with the Local and he was soon the center of an interesting circle. Their goings-on furnished much material for "copy" in the *Plain Dealer*. The paper perked up perceptibly under his frolicsome hand. Then, on January 30, 1858, three months after his arrival, the solemn sheet was placed permanently on the journalistic map of the world by printing the first communication from the hand of "Artemus Ward," which appeared in the following form:

ARTEMUS WARD

"LETTER FROM A SIDE-SHOWMAN

"Mr. Artemus Ward, proprietor of the well-known side-show, writes us from Pittsburg as follows:

"'Pitsburg, Jan. 27, 18&58.
"'The Plane Deeler:
"'Sir:

"'i write to no how about the show bisnes in Cleeve-land i have a show consisting in part of a Calforny Bare two snakes tame foxies &c also wax works my wax works is hard to beat, all say they is life and nateral curiosities among my wax works is Our Saveyer Gen taylor and Docktor Webster in the ackt of killing Parkman. now mr. Editor scratch off few lines and tel me how is the show bisnes in your good city i shal have hanbils printed at your offis you scratch my back and i will scratch your back, also git up a grate blow in the paper about my show don't forgit the wax works.

"'yours truly,
ARTEMUS WARD
Pitsburg Penny

"'p S   pitsburg is a 1 horse town.   A. W.'

"We believe Mr. W. would do well with his show here, and advise him to come along immediately."

The nom de plume, though variously accounted for, in one instance as the misspelling of the cognomen of the Revolutionary general, Artemas Ward, was really a

[24]

ARTEMUS WARD'S "PLAIN DEALER" CHAIR AND TABLE

home product. Waterford, his native town, was a land-grant given to pay claims rising out of Sir William Phipps's expedition against the French of Canada in 1690. The Province of Massachusetts Bay, having failed to collect enough from the spoil of the Acadians to pay the bills, gave away much land. Some of this lay in New Hampshire and the grants were disallowed by that colony in 1739. Maine, being then part of the Bay State, was drawn upon to make good in 1774 to the heirs of past creditors, and Waterford was a slice given to Seth Rice, Stephen Maynard, and John Gardner, "and Artemus Ward is joined" reads the record. Jabez Brown, Artemus Ward's great-grand-father, surveyed the tract in 1783. His grandfather was agent for the Massachusetts owners of the un-settled lands. His father, a surveyor, had much to do with them, so of course their names were familiar to the family. It is easy to conclude, therefore, that in picking a pen-name the young Yankee, chuckling at his shaky work-table in the *Plain Dealer* office, by idle chance was moved to select that of the ancient Boston proprietor.

The whimsy caught popular fancy at once. Further news from the showman was eagerly awaited. It came on February 8th, under a Wheeling date, with another appeal to the editor on behalf of the waxworks, pre-sented in this fashion:

"ANOTHER LETTER FROM ARTEMUS WARD. — Artemus Ward, proprietor of the well-known side-show, writes us again. He writes us this time from Wheeling.

" 'Wheeling, va feby the 3 18 & 58.

"'Gents—ime movin sloly down your way i want
you should git up a tremendus excitement in the
columz of your valerble paper about my show. it nox
the socks off from all other shows in the u. s. my
wax works is the delight of all. the papers sets my
wax works up steep. i want the editers to cum to my
show Free as the flours of may, but i Dont want them
to ride a Free hos to deth. the Editers in pittsburg
air the sneakinest cusses i ever see. they Come to the
Show in krowds and then ask me ten Sents a line for
pufs. they said if i made a Row or Disturbence abowt
it they would all jine in an giv my wax works perfeck
Hel. the editer of the journal said he would Tip
over my apel cart in duble quick time, if i Blowed
round him about hi prises. i put up to ther Extorshuns
long Enough & left in Dizgust. now which papers is
the most respectful in your city. i shal get my hanbils
printed at your offis—i want you to understan that,
but i must keep the other papers in good umer. now
mr. Ed tel me franckly without no disception for disception off all kinds i do dispise. Also git up a excitement in the Plane Deeler sinse i last wrote you
ive Added a Cangeroo two my collecksion of Living
Wild Beasts. it would make you larf to see the little
cuss jump and squeal. if you say anything abowt my
show pleas state my snakes is under perfeck subjecshun.

"'yours truly,
A. WARD.

"'p. S.—my wax works is hard to beet.'"

CLEVELAND

Some of the points in this note, combined with its predecessors, were later put together and appear as "one of Mr. Ward's Business Letters," the first item in *His Book*, in this form:

"Sir—I'm movin along—slowly along—down tords your place. I want you should rite me a letter, sayin how is the show bizniss in your place. My show at present consists of three moral Bares, a Kangaroo (a amoozin little Raskal—t'would make you larf yerself to deth to see the little cuss jump up and squeal) wax figgers of G. Washington Gen. Tayler John Bunyan Capt. Kidd and Dr. Webster in the act of killin Dr. Parkman, besides several miscellanyus moral wax statoots of celebrated piruts & murderers, &c. ekalled by few & exceld by none. Now Mr. Editor, scratch orf a few lines saying how is the show bizniss down to your place. I shall hav my hanbills dun at your offiss. Depend upon it. I want you should git my hanbills up in flamin stile. Also git up a tremenjus excitement in yr. paper 'bowt my onparaleld Show. We must fetch the public sumhow. We must wurk on their feelins. Cum the moral on 'em strong. If it's a temperance community tell 'em I sined the pledge fifteen minits arter Ise born, but on the contery ef your peple take their tods, say Mister Ward is as Jenial a feller as we ever met, full of conwiviality, & the life an sole of the Soshul Bored. Take, don't you? If you say anythin abowt my show say my snaiks is as harmliss as the new born Babe. What a interestin study it is to see a zewological animil like a snaik under perfeck subjecshun! My kangaroo is the most larfable little cuss I ever saw. All for 15 cents. I am anxyus to skewer your infloounce. I repeet in regard to them hanbills that I shall git 'em struck orf up to your printin office. My perlitercal sentiments agree with yourn exackly. I know they do, becawz I never saw a man whoos didn't.

"Respectively yures,
A. WARD.

"'P. S.— You scratch my back & Ile scratch your back."

The showman was next heard from at Columbus, the letter appearing on the 15th, thus:

"LETTER FROM ARTEMUS WARD.—The proprietor of the well-known Side-Show writes us again:

"'KOLUMBUS ohio Febey the 16 18&58

"'Gents—here i am in the kapertal Sity of Ohio. ime gradualy gitting down yr way. as the Poit says, ime on the Winding way mr. Editer. i gut shaimfully uzed up to whealin by a nusepaper. i calls no names but theres a editer in whealin whose meaner than biled vittles. he cums to my show every Night and sets it up Steap in his nusepaper an calls me the erbane an Inderfatergerble Ward, but when i stops gittin my Hanbils struck off up to his offis the pussylanermus cuss changis his toon an abuses me worse nor a injun. he blowed up my wax works and called me a horery heded itinerunt vagerbone. but let it pas. ive bun in the Show Bisness now goin on 22 years an my hed is

[28]

frostid ore with white an ive lernt that peple aint all ainjils in this wurld. their must Be sum black sheap in the flock mr. Editer. But i say an say it Boldly that no man upon God All mitys foot stule can rise an git up an say to my fase that Artemus Ward ever injered no man or woman. my new cangeroo knox the socks off from all Beasts i ever seen. its amuzin to see the little Raskal holler and kick up his legs. heze a Gay one i swear to you. my wax works is the astonishment of the Elittee. yr kolumbus Correspondant had 3 tickets to my Show charged to your offis, he said youd make it rite when i gut my hanbils struck off down to your offis. Several members of the legislater try to cum a Gouge gaim on me and kraul in to my show without Payin, but they aint Smart enough for Artemus Ward. his excellentsee guvner Chase wanted to see my Show gratooitusly, but sez i guvner all must Pay both of hi and low degre. Sez he worthy man i see the forse of yr obserwation and heres ten Sents. the grate man side as he saw my cangaroo. Sez he that chaned Beast remines me of the 3 milyuns an a Harf of our unfortyunate cullered brethren which air clankin their chanes down in the Slaive Ollergarchy. i make it a pint to agre with everybody which cums to my show, so i sez certinly, no dowt abowt it at all— same things ockurred to me numerusly &C. &C. at that he shook me kordyully by the hand an sez he i wish youse wun of my constituunts. you air a hily intellijunt man. i shal go to tiffin from here. i want you to distinkly understan i shall git my hanbils dun at yr offis, but you must git up a tremendus excitement in yr Paper. you scratch my Back an ile scratch yr Back. my Snakes is as harmlis as the new born Babe.

> "'yrs. truly,   A. WARD,

> "'p.S.—Is Haul rent hi in cleveland? Rite by next male to tiffin. A. W.'"

This communication was not used in *His Book*, but the last sentence survives in the Business Letter. Agreeable to promise, the showman was heard from in Tiffin. The letter was local in tone, and included a savage reference to William H. Gibson, an eminent attorney of the town and a leader in the newly organized Republican party, a relative of whom had mismanaged some Ohio state funds in his care, to which the showman made rough allusion. The partisanship of the *Plain Dealer* explains the "shot." Gibson lived to become colonel of the Forty-ninth Ohio Infantry, which distinguished itself at Shiloh and Stone's River, a brigadier-general, and an orator of great distinction. His bones were "berried in Old Seneky," as the letter says he desired, and he stands in bronze beside the Seneca County court-house, within the walls of which he so often sounded oratorical appeals of the highest order. The letter contains the "Judas Iscarrot" story that finally became "A High-handed Outrage at Utica," and is given herewith, less the unkind Gibson reference:

"LETTER FROM ARTEMUS WARD.—Here is another letter from Artemus Ward, proprietor of the well-known side-show:

CLEVELAND

"'Tiffin, Febey the 23th, 18&58.

"'Gentz—I take my Pen in hand to inform yu in regard to my kareer. Ime now in the grate Sity of tiffin. Yu better beleve the peple of tiffin staired sum when i posted my big yeller hanbills up in their town. No sho has bin here for goin on leven (11) years. Frequiently the peple side for amuzement but not a amuzement would cum. The sity is so all fired Big that shows stan no chanse. The hotels is all fust-class and their bills air hyer nor showmen can ford to pay. Howsever Artemus Ward noze no such wurd as fale an i deturmined to storm the Mallerkarf. if i do say it myself imes bold as a eagle. the peple air delited with my show. my wax works is the prase of all. among my wax works is the Lords last supper. the characters bein as large as life. A feller from the east part of Seneky County cum to my show and thot my Judus Iscarrot was alive. Sez he to me, yu jus take that sneakin cuss out this haul er ile smash his hed in. Sez i yung man that air is a wax work. Sez he wax work be darned, thats old Judus Iscarrot and if heze a man he will step out here and fite me. i kan stan a good deel but i gut all fired mad, and sez i yu ornary cuss keep away from my wax works or ile fall on ye. At that he made a lunge cross the table and seised Judus by the neck an dragged him out inter the middel of the haul and kommensed a poundin him. Sez he Judus Iscarrot cant show hisself with impunerty in tiffin by a Dam site. I finerly convinsed the pesky fool that it was a wax work. He larfed and said he would stan the old rye for he and me. Tiffin is a grate sity. It is thickly settled round the meetin-house.

its princerpal institushuns air the meetin-house, hay-scales and William H. Gibson. mr. Gibson is on the legul tide. He tole me his bones wood be berried in Old Seneky. . . . There was a grate competishun atween the Advertiser and tribune to see which should strike off my hanbils. Armstrong has got a kut of a horse with a man holdin onto him as he said he was the only printer in town which could do picktorial bills, so i gut my hanbills struck off up to his offis. i shall be in Cleveland in a few weeks. i want yu should go to the gentlemunly lanlords of the American, Wed-dell, Anjier, and Johnson tavurns and git their proper-sishuns for keepin me. my kompany consists of my-self two boys a forrun Italyun who plays the hand orging, 1 cangeroo, 6 snakes, calerforny bare and other wild beasts two numerous to menshun. Set yr hearts at rest about my Hanbills—i say they shall be struck off down to yr offis an what i say i mean. I shall go to toledo from tiffin.

"'yours Respectably,

ARTEMUS WARD.

"'p. s. ive bin in the show bisness twenty-two (22) yrs.   "'A. W.'"

He wrote from Toledo, another "home town," on March 9th. The letter vividly describes the elopement of the Kangaroo. It was not preserved in his printed works. This is the text as found in the *Plain Dealer:*

"LETTER FROM ARTEMUS WARD.—We have received another letter from Artemus Ward, proprietor of the well-known Show:

CLEVELAND

"'toledo, march 7, 18&58

"'Gentz—For 22 yeres has the undersined bin in the show bisness and i say open and abuv bored that i was never in a more hosspital town than toledo. Awl the peple hear take a interest in my show. The haul where i exhibit is krowdid from "erly morn to dooey eve," as the Poit sez. Several of the fust famerlis of Mawmee sity and White Pidging also cum to my show. My wax works takes the peple by storm. In the langwidge of the Toledo Blaid, "Artemus Ward's wax works air chief de overs of skulptorialastic art." Toledo is a interestin sity. There is probly more promersing and virtuous young men in toledo than there is anywheres. The climit is such that a great many of the mail inhabitants hav to take a gin-cocktale evry mornin afore brekfust. It was hard for them to do it at fust but thay take to it quite nateral now. My cangeroo gut out of his cage the other evenin and run off faster nor a lokomotive. The Common Counsil was in session at the time my cangeroo gut out and when thay heerd of the affectin casyualty they unainimersly parsed the follering preambel and resolushuns:

"""Whereas, This ere Counsil thinks hily of Artemus Ward; and Whereas, it has pleased Devine Providence to cause his cangeroo to escaip; and Whereas, the resunt escaip of a hyeny in Pauldin county and his terriable doins in a grave yard planely shows the awfulness of allowin beasts of pray to roam through the country—therefore be it

"""Resolved, That this Counsil do immediuntly ajurn and assist Mr. Ward for to capter his beast."

"'Accordingly thay did so. Abowt seving hundred (700) citizuns jined in the pursoot. We chased the little cuss clear up to Tremendusville afore we cawt him. It wood hav made you larf to hearn the little cuss squeal and kick up his legs. On our return to toledo abel and eloqunt speaches was maid by several distingwished citizuns, and awl parsed off in the most pleasant stile.

"'My snakes is under perfect subjecshun. Among my snakes is a Boy Constructor, the largist in the wurld. It wood make your blud freeze to see the mongster unkoil hisself. If yu put this letter in the papers i wish you wood be more particlar abowt the spellin and punctooation. i dont ploom myself on my learnin. i shall be in Cleveland befour long and my hanbills shall certinly be struck off down to your offis. Set your harts at rest on that pint.

"'Very Respectively yours,

ARTEMUS WARD.'"

Local appreciation at once greeted the showman. His name and sayings became bywords in the community. Preceding Gray's masquerade ball, held on the evening of March 16, 1858, this circular was distributed to herald a feature of the evening:

"Great Exsitement!! Artemus Ward is arrived in Town with his Big Ellefant Ameraka and by patickelar reqest will B here this evening. Evry boddy must B karful not to git two klost two the quadry pid as he has only bin kaut bout 22 yeeres an aint all togather acquainted with the Humin raise. Artemus houevr has controlle of the animile and will make him kut up sum of his best kapers.

"P. S.   ladys may ryde on the animile at their own risk.

"ARTEMUS WARD.

"N B March the Sixteenth, Aighteen Hundred and Fifty Aight."

Mr. Ward noted the event, with its use of his name and orthography, in a communication, dated from Sandusky, printed in the *Plain Dealer* on March 20th, *viz.:*

"OUR WARD CORRESPONDENCE. — Artemus Ward writes us again:

"'SANDUSTY mch the 10 18&58.

"'Gentz.—my feelins has bin injered by them scanderlus proceedings at the maskeraid Bawl in yr sity. my virtoo and repytashun has bin tampird with by a sekrit organizashun of konsperitors in yr sity which stile theirselves the elefunt klub. Jellus of my grate and brilyunt sucksess in the show bisness (which ive bin into going on 22 yeres), this klub mulishusly undertakes to pull awl the lawrils cut of my Brown, for their own selfish agranndeyesment.

""'Manz inhumanerty two man
maikes kountlis injuns for to moarn."

sez the Poit and heze rite. Jest yu tell them elefunt fellers that the feelings of A. Ward air not to be lazzeratid with impunerty, and if thay kut up much moore capers at my expence thay wont be allowed to

[35]

visit my show when i DOO (put doo in large tipes)
cum to Cleaveland upon no konsiderashun whatsoevir.
ime doin middlin hear in Sandusty. The peple dont
seam to preshiate my wax works, howsever. sez a
leadin sitizen to me sez he pintin to my wax work of
Dr. Parkman, Doo i behold, sez he, the grate Bunyun,
awther of the Pilgrims Progriss, dun in wax? Sez i
skacely. Sez he worthy man what doo yer mean.
Sez i my fren that air aint Bunyin—its Parkman
who was fatally killed by a unprincipled cuss in Bostin
named Webstir. Sez he yu egrejus old ass doo yu
spose i dont know Bunyun. He use to live in Sandusty
and his Pilgrim's Progriss was orijernally printed in
the lokul colum of the Daly Registir. i maid no repli
yit i was all fired mad at the man, i tell yu. sins i
last writ to yu ive addid a panaramy to my show. i
call it a Grand Movin Diarer of Seens in the Crymear.
It takes like hot cakes. my cangeroo continers very
troublesum. He rasis perfeck Hel all the time. he
yells and kicks up his legs from mornin til nite. He
hollererd so outrajusly last evenin that the music of
the handorgin was compleetly drowndid. Ime tryin
to hosswhip the little cuss into subjecshun. Ime goin
to Oberlin from hear and from Oberlin i shall cum to
Cleaveland without no fale.

> "'yours Respectively,
> ARTEMUS WARD.'"

Agreeable to announcement, Mr. Ward visited
Oberlin. The result appeared in the *Plain Dealer* of
March 20th. It is one of his best and, but slightly
modified, appears in *His Book*. Oberlin "konfired"

on him the "honery title of T. K.," of which he was "suffishuntly prowd." Despite his promises to the editor, Mr. Ward evaded Cleveland, and a gap follows in the correspondence. He is not heard from until April 17th, when this letter is given as from Chicago, explaining his failure to reach the Forest City:

"LETTER FROM ARTEMUS WARD.—'Chicago, Illinoy, Aperel the 12, 18&58:—Gents—I took a suddin departer from Oberlin and cum Westwud hoe. I shant be in yr sity for sum time. I trust you will bare up under the disapintment of my not cuming as pir agreemunt, but the fackt is talents and wax figgers air not apreshiatid in yr. sity. The fine arts stan no moor chanse in Cleaveland than thay do amung the wild injines of the far westurn prehayries. I know yu air men of a good many feelins, an your feelins may prehaps be injered at these ere remarks, but thay air true an so i tell yu open an above bored without no disception, an disception of awl kinds i doo dispise from the Bottum of my hart. Stil i may try yr sity on, but as i gaze far back into the Dim vister of the past an remember how i was cleaned out when i showed in yr. sity several yeres ago, i sez to myself, avoyd the Forrist Sity as yu wood a unchaned beest of pray. Tharefore my frends of the editorial corpse, yu must exkuse me. I know yu will be disapinted at not doin my hanbils, but i bleeve you hav soles abuv a few poltry hanbils.

"'Chicago is a grate plase. Awl the sitizens think it is a grate plase. Thay say its futur is brilyunt. Ive looked round considerable an must say i haint diskovered the brilyunt futur yet, but they paternize my wax figgers librally, and thats the mane pint with me. I was told thay kept the brilyunt futur up to the Democratic Press offis mostly, an prehaps thay doo. Thay say the dume of New York is seeled, becoz it is two far off from Chicago. The only rivuls thay acknollidge is Lundun, Pekin and Tiffin. Thare's a hi breeze prevalin here awl the time, which makes the streets dusty. The Statistick editer of the Demercratic Press told me that he chanes his feet to the floor and wares a small grindstun in his hat when he rites statististicks, to avoyd bein blowd away. Lake Mishigan is lokatid on Chicago. Illinoy is also in Chicago. There aint much money here. Corner-lots is the principal currency. Fur instance, a sitizun wants a drink, (which he duz quite frequiently) he takes his map, goze to the serloon, gits his beveridge, an then unrols his map. Which seckshun wood yu like a lot in? he sez two the bar tender. The bar tender picks out the lot he duz desire an the papers air made out on the spot. About awl the muney ive taken is in corner-lots, but i spose it is awl rite, partickerly if thay turn that air brilyunt futur loose pritty soon.

"'Ime greeved to inform yu that my Cangeroo continers to conduck hisself in a owdashus stile. Sich infernul doins as that air beest cuts up i never did see in my born days an dont want to agin. He yells from mornin till nite an kicks up his legs in a stile startlin two behold. Even sinse he was captered by the Sity Counsil of Toledo he has acted outrajusly. Whare next i shall unfurl my Bannir two the Breeze, i know not. Awl plasis air alike two the undersined.

But where ear i Rome my buzzum shall team with
kind feelins for thee.

"'ARTEMUS WARD, T. K.'"

Nothing further appeared from the showman's pen
until May 29th. Then the note was dated from Baldwinsville. It was illustrated with a cut of "Artemus
Ward" from an "Autograph by Ryder," meaning
James F., but drawn by George Hoyt, and described
"Scandalous Doings at Pittsburg," as it appears somewhat modified in *His Book*. In the book the intro-
ductory paragraph is missing. It reads:

"BALDINGSVILLE Indianny
May the 25 18&58

"Gentz—Hears two you o'd fellers and ma your shad-
ders never gro lesser. I spose you have bin a wonderin
whare upon arth the undersined was and what i wus
a doin on, and prehaps the sollum thawt has struck
yu that i had takin my departer from this mundaine
spear and as Hamlick sez, 'Shoveled orf this mortal
Koil,' and seazed two be no moore. Likeliz not yu
hav bin temptid moren once to rite a obitchuary on
Artemus Ward. But surs my time hasent arrovan
yit. Tiz troo my live is in the Sheer and Yeller leef
but while i doo live and hav my bein i maik Bold two
say i shall continner a ornimunt to Sosiety and the
show bizniss, which larst as i heve befour frequiuntly
obsarved i hav bin into goin on twenty-too (22) yeres.

"I rite yu frum my humstid in Baldingsville Indianny. Ime at hum Rekuperatin and preparin fur
the Summir kampain.

[39]

"Hear in the Buzzum of my famerly i am enjoyin myself, at peas with awl mankind and the wimmin folks likewize. I go down to the village ockashunly and take a little old Rye fur the stummucks sake but i avoyd spiritus lickers as a ginral thing.   No man evir

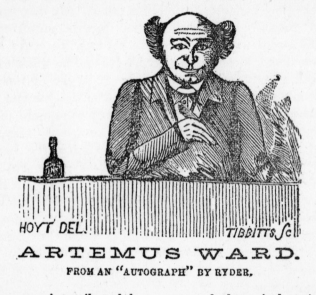

HOYT DEL.   TIBBITTS Sc

ARTEMUS WARD.
FROM AN "AUTOGRAPH" BY RYDER,

seen me intossikated but onct and that air happind in Pittzbug. A parsel of ornery cusses in that mizzer-able sity bustid inter the hawl durin the nite and aboosed my wax works shaimful. I dident obsarve the outrajus transacshuns ontil the next evenin when the peple begun for to kongregate. Suddinly thay kommensed for two larf and holler in a boysterious stile. Sez i good peple whats up? Sez thay thems grate wax works isnt thay old man. I immejitly looked up ter whare the wax works was and my blud biles as

[40]

i think of the site which then met my Gase. I hope two be dodrabbertid if them afoursed raskals hadent gone and put a old kaved in hat onter George Washington's hed and shuvd a short black klay pipe inter his mouth. His noze thay had paintid red and his trowsis legs thay had shuvd inside his butes. My wax figger of Napoleong Boneypart was likewize mawltratid. His sword was danglin tween his legs, his cockd hat was drawn klean down over his ize and he was plased in a stoopin posishun lookin zactly as tho he was as drunk as a biled owl. Ginral Tayler was standin on his hed and Wingfield Skott's koat tales were pind over his hed and his trowsis ware kompleetly torn off frum hisself. My wax works representin the Lords Supper was likewize aboozed. Three of the Postles ware under the table and two of um had on old tarpawlin hats and raggid pee jackits and ware smokin pipes. Judus Iskarriot had on a cocked hat and was apperently drinkin, as a Bottle of whisky sot befour him. This ere specktercal wuz too much fur me. i klosed the show and then drowndid my sorrers in the flowin Bole.

"Probly ile rite you agin befour i take my departer on the Summer kampain.

"Very Respectively Yures,

ARTEMUS WARD, T. K."

The Hoyt woodcut was used occasionally afterward to lead the letters. It was a very early example of newspaper illustration. The *Plain Dealer* sometimes used other specimens of his work carved on the block by a local engraver named George W. Tibbitts.

The half-thought crudities and incongruities now began to shape themselves for a wider call. The next letter in order was ostensibly from Cincinnati, and without title, but became "Wax Figures *vs.* Shakespeare" in *His Book*. It was printed in the *Plain Dealer* on July 10th. This was followed on July 16th by a "Fourth-of-July Oration" supposed to have been delivered at Weathersfield, Connecticut, by Mr. Ward. He hinged it on the annual celebration held there by Henry C. Bowen, whose custom then and for many years later was to have some celebrity sound a high note on the occasion to a distinguished company and the neighbors about his country seat. It was an extremely able "oration," better by far than most of the serious ones usually given at the place, and lifted him still more into the lime-light. There was a lapse from this to September 6th, indicating a lengthy vacation, when "The Atlantic Cable in Baldwinsville" appeared. This was an account of a "celebrashern" in honor of the first laying of Cyrus W. Field's line under the Atlantic, which broke down after transmitting a single message. It ranks with the best of his productions. A visit to the Free Love Colony at Berlin Heights, Ohio, published on October 11th, was another very successful letter. The showman was not heard from again until December 13th, when the celebrated essay, "Among the Spirits," appeared. There was a further absence of communication after this date until February 2, 1859, when a note came from Baldwinsville, indicating that the Local had been among the lost for some time, Mr. Ward furnishing the pleasing news of his discovery:

CLEVELAND

"OUR LOCAL HEARD FROM

"'baldinsville febuary 1 18 & 58 no 9.

"'deer sur, i larn a reward is gin out fur the capter uv mister broun. ile fetch the kus back and no questions ast—ive had trubel a nuf with him a reddy, when i got mi waxworx uv franklin smasht and spilte tha tole me he was jes the wun 2 pla Waxworx til i cood git a nuther Main, so i cum 2 klevlin and found him in a religus meetin where he had no frenz, and sur, i druther got a lejin uv wild snaiks and kangaroos on the karz than him, but i got him on, and had 2 send rite off fur pants fur boath uv us afour the conducter wood start, Wal we got saif 2 oblin and thare we got off and went behind the shed to change britches, coz mine was 2 small, and hizen 2 big, jes then peck hearn How it was and in the wurds uv the lamented mister Paul.

""At once there rows so wild a yel within that dark and dismal del as All the imps frum heven that fel had razed the battel kry uv hel,

""""Felons 2 the resku!!
Felons 2 the resku!!
God and mi rite!!'

""""daten forever! daten, daten! mis daten!"—parenthesis, u see ime a skoler, parenthesis, what he ment by callin out mis daten i dunno—In 2 minits he had moren 20 thousin niggers, white and black after us, broun sed he druther fall in mi hans than theirn so a4 we got a toe into tother trouses, we cut for the cars and lost both pare, and not likin to go in the cars this way, we shot under and got on the trux, now sur ive been in sho bisness 22 years, ive showed bares, and kangaroos and snakes and other sich animals, but this capt all i ever see. Ma be we didnt have a time a4 we got 2 baldinsville, but weve had a wus time sens, a purty waxfiger he makes snickering every time any 1 sez "franklin looks natral," i tride him 2 take care of the kangaroo but which had the wust time i dunno. No mr editer ime BEET for the fust time in my life, and ile bring the Kus back and no kuestions ast.   yours,

ARTEMUS WARD.'"

At this day all the above is enigmatical. February 14, 1859, the *Plain Dealer* carried the letter from Baldwinsville describing the "Showman's Courtship" —in which the sweet object of his affections is named "Susanner." This was changed in *His Book* to "Betsey Jane," the permanent appellation of the sharer of his joys and sorrows. There was no letter in March, but April 25th the paper printed "Artemus Ward Sees Piccolomini," that lady being then the reigning star of the operatic stage. Nothing more appeared until November 12th, when "Joy in the House of Ward" came out—well waiting for—reciting, as it did, the coming of "The Twins," or "two episodes," as he termed them!

The *Plain Dealer* files disclose no further communication until April 21, 1860, when "Artemus Ward Encounters the Octoroon" appeared. June 1st gives us his vision of Adelina Patti, then in the first blush of her lovely youth, the last item to appear over his signature.

III

IN the day's work, besides joking the citizens, picking up police and court items, the flotsam and jetsam of city news, and recording the showman's adventures, the Local answered mythical correspondents with replies calculated to jar the readers. His "copy" wandered in all directions, noting current events elsewhere, and inventing them when dull, with plenty of playful paragraphs affecting his contemporaries.

A freak in the column which excited much amusement in the city, especially in the newspaper-offices, was the publication in the *Plain Dealer*, January 28, 1859, of "The Three Tigers of Cleveland Journalism," purporting to be contributions on moral questions, most immorally written, and ascribed to the grave editors of the *Press*, *Herald*, and *Plain Dealer*. The articles with their prelude follow:

"A NOVEL AND UNIQUE FEATURE
THE THREE TIGERS
OF
THE CLEVELAND PRESS
ALL
WRITING FOR THE PLAIN DEALER!

"It is with no ordinary emotions of pleasure that the Local Editor of this paper announces the entire success

☞ VERITAS. — Many note the same error. Mr. Key. who wrote the "Star Spangled Banner" &c. was not the author of "Hamlet" or Hogarty. He wrote the former Scavenger and assisted in "The Female Pirate" — but did not write Hamlet. Hamlet was written by a celebrated but unscrupulous man named Mackett Speare who bid us persisted for not using slep?"

☞ Young clergymen. — Two pints of rum, two quarts of hot water, tea-cup of lemon, sugar and a banana. Stir in nutmeg, Stir thoroughly and drink while warm.

FACSIMILE COPY OF TWO "PLAIN DEALER" PARAGRAPHS

of one of the most stupendous newspaper achievements on record. This evening's paper contains the achievement. Below is the achievement. We invite the particular attention of the American people, irrespective of party or sect, to the achievement. Other achievements have been achieved, but they were as molehills to mountains beside this one—which is undeniably a stunner.

"In this evening's PLAIN DEALER the Three Tigers of the Cleveland Press furnish our column, for this occasion only, with original communications, written expressly for us. Bonner's hiring the Three Lions of the New York Press to write for the *Ledger* did not suggest the idea to us. Far from it. We thought of the idea long ago. Besides, our writers are Tigers while his are Lions. For these Tigers to lie down together is nothing new, for if they are themselves to be believed (as we know they are) they have been doing that for several years. That is not the point. The hugeness of the thing consists in our being able—we, an inexperienced young man and born of poor but respectable parents—to bring these three ferocious Tigers together! The enormous expense of the thing —the many sleepless nights we have passed thinking of the thing—how we have racked our brain pondering on the thing—need not be told. Suffice it to say, in the language of the Duke of Wellington at the close of the Battle of Waterloo, 'THE THING IS DID!'

"From the pen of the veteran editor of the Cleveland *Press*, J. A. Harris, Esq., we have an able and eloquent essay on Prize-Fighting.

"Mr. Benedict, of the *Herald*, furnishes us with a

beautiful paper on 'Dress, Etiquette, &c,' on which he is admirably competent to speak. He also furnishes us with a juvenile poem which now appears in print for the first time.

"From Mr. Gray's felicitous pen we have an affecting article 'On the Evils of Dancing,' and also a Juvenile Essay of marked merit 'On the Elephant.' Enough said.

"'PRIZE-FIGHTING. AN ESSAY

By J. A. HARRIS

"'The late "mill" between Messrs. Morrissey and Heenan at Long Point, Canada, (to which bleak and dismal spot, to the shame of America be it said, they were ruthlessly driven by our infamous laws,) has directed attention afresh to the noble and muscle-developing sports of the Ring. How that contest resulted, my readers all know, and I presume none of them doubt that had the Benecia Boy not mistaken a post for Mr. Morrissey's "mug," the result would have been different. I shall always censure the Hon. Aaron Jones, albeit he is a high-toned gentleman, for throwing up the sponge at the time he did. Morrissey was nearly as far gone as Heenan, and the latter should have been brought to the scratch, and kept there. Heenan should not have peeled unless he intended to conquer or die. This pretending to be a feller unless you are one don't suit me. Let my young readers ponder this well. Morrissey and Heenan are both young and if they take care of themselves I think they have a brilliant future before them. But to the subject proper:

"'Prize-fighting was an institution as early as 1602. The assertion of Henry Ward Beecher in a late number of the *Independent* that the phrase "traveling on your muscle" originated with the Dutch of Tipperary is incorrect. Wm. Shakespeare, a colored dramatist of some note, wrote a temperance drama in 1603, while he was a student at Oberlin College, entitled, "A Glance at New York." In this drama Lady Macbeth says to Claude Melnotte, "Wherefore perspirest thou so?" "Because, my Lady," returned Claude, "I've been traveling on my muscle." I may add that Henry Wadsworth Longfellow, the well-known author of "Hiawatha" and "Old Bob Ridley," while traveling through Greece with a load of tinware in 1602, also heard this same expression used freely by the peasantry. He has made entertaining mention of it in his interesting "Life of the Broughton Chicken, or the Hero of a Hundred Fights."

"'To further convince my readers that the prize ring was an institution at a very early age I will state that Socrates (or as he was familiarly called, "Sock,") acted as a bottle-holder at a very lively fight when he was only nineteen years of age.

"'The Prize Ring is new in America, but it must grow. We have no Tom Sayers or Tipton Slashers, it is true, but we have Hyers and Heenans, to say nothing of the many members of our National Congress who give great promise of future usefulness in the Ring, and who are already brilliantly gifted in impromptu fights. Let the friends of civ-

5

ilization not despair of the Prize Ring in America.
No, not a despair!'

"'DRESS, ETIQUETTE, &c.

By George A. Benedict

"'An elegantly dressed and polished man is my
especial admiration. Whether I have signalized myself in this way or not, modesty forbids me to say.
But I have no sympathy with those men who go
around with their shirt-collars all rumpled up, who
recklessly jam their hats onto their heads, who
seldom black their boots, and who do not keep their
hair properly oiled and brushed. The low and vulgar
may sneer at these things, but, gentle reader, they
are as indispensable to the real gentleman as the
bright day-god is to the new - mown hay. Every
man should have five suits of clothes, three of which
should be broadcloth with a gloss to it. All should
read Chesterfield the moment they have mastered the
Revised Statutes of Ohio.

"'Be polite. Use polished language. Avoid vul-
garisms. How often are my nerves shocked by hearing
some vulgar person sing out, "How are you, old Boy!"
How much better were it to exclaim, "My ancient
youth, how fares it with thee?" Again, "You can't
come it, old hoss!" Why not say, "You will experience some little difficulty in consummating your
machinations, thou elderly equinal quadruped"? Again,
"A dead cock in the pit." Rather say, "A defunct
male fowl in the parquette." Avoid these boorish
provincialisms altogether. Be prepared to gracefully

remove your hat when you enter the society of ladies or encounter Federal Office-holders. In a word, be genteel. I should like to continue these observations to a much greater length, as I am paid by the line, but engrossing duties prevent my so doing. I will close by presenting my readers with a few valuable recipes for the adornment of their persons:

"'HAIR-OIL.—Take two kegs of hog's lard and boil to the consistency of mush. Stir in whisky and musk. Bottle tight and apply when hot with a currycomb.

"'PERFUMERY.—I hope my readers appreciate the necessity of being sweet-scented. Musk is an exquisite perfume, the best, in fact. I souse not only my pocket-handkerchief in musk-water daily, but my boots and overcoat, also, and would advise my readers to adopt the same system.'

"A FRAGMENT

"(It is proper to state that the following poem was written by Mr. Benedict at an early age of his infancy and was not intended for publication. It is, nevertheless, distinguished by very peculiar genius.—LOCAL ED. P. D.)

> "Uncle Simon he
> Clum up a tree
> And looked round to see what he could see:
> When present-lee
> Uncle Jim
> Clum up beside of him
> And squatted down by he.

THE END.

ARTEMUS WARD

"'ON THE EVILS OF DANCING
By J. W. Gray

"'Dancing is a great evil, and destroys more people than War, Pestilence, and Famine. Yet how many thoughtless people whirl in the mazy dance as often as two times a week. To these misguided persons no sounds are so captivating as those made by the men of sin who rub the hair of the horse to the bowels of the cat. These persons cannot sit down quietly of an evening by their firesides, and derive pleasure from reading Rollin's *Ancient History* or the Debates in the Washington *Globe*. They have no taste for Tracts and Tax-lists. Their minds are continually upon the sinful dance. I say sinful dance, and say it boldly! I have entertained these opinions from boyhood. I stand where I always stood. When a young child I wrote the following composition on the evils of dancing:

"'"ON DANCING.—Some people think Dancing is right but I do not. I think dancing is wrong. People who go to balls lose their night's rest and get up in the morning feeling very bad and cross. My advice to all is not to dance on no occasions whatsomever."

"'I am no more Gray now than I was then, although I am somewhat older, and time and an intimate acquaintance with the man who danced himself into the middle of next week have only more strongly convinced me of the correctness of those views.

"'The charge of inconsistency cannot be brought against me. In the Daily *Plain Dealer* of June 19, 1776, I expressed these same views in reply to a scurrilous article in the *Herald*.

"'Frown indignantly upon the first attempt that is made to induce you to dance. Studiously avoid the ball-room; but if you MUST go there, and you DO dance, I entreat you to shake a lively foot.'

"'ON THE ELEPHANT
(Written in childhood.)

"'The Elephant is the largest animal in the world. He eats hay and cakes. You must not give the Elephant tobacco, for if you do he will stamp his great big feet on you and kill you dead. Some people think the Elephant is the most noblest animal in the world, but as for me, give me the American Eagle.

"J. W. GRAY HIS PEACE.'"

Many tales survive of the Local's life in Cleveland. He kept the city interested in his doings as well as its own. One night, being too restless to sleep, he induced A. Minor Griswold, his rival Local of the *Democrat*, to wander about with him in search of something funny. Nothing was found. Then they recalled that a rather eminent English elocutionist had reached town, and decided to visit him. It was chilly and the hour very late—or, rather, early. They located the victim's room at the hotel and pounded upon the panels until admitted. Inside they told the shivering artist that they were the critics of two local publications and regretted that pressure of business compelled them to call at such an hour. He begged them not to mention it. They gravely asked if he would oblige with some samples of his talent. The floor was cold, so he stood on the bed and gave the "Charge of the Light Brigade," then new, with as much spirit as his chattering teeth would permit. He was warmly applauded. Then Artemus said, sadly, that there was one touching little thing which, if he could hear it rendered as only the artist could do it, he would feel that his life was brighter, to wit, "The Boy Stood on the Burning Deck." It was reeled off. Wiping his eyes, wet with mourning for the fate of the faithful but foolish Casabianca, he bade the elocutionist good night. Outside, the scamps chuckled with glee at the thought of the solemn, shivering figure on the bed and went away comforted. They paid for their joke with excellent notices and kind attentions afterward.

"When A. Ward was in Cleveland," said David Ross Locke (Nasby), who had served the *Plain Dealer* as compositor and reporter, talking in after-years, "he was the greatest man there. Nothing could be done without him. He was a jolly, jovial soul and a true friend."

Usually the Local delighted in his daily task of rounding up Cleveland, but sometimes he became weary of the load, as this paragraph shows:

"EDITING.—Before you go for an editor, young man, pause and take a big think! Do not rush into the editorial harness rashly. Look around and see if there is not an omnibus to drive, some soil somewhere to be tilled, a clerkship on some meat-cart to be filled, anything that is reputable and healthy, rather than going for an editor, which is hard business at best. We are not a horse, and consequently have never been called upon to furnish the motive power for a threshing-machine; but we fancy that the life of the editor, who is forced to write, write, write, whether he feels right or not, is much like that of the steed in question. If the yeas and neighs could be obtained we believe the intelligent horse would decide that the threshing-machine is preferable to the sanctum editorial."

He became very intimate with the Griswolds, Henrietta, the better half of his rival Local, being a bright and interesting young woman. Griswold received two dollars a week more pay than Artemus, which, presumably, took care of his wife, though A. W. used it as an excuse to borrow from Griswold's wardrobe on state occasions. Mrs. Griswold, still living at Cadott, Wisconsin, in 1919, recalls his coming one evening to escort her to the theater with his coat closely buttoned up to his chin. When questioned as to the occasion for this, after much evasion he admitted that his only good shirt was in the wash. "I told him to go into the bedroom and take one of Mr. Griswold's two clean ones or I would not go out with him. 'All right, Sister Henrietta,' was the cheerful reply. I always acted as a sister toward him, doing his small mending and fixing up. His best coat was of dark bottle-green cloth, very short as to sleeves and tight across the back. His meager stock of clothes was a continuous source of comment. In after-years, when both he and my husband became prosperous, we had many a laugh over the old Bohemian days."

He roomed for a good part of his stay in Cleveland on the fourth floor of the old post-office building, located on Water Street, with Jack Ryder as a companion. The windows commanded a fine view of the lake and of the country bordering the west bank of the Cuyahoga, now grim with smoke-stacks and rusty with heaps of iron ore. Three or four chairs, a pine table, and a sofa of more than respectable age formed the "sitting-room" furnishings. Here he did much of the work that brought him fame. Sunday was his "day off," in newspaper parlance, and on the mornings he usually had a roomful of callers, who loafed and listened to the reading of comic copy. Here came Charles W. Coe, James F. Ryder, John B. Lester, Charles E. Wilson (cashier of the *Plain Dealer*), George Hoyt and James Brokenshire of the staff, and other lights of the Cleveland of that day. His Sunday-school was celebrated in its way, the "teacher" furnishing most of the entertainment and usually overflowing in quantity. He liked to sermonize and discuss nature and philosophy, usually in terms of burlesque, like this example, provided by one of his auditors:

"It is susceptible of absolute proof," he solemnly declared, "that a ball will run down an inclined plane, and yet how few people there are who know it! An earthern bowl dropped from the roof of a three-story house, if it strike a stone pavement, will be shattered into many pieces. A bean-pole, legitimately used, is an instrument of good, yet if it be sharpened at one end and run through a man it will cause the most intense pain and perhaps produce contortions. The wick of an unlighted candle may safely be manipulated, but if you light that wick and thrust your hand into the blaze and keep it there half an hour a sensation of excessive and disagreeable warmth will be experienced. A dozen wrought-iron nails may be dashed violently from the steeple of a large meeting-house to a brick sidewalk and sustain no injury, but the same experiment with a dozen clay pipes will result differently.

"The effect upon the sidewalk in either case, however, will be the same. You may lie down on the ground and let a kitten walk over you with perfect safety, but if you put a heavy dray-horse in the place of the kitten you will immediately experience a disagreeable pressure. Hasty pudding and milk are a harmless diet if eaten moderately, but if you eat it incessantly for six consecutive weeks it will produce instant death. You gaze with indifference upon a bull when he is placidly eating grass in a pasture, but if the animal becomes infuriated and attempts to assist you over a rail fence with those horns they immediately become objects of a deep-seated disgust. On the same principle we can easily hold in our arms an infant, and experience delight in doing so; but it would be very difficult for us to perform a similar experiment with a corpulent old gentleman who is in a state of unconscious inebriety, while the delight afforded by the performance in this instance would hardly be worth mentioning. All these things seem wonderful at first blush, but science makes them as clear as clear can be."

These propositions, addressed to his visitors as "Mine Ancient Pistols," were delivered with a gravity that was wholly delicious.

On another occasion he read a poem with this introduction: "A few weeks ago, one Julian Czar Teed fell from the belfry of the Methodist meeting-house at Charndon, in Geauga County. He struck the roof in his fall and bounded off to the ground. Singular to

say—he was not killed—'on the contrary, quite the
reverse.' His fall was truly touching, but he sends a
poem about it that is much more touching than his
fall. It seems that he went into the belfry to toll the
bell for a funeral. But here is the poem:

I

"In Charndon, when the sun was low,
Julian Czar Teed to church did go,
To swing the bell-tongue to and fro,
    To tell us of the funeral.

II

"But soon we saw another sight,
For in a fit Czar took a fright,
Not having all his senses quite,
    He tumbled off the belfry.

III

"A boy while passing heard the sound,
And turned his head and gaped around,
Saw Julian lying on the ground,
    Smashed up extensively.

IV

"His sister saw the awful sight—
Her face with terror soon turned white,
And running up the hill told Dwight,
Who threw his bottle with his might,
    And ran away most frantically.

V

"While sprawling on the ground so low,
The crimson tide began to flow,
And people running to and fro,
    Cried, 'tis a dire catastrophe.

VI

"Wonder of wonders 'tis to tell,
No bones were broken when he fell,
And now he's up and doing well,
    As he was formerly."

BOHEMIAN DAYS

Occasionally he indulged in verse in the local columns. In after-years he alluded modestly to this talent, which he used sparingly, but insisted that upon occasion he could "jerk a poem equal to any of them *Atlantic Monthly* fellers." This is a specimen:

"LOSS OF THE GOOD SHIP *POLLY ANN:* A PATHETICAL NAUTICAL BALLAD

I

"As the good ship *Polly Ann* was sailing
   Across the briny, briny sea,
She sprang a leak, and no kind of bailing
   Could save or could save she;
For she went down to the bottom of the sea—
    The sea, the sea, my boys,
With her cargo, and old Captain Grives,
Being the total loss of the good ship *Polly Ann* and fourteen
   hundred lives.

II

"Captain Grives was a gallant old man,
   Gallant, gallant was he;
He drank his rum from a large tin pan,
   Jovial and jovial was he.
Says he, 'My boys,' when the storm was ragin',
   'Farewell to our friends and wives,
For we're goin' down in waters very surgin',
   Being the total loss of the good ship *Polly Ann* and fourteen
    hundred lives!'

III

"Then up did speak the brave first mate,
   And a nice-spoken man was he;
Says he, 'Ere we go I've a suggestion for to make,
   To make, to make,' says he;
   'Ere this vessel goes down and we all do sink,'
'That's very well said,' says the good Captain Grives,
So he filled up his pan; the brave seafaring men proceeded to individually and collectively imbibe and the unfortunate vessel went down, being the total loss of the good ship *Polly Ann* and fourteen hundred lives.

IV

"Previous to which the second mate he spoke,
His name, and his name was Brown;
He says, 'With deep grief do I very nearly choke
At the idea, the idea of going down—
While ashore my Betsy cleans the dishes,
Likewise the spoons and the knives,
I shall be food for the pesky old fishes,'
And I regret to say that he was; being the total loss of the
good ship *Polly Ann* and fourteen hundred lives.

V

"And now young men of high and low degree,
Your attention, your attention I ask;
Never leave the land for a life upon the sea—
'Tis a very, a very sad task;
You'd far better plow, you'd far better mow,
Than to go, to go for a sailor,
Never leave the land—don't a sailing go,
For fear you may suffer the same melancholy and harrowing
fate that befell the gallant Captain Grives, his energetic
and worthy crew, and the very valuable cargo on board
the ill-fated vessel; being, as I have already informed my
readers, the total loss of the good ship *Polly Ann* and
fourteen hundred lives!"

Colored people always fascinated him and he was a
frequent attendant at an assembly-room on the corner
of Seneca and Champlain streets, where most of their
festivals were held. Here, too, came many citizens
of the period, when the black folks were the center
of political interest, to patronize the fairs and suppers
given in aid of the church. Artemus rarely missed
one of these, though the local editor of a Democratic
pro-slavery paper. In truth, he was not a very solid
partizan and his kindly side overruled his political
opinions. He was very generous with space in
noticing the affairs and correspondingly popular with

the colored congregation, which worshiped in the edifice at the corner of Ohio and Brownell streets. A revival here always brought Artemus to the scene. The "flood of grace" thrilled him, led as it was by the fervid appeals from the pulpit. On one occasion he was moved by an especial effort to walk up the aisle and give the clergyman a congratulatory hand-shake.

Besides the theater, the lecture, the concert, and the circus in season he liked to visit a road-house in East Cleveland kept by a genial giant named Abner McIlrath. Buggy-rides in the summer and sleighing-parties in winter usually ended at Abner's, where there was always a good meal waiting and something cool or hot on the bar, according to season. In summer there was a table under the vine-covered arbor, and in winter guests were served in a great room facing the bar, where hickory logs blazed and crackled in the fireplace, while Abner added to the solid entertainment with his views on men and things, cleverly pumped by the Local, to the delight of the company. The staffs of the several newspapers were often gathered here as well as the pleasant young people of the city. McIlrath owned a tame bear, with which he was wont to wrestle, and which, without success, he would try to persuade Artemus to hold. Dances were held at the inn, led by John Van Olker's orchestra, in which the Local joined with great energy, his long legs enabling him to execute marvelous steps.

The vagaries of the Local were not relished by Mr. Gray, the editor and publisher of the *Plain Dealer*. His "stuff" was traveling and making the *Plain*

Dealer famous, but the repute of the writer grew faster than that of the paper, to which, in the slow-going time, he was something of an embarrassment. Then he was none too industrious, and to Mr. Gray, like most proprietors, cleverness was a poor substitute for exertion. Besides, there was a strong intimation that more salary would soon be required than the petty amount doled out weekly by the cashier, though the original ten dollars had been expanded to twelve dollars, and then to fifteen dollars, after two years of service. He refers to this sum in a letter introducing a Cleveland friend to his mother, written in more prosperous days, reading:

"Mother: This is Charles W. Coe, wno was as much my friend when I was worth fifteen dollars per week as now."

The idea of becoming a public entertainer was working in his mind. He made stray jottings of idle thoughts from time to time, and, leaving some of these on his work-table, they were noted by Mr. Gray, who wanted to know why they were not in the paper. When informed it was material to be used in a lecture, he expressed his dissatisfaction and also some scorn at the notion that his Local could do anything successful in that line.

In the fall of 1860, through the initiative of Charles Hallock, later of *Forest and Stream*, Artemus engaged with *Vanity Fair* in New York to duplicate his copy to its pages—thereby to become a pioneer in syndicating humor, a present-day industry largely developed. He was to get ten dollars for each article so reproduced. This further displeased Mr. Gray, who

ARTEMUS WARD AND A. MINOR GRISWOLD AT McILRATH'S
(McIlrath in the doorway)

thought that all outgivings and incomings belonged to the *P. D.*

The Local deemed Artemus Ward's letters a by-product of his own, to do with as he pleased, and, as a result of the difference, cut off the supply. The friction long developing came to a head at this action. He offered to remain and give the paper his undivided output for twelve hundred dollars a year! To this Mr. Gray would not accede. Wearly of the irksome conditions and the poor pay, having perhaps a timid vision that he belonged to a broader field, he retired from the *Plain Dealer* with the issue of Saturday, November 10, 1860. The column contained a farewell note, reading:

"VALE

"The undersigned closes his connection with the PLAIN DEALER with this evening's issue. During the three years that he has contributed to these columns he has endeavored to impart a cheerful spirit to them. He believes it is far better to stay in the Sunshine while we may, inasmuch as the Shadow must of its own accord come only too soon. He cannot here, in fit terms, express his deep gratitude to the many, including every member of the Press of Cleveland, who have so often manifested the most kindly feeling toward himself. But he can very sincerely say that their courtesy and kindness will never be forgotten.

"The undersigned may be permitted to flatter himself that he has some friends among the readers of newspapers. May we meet again!

"CHARLES F. BROWN."

The *Plain Dealer* itself, bade him good-by in kindly terms:

"Our associate, Mr. Brown, has had a 'louder call,' as the Reverends would say, and goes to a larger city, where he can enlarge his sphere of usefulness. To do the Locals for a daily paper in a city like this is a drudgery, cramping to such a genius as his, and we cannot blame him for aspiring to a higher position. It is the lot of our Locals to rise in the world. Bouton built himself such a reputation while with us that he went to New York and is now the City Editor of the *Journal of Commerce*. McLaren, another Local, is now preaching the gospel; and Brown is destined to become either a minister or an author, perhaps both. Our relations are now and always have been of the most agreeable kind, and we part with him with many regrets."

His rivals in the local field bade him generous, regretful farewells, that in the *Herald* of the same morning reading:

"GOOD-BY, ARTEMUS.—We understand that the connection of Mr. C. F. Brown with the *Plain Dealer* terminates this evening. Mr. Brown, we learn, intends removing to New York, where he has an engagement as contributor to *Vanity Fair*, in whose columns he will continue his celebrated 'Artemus Ward' letters.

"As a writer of spicy paragraphs and humorous articles, Mr. Brown has won wide-spread and deserved celebrity, and we congratulate him on the prospect of more extensive remunerative fame which lies before him. At the same time we shall miss him from the corps of Cleveland journalists with regret. For the past three years we have been intimately acquainted with him, and, though attached to rival journals, our acquaintance has always been of the most friendly nature. Though often firing 'paper bullets of the brain' at each other, never, to our knowledge, was one of them winged with malicious purpose. Mr. Brown has won many personal friends in this city, but none who will more sincerely regret his departure than we do, or more heartily wish him success in his future career."

The *Leader* echoed the sentiment on the same date, saying:

"FROM CLEVELAND TO NEW YORK.—Charles F. Brown, the original and genuine Artemus Ward, who for three years has given spice, life, and celebrity to the Cleveland *Plain Dealer*, has dissolved his connection with that paper, and is about to remove to New York, where he will write exclusively for *Vanity Fair*, the *Punch* of America. We cannot let him go without a slight but hearty recognition of kindly feelings for him, expressed, not simply for ourself, but in behalf of the people of Cleveland who have known him as a genial companion, a kind-hearted citizen, and a dashing, humorous writer. His 'letters' have been read and laughed over far and wide, and will now be still more widely circulated.

"Charlie, we are sorry to say good-by, but we know you won't forget Cleveland, and you won't be above your old friends. You will live, as you have lived in Cleveland, upon the injunction of your own Artemus, 'If you would be virtuous, be happy,' and in so doing you will win and keep lots of friends. We shall miss you here upon the reportorial and editorial staff, but you will have a pleasanter berth than life upon a daily newspaper will ever afford.

"You have worked your way high up the slippery side-hill of success; go on and reach a higher point, and then, when you can stop and take a pleasant backward view over the valley of mediocrity, and rest awhile in one of the arbors prepared for the delectation of those who have toiled well and fought bravely, none will be more ready to take you by the hand and cry you good speed than those who have known you here, and the 'we' who writes these lines."

Though but three years in the employ of the *Plain Dealer*, he had so thoroughly identified himself with the paper as to be a permanent asset in its repute, and so endeared himself to the community that his memory remains in lasting affection. The bust carved by Geflowski stands to-day in the magnificent home built for the *Plain Dealer* by the late Liberty E. Holden, under whose ownership and with the guidance of Elbert H. Baker the paper has become one of the great journals of the world. Curiously, Mr. Holden came from Sweden, Oxford County, Maine, the next town to the west from Waterford, A. W.'s birthplace, and their boyhood days ran parallel. Joseph W. Gray died in 1862, and by another coincidence in relationship, William W. Armstrong, who had first employed Artemus in Tiffin, became the *Plain Dealer's* owner in 1866, continuing until Mr. Holden and his associates acquired the property in 1885. The latter established a morning edition March 16th of that year, and July

15, 1905, extinguished the evening issue. It is now the only morning paper in Cleveland.

Cleveland attentions to A. W. have been many. He figures in all local histories. James F. Ryder's book *Voightlander and I in Pursuit of Shadow-Catching* gives him a full chapter. The Rowfant Club issued a volume of his letters to Charles E. Wilson, cashier of the *Plain Dealer*, during his time with the paper, in 1900, and the journalists of the city have an Artemus Ward Press Club. The table and chair used by him in the editorial-rooms of the *Plain Dealer* are preserved in the Museum of the Western Reserve Historical Society, together with the original of the cartoon drawn by George Hoyt, his associate on the paper, depicting the showman and his kangaroo.

IV

NEW YORK—"VANITY FAIR"

WHILE the purpose to invade New York, as stated in the farewells, was uppermost in his mind, the adventurer had no engagement with *Vanity Fair*, beyond the ten-dollar weekly letter, and he did not at once take the direct road for the metropolis, but became advance agent and business associate with Ossian E. Dodge, who gave a musical mélange on the circuit. He was to arrange dates, help out on the stage when need be, and receive twenty-five dollars per week for his services on a tour which ran across Ohio, Indiana, and Illinois. Dodge had years before elevated himself into public notice by becoming the highest bidder for a ticket to Jenny Lind's first concert in Boston, paying six hundred and twenty-five dollars in a fierce competition. He then caused to issue a lithograph showing the unctuous P. T. Barnum, the song-bird's manager, gracefully introducing the lady to Ossian E. Dodge. This prominence gave him a considerable vogue, which was on the wane when Artemus Ward joined his fortunes. According to J. T. Trowbridge, who held his hat for him in Boston at the time of the Lind auction, Dodge was "a singer of comic songs and a giver of entertainments in which he was the sole performer. His comic powers consisted largely in grotesque grimaces, and the feats of a voice that could go down and down into the very sepulchers

[68]

of basso profundo, until the hearer wondered in what ventriloquial caverns it would lose itself and become a ghost of sound."

Artemus started on what was to be a brief venture, gaily enough. He was first heard from at Lima, Ohio, under date of December 7th, when he wrote thus to his friend Charles E. Wilson:

"Send all letters, papers, etc., that may have come to me at Russell House, Detroit, immediately. I presume that *Vanity Fair* has sent you $20. Please write me at Detroit immediately, giving all the news. Have had a first-rate time, but may want you to send that on soon. Will see at Detroit, and will write you from there."

The twenty dollars was due on the first two letters to *Vanity Fair*, "Artemus Ward Visits Brigham Young" and the profound essay on "Forts." Wilson replied at once, with "all the news," among other items of which was the fact that Griswold had taken his place in the office. He replied from Detroit, December 11th:

"Your favor with several other favors reached me this evening, and were most gladly read. A man don't know how good letters are until he is among strangers, tho. I am scarcely among strangers, after all. I find friends all around—enthusiastic ones. Here they are very numerous.

"*Vanity Fair* should send you $20. I shall write him again. I think Derby & Jackson will publish for me. Since I left Cleveland I have had several overtures from N. Y. publishing-houses—or, rather, I found letters from several on my arrival here. I shall go on in about a month—perhaps less.

"I have a letter from my mother. She is deeply afflicted, as I anticipated, and her troubles are more nor what she can endure. She has been this way before and I guess she'll come out all straight. She says she hasn't received a single paper I sent her containing accounts of my presentation, &c. For God's sake, if you love me, send her a *Leader*, *Plain Dealer*, and *Herald* what had said accounts. Direct Mrs. Caroline E. Brown, Waterford, Oxford County, Maine. She says my papers probably went to Waterville, which I cannot understand. Please get the direction right. I am troubling you much, but will repay if I ever can.

"I paid Hoyt a day or two before I left. I am certain of this. I regret to say that his recollection is not very clear in regard to matters of this kind. I borrowed $2.00 of him once, but when I went to pay him he said he had never loaned it to me! I succeeded in forcing it upon him. He can sculp first rate, but his memory fails him in money matters. As for McGuire, tell him the Panic has got me, and that I ain't worth a d—— or a dollar. Tell him there is some mistake about it.

"I have advertised Dodge big here. He told me to sink one hundred and fifty dollars, and have sunk it. If anybody can sink a hundred and fifty dollars quicker than I can, I should like to see him. In some respects this trip will do me good. I feel more healthy and I have formed many valuable acquaintances. I will write you again from Jackson or 'long there somewhere. I shall write to *Vanity Fair* at once, about money. Love to Less. Who copies the Wards in the *Plain Dealer*?"

Like the very prudent New England person that she was, his mother was naturally "upset" at his departure from a regular job and feared a period of instability with incidental hardships. It is to this that he refers in his note. She had visited him at Cleveland and was pleased with his friends, his surroundings, and his position in the town, so her disturbance was quite natural.

Dodge was very "near" in money affairs, and his advance agent was not well furnished with funds for his own use. The one hundred and fifty dollars seems to have been sunk too deep for rescue. What blew up the relationship is not revealed, but the period of road work soon ended. A letter to Wilson from Chicago, dated December 22d, tells of the parting:

"I have cut loose from the Concert business. I packed Dodge's baggage very carefully at Niles yesterday, had it safely stored away subject to his order, wrote him that sickness in my family demanded my immediate presence at home, and came on here last night. On the cars I encountered the Chicago Academy of Science, some 100 ladies and gentlemen, who were returning from an excursion to Ann Arbor. They made an immense splurge over me and elected me an honorary member of the society amidst 'loud applause.' I returned thanks in a 'few brief remarks.' The Chicago papers will doubtless have accounts of it. The Society is composed of eminent geologists, astronomers, etc.—first-rate people. Devilish pretty girls among them, too. I go to Pittsburgh on Monday—thence to Philadelphia and thence to New York. I have money enough for the present but may want you to send on the *Vanity Fair* fund (I take it for granted Stephens has sent you pay for three letters) at Pittsburgh. I will write you from that place. Just write me at once, please, at Pittsburgh, care of *Chronicle* office, giving all the news, but don't send the money until I write for it.

"You know what a vindictive devil Dodge is, and I expect he will raise a jolly breeze over my leaving him, tho. I can't see wherein I have acted dishonorably. I rely on your assistance in setting me right before my Cleveland friends, provided Dodge (as he may) tries to make them think I acted dishonorably toward him. But the folly—the madness, of continuing with him grew every day more and more apparent, and I determined to cut loose at all hazards. If he is wise he will be satisfied with the explanation I gave him. All this is, of course, strictly confidential, between you and me.

"I have had a nice time during my trip. Have made many valuable friends, seen a new and splendid country, and picked up withal numerous good things. My last letter in *Vanity* ('Seeing Forrest') was rather flat, but I think my next one will be fair. It should appear next week.

"How are things in Cleveland? What's the news generally? Love to Less—be sure and write me at Pittsburgh on receipt of this."

At Pittsburgh he fell in with Sanford's minstrels and, putting on burnt cork and thumbing a stringless banjo, he sat in the horseshoe and chaffed the end-men, to the delight of the audience, then headed for New York, *via* Philadelphia. His further adventures are described in a letter written to Wilson from New York on January 2, 1861:

"I got your letter and those you forwarded at Pittsburgh. From Pittsburgh I went to Philadelphia, where I met Dixey of Sanford's troupe, who made me stay two days with him at his house. He lives in elegant style, has a nice wife and little girl, and altogether I never spent a happier two days. All the railroad fare I had to pay between Chicago and New York was seventy-five cents from Brunswick, N. J. The conductor to that point 'deadheaded' me at the special request of S. S. Sanford, 'delineator of negro character.' So you see it is a good thing sometimes to have friends among 'nigger singers.' In addition to this good luck I must mention that Ed. Bacon, formerly C. & P. R. R. and now general ticket-agt. at Pittsburgh, gave me a diamond ring worth sixty dollars when I parted with him. Well, here I am at last. I arrived at four o'clock Tuesday morning and went to bed. Got up at one and went up-town. Couldn't see anybody and felt blue. Went to bed early. Got up this morning and went to *Vanity Fair* office. Good fellows—glad to see me. Talked ten minutes with them and made a permanent engagement at twenty dollars a week as one of the editors of the paper. Mr. Leland is editor-in-chief. First-rate fellow, I judge. I am to be there promptly at ten o'ck A.M. and go away at half past three. I am to read all the exchanges and cut out everything of which anything can be made. Am to write what I want to and 'Wards' when I feel like it. As you will see, this will consume only a small portion of my time, and I can doubtless make ten dollars or so a week extra writing for other papers. At least, I am told I can. I shall board where I now am (the Western Hotel) for the present—seven dollars a week with good room. I think I can live cheaper than this when I learn the ropes, but the landlord is a particular friend of mine and will treat me princely. I am already on the free-list at the minstrels and circus. Shall 'fetch' the theaters directly. . . . I have thus told you all about myself. I am certainly a lucky cuss. I don't under-stand it myself, but it is so. Things are new to me here now, and I shall proceed cautiously. But as soon as I get started I will make things whizz, so to speak. I intend to know everybody on Broadway in about six months. I shall withhold my book for the present, until the d—d panic subsides. Have you heard from Dodge yet? Is he 'howling' anywhere yet? I shall write him a long, explanatory letter to-morrow.

"I am speaking of myself principally in this letter, I see, but I know you feel an interest in my movements and I feel so elated over my prosperity that I can't restrain a little self-satisfaction. Give my love to Lester. Tell him he's a splen' feller from a legal point of view. I have heard of him in foreign lands. Won't you have this notice published in the *Plain Dealer?*

"'CHARLES F. BROWN.—This gentleman, widely known as the former local editor of this paper, has at last reached New York and joined the editorial staff of *Vanity Fair!*'

"As I don't like to make the request myself, I will feel obliged if you will copy the above and hand it in."

The notice appeared in the *Plain Dealer*, and Cleveland was for the first time apprised of his whereabouts. He could have joined the rosy fortunes of the New York *Ledger* had he wished. Robert Bonner, its prosperous proprietor, offered him what was then a handsome sum for a weekly letter from the showman. He very wisely declined. "I needed the money badly," he said afterward, "and the offer was tempting, but I wasn't fool enough to accept it. To try to grind out an Artemus Ward column each week would have resulted in the dreariest drivel and would have ruined forever what little reputation I had made."

In truth, he was not constituted to produce humor as a trade. With him it was spontaneous, effervescing, bubbling without effort, seeming often to repress more than was allowed to escape. There was, too, perhaps, a desire to stand alone and not compete with the vivid romance in the *Ledger*. For one thing, he may have had a lurking spite against Sylvanus Cobb, Jr., the *Ledger's* chief contributor. Cobb's father was a native of Norway, Maine, and the great Sylvanus made the town his home for the decade in which both he and Artemus were rising stars. That he had some feeling in his mind—perhaps the relic of a boyhood snub—is shown in the showman's frequent references to Cobb, in one of which, when under the undue excitement roused by an overload of New England rum, he knocked a small boy down, picked his pocket of a New York *Ledger*, and "wildly commenced reading Sylvanus Cobb's last Tail."

Vanity Fair had been established December 31, 1859, by Frank J. Thompson, as a comic weekly, with Louis H. Stephens as publisher, something on the lines of the London *Punch*, which it resembled in form and make-up. William A. Stephens was editor; Henry L. Stephens, art editor. New York of the day possessed a sort of literary Bohemia, where bright souls burned themselves out as fast as the strength of their constitutions would permit. A lively group of these centered in the office of *Vanity Fair*, to which they contributed everything but prosperity. Seeking to evade frowning disaster, Mr. Stephens engaged Charles Godfrey Leland, then a latent "Hans Breit-mann," whose fame had not come forth, but who had been in charge of P. T. Barnum's ill-fated *Illustrated News*, and had earned a status as an editor on the *Philadelphia Bulletin*. He took firm charge of *Vanity Fair*, to the disgust of Bohemia. This is Mr. Leland's own version of Artemus Ward's coming, taken from his autobiography:

"*Und noch weiter*. There was published in New York at that time (1860) an illustrated comic weekly called *Vanity Fair*. There was also in the city a kind of irregular club known as the Bohemians, who had been inspired by Murger's novel of that name to imitate the life of its heroes. They met every evening at a lager-beer restaurant kept by a German named Pfaff. For a year or two they made a great sensation in New York. Their two principal men were Henry Clapp and Fitz-James O'Brien. Then there were Frank Wood and George Arnold, W. Winter, C. Gardette, and others. Wood edited *Vanity Fair*, and all the rest contributed to it. There was some difficulty or other between Wood and Mr. Stephens, the *gérant* of the weekly, and Wood left, followed by all the clan.

I was called in in the emergency, and what with writing myself, and the aid of R. H. Stoddard, T. B. Aldrich, and a few more, we made a very creditable appearance indeed. Little by little the Bohemians all came back, and all went well.

"Now I must here specify, for good reasons, that I held myself very strictly aloof from the Bohemians, save in business affairs. This was partly because I was married, and I never saw the day in my life when to be regarded as a real Bohemian vagabond, or shiftless person, would not have given me the horrors. I would have infinitely preferred the poorest settled employment to such life. I mention this because a very brilliant and singular article entitled 'Charles G. Leland l'ennemi des Allemands' (this title angered me), which appeared in the *Revue des Deux Mondes* in 1871, speaks of me by implication as a frequenter of Pfaff's, declaring that I there introduced Artemus Ward to the Bohemian brotherhood, and that it was entirely due to me that Mr. Browne was brought out before the American world. This is quite incorrect. Mr. Browne had made a name by two or three very popular sketches before I had ever seen him. But it is very true that I aided him to write, and suggested and encouraged the series of sketches which made him famous, as he himself frankly and generously declared, for Charles Browne was at heart an honest gentleman, if there ever was one; which is the one thing in life better than success.

"Mr. Stephens, realizing that I needed an assistant, and observing that Browne's two sketches of the Showman's letter and the Mormons had made him well known, invited him to take a place in our office. He was a shrewd, naïf, but at the same time modest and unassuming young man. He was a native of Maine, but familiar with the West. Quiet as he seemed, in three weeks he had found out everything in New York. I could illustrate this by a very extraordinary fact, but I have not space for everything. I proposed to him to continue his sketches. 'Write,' I said, 'a paper on the Shakers.' He replied that he knew nothing about them. I had been at Lenox, Massachusetts, where I had often gone to New Lebanon, and seen their strange worship and dances, and while on the *Illustrated News* had had a conference with their elders on an article on the Shakers. So I told him what I knew, and he wrote it, making it a condition that I would correct it. He wrote the sketch, and others. He was very slow at composition, which seemed strange to me, who was accustomed to write everything as I now do, *currente calamo* (having written all these memoirs, so far, within a month—more or less, and certainly very little more). From this came his book.

"When he wrote the article describing his imprisonment, there was in it a sentence, 'Jailor, I shall die unless you bring me something to eat!' In the proof we found, 'I shall die unless you bring something to talk.' He was just going to correct this, when I cried, 'For Heaven's sake, Browne, let that stand. It's best as it is!' He did so, and so the reader may find it in his work."

There is an after-memory of Artemus in Leland's Ballads, where, in a rhymed account of a printing-

office dispute over the meaning of Breitmann's verse,
only one voice was lifted in its favor, that of the proof-
reader, who asserted his view thus:

> Den a proof-sheet veller respondered,
> For he dink de dings vos hard,
> "Dat is shoost like de goot oldt lady
> Ash vent to hear Artemus Ward

> "Und say it vas shame de beople
> Vas laugh demselfs most tead
> At de boor young veller lecturin'
> Vhen he tidn't know vot he said."

The office of *Vanity Fair* was located at 100 Nassau
Street. Subsequently it removed to No. 116 on the
same thoroughfare, where it finished its career. The
new editor's duties were considerable. He handled
"copy," furnished head-lines—very good ones—wrote
odd jokes, improved others, and searched the exchanges
for points. The paper usually consisted of twelve
two-column quarto pages, twelve by sixteen inches.
The make-up and typography were neat and the illustrations, mainly by Henry L. Stephens and Edward F.
Mullen, of the very best grade of comic art. These
were carefully engraved on wood by Bobbett and
Hooper, famous workers in their line. The policy
of the paper, at this distance, seems to have been
most sane and orderly. During the period of secession
and before the outbreak of hostilities it reprehended
the extremists on both sides. Where it failed was in
its refusal to accept slavery as an issue and in its
appeal to good humor and common sense in seeking
to ward off the crisis. *Vanity Fair* wanted to save the

country by getting rid of the fire-eating Southern politician and side-tracking the negro—an impossible solution, as the event proved.

In a second letter to Wilson, dated January 9th, the adventurer grows exultant over the rapidity with which things were coming his way:

"The letter I sent you several days since doubtless reached you and I hope to get an answer shortly. I now write to ask you to hunt up, cut out, and send me my burlesque description of the play of 'John Brown,' which was brought out about a year since, I think at the Cleveland Theater. Send also in same letter the check Stephens sent to you. I want to bank an even hundred here as a reserve fund, and find I am short that amount (ten dollars).

"My book will positively appear in the spring, published by Derby & Jackson, 498 Broadway, and unquestionably the best house in the city. They sent their agent to me almost as soon as I reached the city, and to-day I had an interview with Mr. Derby. I have not closed with him, but he speaks in the most encouraging manner of the enterprise, and they all tell me he will make me a good offer. From his anxiety to publish for me I am confident he regards the success of the book a sure thing. I showed him Hoyt's illustrations and he said they were capital— better far than those in *Vanity Fair*. Tell Hoyt this. It was a very high compliment, as Derby is confessedly at the head of the book business here.

"I am all right. Get along just as easy as rolling off a log. I dare not tell you all the fine things that have happened to me, for fear you may think I blow, but I certainly start out here under brilliant auspices. Instead of asking favors, they are offered to me. Hence a situation was offered me by *Vanity Fair* and Derby made extra efforts to get me to promise my book to him. This is pleasant.

"By the way, *Vanity Fair* is set up by girls, and the printing-office is next to the editorial-office. They are devilish fine girls, and I took two of them to Bryant's last night, but I am a man of strict honor. Write soon."

Bryant's was the famous home of black-faced minstrelsy, then at 472 Broadway. Even at this distance one is inclined to envy the girls their evening's outing. A postscript appended to this letter acknowledges the receipt of one from Wilson and gives a little glimpse of the friction with Gray, as it says: "It is utterly unaccountable to me why Gray should have any ill-feeling toward me. But let it slide. . . . Since writing the above I've seen Derby again. He wants to see the 'Three Tigers of the Cleveland Press.' Will you also hunt that up and send it? I am a heap of trouble, I know, but can't help it. Will do as much for you if ever I can.

Artemus fitted instantly into the new surroundings. The atmosphere and the habits of the city pleased him. There was plenty of good company from the stage, the press, and the pavement. Writing to Wilson, on January 22d, he once more voices his satisfaction:

"I'll send for my trunks soon. Let that slide. I am now rooming with the publisher of *V. F.* at No. 28 East Twenty-eighth Street. We have a parlor, bath-room, closets, fire, gas, and breakfast sent to room for

7

four dollars a week each. Our dinners we get down-town, a shilling getting a beefsteak pie or a piece of baked beef. . . . I mention these things so that if you come on here by and by you will come to the office and go home with me. I can keep you like a fighting-cock for a few shillings a day. Such beef as we get at Crook & Duff's you never saw since God made you. Tell Less I got his papers and will write him soon. He is your nephew and an ornament to his sex. I see people from the West occasionally. They come up to the office in large numbers sometimes, much to my gratification. I am glad Alphonsus is exerting him-self. A man ought to for six dollars a week.

"I shall go to Fall River Saturday by boat. The factory-owners will probably turn out and receive me with the band. Give my love to J. B. Altho' an English wretch, he is one of the best men I ever knew, and I hope he will live to expectorate on the tombs of all his enemies, if he has any.

"Ever of thee,   A. WARD."

"J. B." was James Brokenshire, one of the *Plain Dealer* staff with whom he had dwelt in happiness during his term with the paper. "Less" was John B. Lester, brother-in-law of Senator John P. Jones, of Nevada. The trip to Fall River was taken to meet his brother Cyrus, then holding an editorial position in that city.

February 2d, he wrote again to Wilson, quite cheerily:

"Your last came duly to hand. I haven't seen Brown yet—called once, but he wasn't in. Shall see him sure.

"Tell Jule I have 'gone back on' suppers, the vigorous meals I absorb at 3 P.M. daily being entirely adequate for my sustenance. I 'reach for the bread' just as I did in the palmy days of Wilson's tavern, and pour out my own tea—scalded a waiter the other night pretty bad, but he excused me.

"I go East first of March to see Caroline. Going or coming I shall visit Willimantic. Shall go to 'Moosup' likewise, as I must see 'Orry' and Jenny.

"Caroline is getting reconciled to my change of location. Her late letters are quite cheerful.

"Now I blush as I write it—I feel that I am coming it altogether too strong on you—but do hunt up my 'Three Tigers of the Cleveland Press' and send it in a letter. The piece was not in the bundle Less sent. The piece is valuable to me. In short, without the piece I shall be unhappy, and prithee send her on. Set some of the boys in the mailing department to work hunting it up, and my children's children shall lisp your name with heartfelt affection. Bully boy! As I was quietly taking some coffee and cakes with Henry Ward Beecher at Smith's in Chatham Street, the other night, after the Bowery was out, he accidentally alluded to you. 'Wilson,' says he, 'is a young man of much promise. He is a good bookkeepist and his balance-sheets are always correct. I like Wilson.' He also spoke of Less, but I am sorry to say he was not very complimentary. 'Lester,' says Mr. Beecher, 'will come to the gallows in about two years if he keeps on.' 'What do you think of Brokenshire, Henry?' says I. 'A good man, sir,' said Mr. Beecher—'a very good man indeed, tho' he's a d—d Englishman.' On getting up, Mr. Beecher insisted on allowing me to pay for the coffee and cakes—twelve cents.

"I anticipate considerable fun in my forthcoming trip to the East, tho' my stay will necessarily be short.

"By the way, love to the ever-blooming Briggs. Shall write him soon. Did he get the sixteen million dollars and box of jewels I sent him the other day?

"Send the 'Tigers.' I shall soon cease troubling you, I hope. And now farewell. A fond embrace. A few natural tears, and some wild groans! There, there, it's over now. Adoo! Adoo!"

"Caroline" was his mother. "Jenny" was Mr. Wilson's sister, and "Orry," Doctor Briggs, her husband.

Meanwhile, things were not going well with *Vanity Fair*. Leland, who was a strong abolitionist, saw in the rapid secession of the states need of harsh dealing with the "erring sisters," and wished to make the paper radical in its insistence on stern measures. Thompson and Stephens, both Democrats, loyal and faithful to the Union, were still hopeful that some way out would be found. Leland's feelings came to a head on the firing on Fort Sumter. He resigned and, going to Boston, started the *Continental Magazine* with the aid of an "angel" and was radical to his heart's content—often too much so for the Lincoln administration, which he tried to drive rather than serve. As the result, Artemus was given his place on *Vanity Fair*. He notes the promotion in a letter to Wilson, written May 16, 1861:

"I must trouble you again. Will you forward my trunk and box at once by U. S. express? If Barney is still identified with that institution perhaps he can 'deadhead' them through for me, if it is convenient for you to see him. At all events, please forward at once. I hate to bother you, but there is no one else upon whom I can call.

"The times are rather severe, but we shall weather the gale. My publishers are holding the 'Ward' book back in the hope of better times. It would be folly to issue it now. I am now the managing Ed. of *Vanity Fair* and my duties have materially increased. Contrary to my expectation and hope, I shall be unable to visit the West this season. New York is severe on a man's feelings in summer-time, but I think of taking board in Rahway, N. J., for the summer. It is twenty miles distant, a delightful village, and abounds in female society of first-class moral character, the refining influence of which I have already felt. I am popular in Jersey. They like me for my winning ways.

"I am making influential friends fast. I have altered my views of some things and have courted the friendship of men whose friendship is worth having. I have eschewed fast society and was never so steady in my life. Indeed, I am compelled to be. Promptness and faithfulness in business here are implicitly demanded. It is the greatest mistake in the world to suppose that a man can raise the d—l in New York and still occupy a responsible business position. I have not made anything stunningly gorgeous in the way of money, but I believe my prospects are good. I should be rejoiced to see you here, and to pay you back a few of the many kindnesses you have shown me in 'the happy days agone.'

"I am more and more convinced that I acted wisely in leaving Cleveland. I had accomplished all I could there. It is a wild, mad jumble here, but those who take care of themselves usually come out all right.

"Love to the office generally. I sincerely and very deeply sympathize with Brokenshire in his great misfortune. I never read of any similar accident which affected me so much. I thought of writing him a letter of condolence, but hesitated for fear it might be out of place to do so. I respect him far more than he may have been led to believe by my eccentric bearing towards him. He is a man, and I have often envied him the noble qualities of head and heart with which he is so decidedly gifted. You must sadly miss his sunny presence in the office. I hope he is improving fast— I know he bears it gallantly, hopefully—like a true man as he is. Will you do me the favor to tell him how sincerely I sympathize with him?

"How's J. W.? and the deacon? and Gris? Stow and the rest. I see Bouton occasionally. He speaks in the most flattering manner of Gray.

"Please attend to the request expressed in the beginning of this—write a good long letter."

For the moment he was very busy with his pen, as well as paste-pot and scissors. Besides the intermittent letters of the showman, and the minor jests, he contributed an occasional local sketch, such as "East Side Theatricals," printed March 23, 1861, and a bit of travel experience in "Maine in March," an echo of his visit to his mother anticipated in the Wilson letter of February 9th, found in the issue of April 20th. This told the story of his voyage from Portland to

Boston—in his mind—as because of storm the boat remained at the dock all night. Both were signed "Alphonso the Brave" for no particular reason that now appears. By their flippant tone, yet never failing to make a point, it would also seem that he wrote some of the short book reviews that appeared with more or less regularity in the paper. For example:

"*The Life of Major John André*, Adjutant of the British army in America. By Winthrop Sargent. It is as the well-known author of a comic ballad entitled 'The Cow Chase' that Major André achieved a brilliant reputation, and eventually secured himself this first-rate notice in *Vanity Fair*. We are sorry to learn he got into some trouble about something somewhere in the road up towards the old Dutch church at Tarrytown, which caused him to be hung, but are still glad that he became so distinguished as to merit the compliment of a biography from so excellent and elegant a writer as Winthrop Sargent—a gentleman who was, we understand, Governor of Massachusetts. Go thou and do likewise."

He occasionally answered correspondents in the old *Plain Dealer* style, toned down and refined. Here is a group of samples:

"Equus.—Our paper is not a sporting journal, and for any information about the pedigree of the Mare Imbrium you might as well ask the Man in the Moon."

"A. P. A.—The slang you speak of, 'Get him where the hair is short,' is of very ancient origin, and is profanely supposed to have been the exclamation of one Delilah, as she waved her shears in triumph after clipping off the last lock of Samson's hair. It has been a byword among the Philistines ever since."

"BUTCHER BOY.—Isn't it always a poor rule that won't work both ways? By no means. For instance: a dollar's worth of beef can always be had for four quarters, but it does not follow that four quarters of beef can always be had for a dollar."

"L. S.—*Quid Washingtonæ facium? Mentiri nescid* is a Latin quotation slightly varied from Juvenal and was the noble reply of Bennett (of the N. Y. *Herald*) to his friends, when advised to go to Washington on the Fourth of March and make his peace with 'Old Abe.' The translation is: 'What shall I do at Washington? I cannot lie!'"

May 24, 1861, he wrote Wilson, saying.

"I suppose Less is with you yet, or is he in the post-office? He seems to have forgotten me. Tell him to either write or go to the devil. Much obliged for my trunk. If the expressage cost anything send bill or dig till I see you. I have authorized you to draw on me for any favors I can do you here. Will tear my shirt for you if necessary. New York is beginning to scorch me. They say it is blazing hot here in the summer, so as I said I shall hie me away to Jersey, to Jersey, ere long, amid the flowers, lambkins, and the pretty little birds. Well, I will, hoss. Is it a fact that Hoyt, the sculptist, has gone to the wars? I don't know how it is, but something within tells me, in a still, small voice, that I am better adapted for the Home Guard than anything else."

The summer developed hard times for *Vanity Fair*. The war absorbed popular attention. A comic paper to succeed must belong to the opposition. Adulation and political supporting have no place in its vital system. In such a time opposition could not thrive. Artemus enjoyed the editorship, but had no heart for details, and least of all for financiering, which the sheet sadly needed. A little glimpse of the situation is afforded by William Dean Howells, who, pausing in New York en route to his consulate in Venice, in 1861, failed to collect for some verses he had sold to the paper. "I sailed without the money," he records, "but I hardly expected that, for the editor, who was then Artemus Ward, had frankly told me in taking my address that ducats were few at that moment with *Vanity Fair*."

Artemus himself labored at high pressure on routine work and, in addition, let his fancy range in the concoction of burlesque romances, making fun of the high-flown French style then being aped by popular New York story papers. Several of these are to be found in his works, along with others which were not published until they appeared in book form. These efforts were echoes of the distant days of *The Carpet Bag*, in whose columns numbers of such parodies made frequent appearance and were the undoubted source of his inspiration. Two of the *Vanity Fair* "romances" were never reproduced from its columns, "The Fair Inez; or, The Lone Lady of the Crimson Cliffs, A Tale of the Sea," which began July 27, 1861, and ran through five numbers, and "Woshy-Boshy; or, The Prestidigitating Squaw of the Snakeheads," started on November 2d, following. In the first "romance" he took liberties with the names of some of his Cleveland friends, including C. W. Coe and Doctor Briggs, besides putting Wilson and Jack Ryder in as members of a pirate crew. In the last chapter, after the manner of writers of romance, he "accounts" for the future of his heroes: Dr. Briggs [his friend Wilson's brother-in-law] is a dentist in Moosup, Ct., and is a fine operator upon human gums. Mr. Coe unintentionally dislocated his neck a few years since, by falling from a scaffold in Illinois, a rope being twined about his neck at the time. There was a large crowd present, including the sheriff of the county. Charlie Wilson is publishing a daily in Waterford, Maine, having more subscribers than he knows what to do with. Old Jack Ryder renounced the sea and accepted a professorship in Oberlin College. He also conducts a concert-hall in that place, refreshments being handed around by beautiful Moorish maidens.

Edward F. Mullen, Frank Wood, and Charles Dawson Shanly, of the *Vanity Fair* staff, were used as incidental characters in "Woshy-Boshy."

After midsummer the employment grew irksome and the prospects for the paper were discouraging. Artemus, unused to confinement, pined for more outdoor life. He slipped away for a journey that took him as far as Louisville, appeasing *Vanity Fair* with a single contribution, but an especially good one, in the "Interview" with Prince Jerome Napoleon. During the excursion he paused at Cincinnati, where he picked up an acquaintance destined to be of much use to him in his growing career, Dr. E. P. Hingston, who was in time to become his skilful agent and manager. Hingston, riding in a train that was stumbling across

Indiana and Ohio toward Porkopolis, commenting on
the slowness of the locomotive to a fellow-traveler,
received the response that this was "Artemus Ward's
road"—the one to whose superintendent he applied for
a pass in the guise of an editor and was refused this
wise:

"'You a editor?' he axed evijently on the pint of
snickerin.

"'Yes, sir,' sez I, 'don't I look poor enuff?'

"'Just about,' sez he, 'but our road can't pass you.'

"'Can't, hey?'

"'No, sir—it can't.'

"'Becauz,' sez I, lookin him full in the face with a
Eagle eye, 'it goes so darned slow it can't pass anybody!'

"Methinks I had him then. It's the slowest Rale
Road in the West. With a mortifiled air, he told me
to git out of his office. I pitted him and went."

After reciting the tale the traveler, who knew
Artemus Ward, advised Hingston, whose latent interest
had been aroused, that he was to be in Cincinnati that
evening and offered to introduce him, a promise
that was kept at the Burnett House. The rather
literal Englishman had expected to find a burly ex-
hibitor of snakes and waxworks, and was duly astonished to meet a gentleman. Here is his account of the
meeting:

"I expected to see an elderly man with a shrewd face
and 'busy wrinkles round his eyes,' like those of Tenny-
son's miller; a man of cunning look and rough exterior,
who had mingled much with the world, and who, by
travel and long experience of the rough-and-tumble

life of a showman, had qualified himself to be the Mentor to so inexperienced a Telemachus as myself. No trace of my ideal presented itself in the gentleman to whom I was introduced. He was apparently not more than twenty-five years old, slender in build, frank, open, and pleasant in demeanor, with ruddy cheeks, bright eyes, and a voice soft, gentle, and musical. Instead of an old showman I saw a young man who, judging from his appearance, might have just left college. Instead of the sort of person usually found traveling with a waxwork exhibition, I met a gentleman who might have passed for a youthful member of one of the learned professions. Feeling some doubts about my having been introduced to the right man, and half suspecting that I was being made the victim of a hoax, I asked, hesitatingly, if the gentleman was really Mr. Artemus Ward.

"'This is my friend Mr. Charles Browne, who pleases to call himself Artemus Ward,' replied my introducer. 'I'll vouch for him, but not for his show. As for his kangaroo, I don't go anything on him.'

"Very little time elapsed before we were on terms of chatty acquaintance. Presently Artemus Ward interrupted the conversation to inquire whether or not I was an Englishman. I replied that I was, when he again offered to shake hands, and said, half in earnest and half in jest:

"'I like Englishmen; this is the hotel your Prince of Wales stopped at when he came through here last summer. By the by, how is the prince? Give my compliments to him when you see him. Suppose we go down and hoist to him.'

"'To hoist,' or to give the pronunciation more closely, 'to hyst,' is, in American parlance, to indulge in a drink. The bar of the Burnett House is downstairs. Thither we adjourned, and after duly toasting the health of his Royal Highness in some very excellent Bourbon, the genial 'showman,' addressing me, said:

"'My friend and I are going round to see the shows in Cincinnati to-night, and we mean to visit the Infernal Regions. Will you join us?'

"'Willingly,' I replied; 'but pray what are the Infernal Regions?'

"'Don't be frightened. Come and see.'

"Thus it was that I first met Artemus Ward."

Before visiting the Infernal Regions the pair saw Tobin's "Honeymoon" at Pike's Opera House—"every brick of which was whisky and all the mortar pork." The play was poorly performed, the Duke of Aranza being worse than usual. The wretched acting, so bad as to be almost burlesque, kept Artemus rocking with pent-up mirth. At the drop of the last curtain he gravely said to Hingston:

"I am going over to your country some day, and I shall want you to introduce me to Mr. Tobin."

The amazed doctor replied that Tobin had been dead for fifty years.

"I am sorry, indeed I am sorry," said Artemus, sadly. "I wanted to see Tobin very much. Mr. Tobin has done me a great deal of good in time; Mr. Tobin has been very kind to me. Whenever I have wanted to see any bad acting I have always found it when the 'Honeymoon' was on the bills; whenever I've had to report an amateur performance or take a young lady to the play, I have been sure to see the 'Honeymoon.' Much honeymoon is on my brain. It oppresses my heart, and I have hoped one day to be able to go to England just to call on Mr. Tobin to say how grateful I am—and to kick him!"

The night was long. The party went, after the "Honeymoon," to Wood's Theater in Vine Street, in search of more diversion, which, not appearing, they journeyed by way of the National Theater to the promised Infernal Regions, a gruesome housing of waxworks, worked in pantomime. The animated figures, with the clanging accompaniment of horrific noises, thrilled Artemus with delight.

"They feel at home in their parts," he said of the figures and their manipulators. "It's the best show in Cincinnati."

The next day was Sunday, and, starting down Race Street, Hingston met Artemus in front of the Unitarian chapel. At the suggestion of another chance acquaintance they went in. Moncure D. Conway was preaching a sermon denouncing Lincoln for not taking a more aggressive attitude toward slavery, supporting Gen. John C. Fremont's policy in Missouri, which the country at large was not then prepared to indorse—though finally coming to the Pathfinder's radical view. Artemus did not like the sermon and came away shaking his head in excited dissent. Conway did not, of course, know he was in the audience. Six years later they were to meet again, and it befell that to Conway came the duty of laying his body in the earth.

Ward and Hingston took a run down the Ohio River

to Louisville on the *Major Anderson*, a mail-boat named after the defender of Fort Sumter. It was a joyous trip, punctuated with many cocktails and smoothed with the flow of choice Catawba from Nicholas Longworth's cellars at Cincinnati. Hingston was advance agent for some entertainment—he does not tell us what—and Artemus attended him while he went about distributing advertising matter and adjusting details, reveling all the time in talk of the showman's trade.

"I understand that you are used to managing shows. Suppose some day you manage me," he observed.

Hingston was puzzled to know what there would be to manage.

"A moral lecturer," replied Artemus, with much gravity. "There's nothing else to be made of me but that, and you must take me to England and Australia."

They parted, Hingston continuing with his attraction and Artemus returning to New York by way of Cleveland, Buffalo, Rochester, and Corning. The Rochester *Union* noted his passage, though he did not pause, having "wasted a day at Buffalo looking at the county fair." He spent four days in Corning visiting some unnamed friend, and reached New York to write Wilson on September 26th, evidently having a debt to the latter in mind:

"In a very short time, say four weeks, I will square your account. But if you must have it before then say so, and I will dig it up for you or perish in the attempt. So much for that. I feel first rate. My trip did me good. New York is lively enough for practical purposes, the many rumors to the contrary notwithstanding. In regard to my orders on the Mercantile and Westchester, I haven't seen the latter yet, but I called on the former. He was angry and said the work had done him more harm than good. Among other remarks he said:

"'Damn the papers, all of 'em!'

"I said 'certainly,' but invited his attention to the fact that his signature was attached to the document in a regular business way, and that I couldn't well perceive how he could repudiate. He said I might come and board it out, but, as his face was flushed with anger, I don't think I shall. I am afraid he will make it too lively for me. . . . If ever I start on another pleasure tour without plenty of money, I hope some one will kill me."

Meanwhile, the idea of giving a "show" grew stronger in the humorist's mind. He saw no future for the paper or himself if he stuck to it, and began the preparation of a "piece." He was cheered in pursuing his purpose by the Bohemian congregation to which Mr. Leland has referred. Henry Clapp, Jr., around whom the wits and writers gathered, was a native of Nantucket, where he was born November 11, 1814, and had been for some years a figure in the fugitive-literature-making of New York. He had established the *Saturday Press* in 1858 as a literary journal, with a pungent editorial side that took many liberties with the city and its denizens. He was for a time secretary to Albert Brisbane, the disciple of Fourier, advocate of a socialistic state, father of the Arthur Brisbane of our day, a son of his elder years. The meeting-place of Clapp's followers was in a café kept by Charles Pfaff in

NO. 647 BROADWAY, NEW YORK

(Where Pfaff's "Bohemia" was located)

the basement of 647 Broadway, on the west side, near Bleecker Street. Fifteen years later, in the middle 'seventies, 647 became a loafing-place of my own, as a small boy, fascinated with books, for here James Miller, the publisher, then had a fine book-store, of which I had the run and where I spent many days of delight. Pfaff's was, of course, gone. Mr. Miller used the basement for storage and packing. Occasionally I descended to its depths, but, alas, I did not know this had been Bohemia! I mention it only as another co-incidence in my circling about Artemus Ward.

The group which welcomed him included Thomas Bailey Aldrich, brought there by his friend William Winter, so long the dramatic critic of the New York *Tribune;* Fitz-Hugh Ludlow, the "Hasheesh Eater"; Charles Dawson Shanly; Edward G. P. Wilkins, dramatic critic of the *Herald;* Frank Wood, who had preceded Leland as editor of *Vanity Fair;* Charles D. Gardette, author of "The Fire Fiend"; N. G. Shepard, a long-since-forgotten poet; Fitz-James O'Brien, the gifted author of "The Diamond Lens" and "The Wondersmith," two tales that thrilled the readers of the *Atlantic Monthly* in the early 'sixties; Henry Neil, a working newspaper man; George Arnold, wit and poet, and Walt Whitman, with five years of "Leaves of Grass" behind him, posing much in flannel shirt and sombrero, roughly unpleasant, and plainly on exhibition, before his services as a war nurse and a stroke of paralysis had softened him into the good gray Poet. "We were all very merry at Pfaff's," wrote Aldrich in his poem "At the Café," printed in the first number of *Vanity Fair.* This rude Bohemia, its bar damp with

8

beer suds, sawdust floor, and bare tables, had also a queen, "Ada Clare," the name chosen by Jane McElheney to grace some slight poetical and literary efforts in the *Saturday Press* and other publications. Poor girl! It was her fate to die in terrible agony from the bite of a mad dog. She was seized with the hydrophobia while on a train returning from a visit to Ohio

FITZ-JAMES O'BRIEN (IN UNIFORM)
(From a *Vanity Fair* "comic" by Mullen)

in 1872, and suffered incredible torture. O'Brien was the greatest genius and strangest personality of them all. At times he was without a permanent place of abode, but, being equipped with a bunch of pass-keys to the lodgings of his fellow-Bohemians, slept in the bed that was most convenient at the time he felt the need of slumber, occasionally to the surprise of the friend who came in late and found his single couch occupied. He volunteered with the Seventh Regiment when the war broke out, and by the chance of a delay in the mail secured a place on the staff of Brig.-Gen. Frederick W. Lander, for which his fellow, but more orderly, Bohemian, Thomas Bailey Aldrich, had been selected. He was mortally wounded at Cumberland, Virginia, February 16, 1862, and died April 6th. Henry Clapp, who disliked both Aldrich and O'Brien, remarked on the first news that "O'Brien had been wounded in Aldrich's shoulder."

Artists of growing fame were often added to the company: Launt Thompson, George H. Boughton, Wilson Fisk, Edward F. Mullen, Frank Bellew, and Sol Eytinge, Jr. To such associates Artemus Ward came as one to the manner born. The evenings were gay with converse and many libations of Pfaff's brew. To W. D. Howells, pausing gingerly for a moment at the door, it seemed a cheap and vulgar Bohemia, quite unworthy of his interest. But it was not that. Clapp had talent and insight. The members were men of genius, kinsmen in the world of light, who came here to meet their brothers. That it became a bit of an exhibition-place was only natural—this is the fate of all Bohemias, from Murger's Latin Quarter to Marie's in McDougal Street. The world will not let Bohemia alone, and it smothers in a crowd.

To this Bohemia it was that the adventurer turned for encouragement on the lecture idea and found it. The ever-hopeful wits and chance-workers saw always something better beyond. The fortunes of the paper were obviously low and the platform held out rainbow

promises. There was a craving for oratory and monologue. Henry Ward Beecher and Edwin Hubbell
Chapin from the pulpit; Wendell Phillips, Anna Dick-
inson, and John B. Gough from the oratorical side,
with scores of lesser lights, were appearing on the
scene. To join he needed only a manager, some dates,
circulars, and a dress-coat. The last two were easily
had, the former not so facile.

Artemus fussed around, stringing together old jokes
from the *Plain Dealer's* local column, stories picked
up about town, on the road, and in Bohemia, and new
thoughts, conjured up with a subject on his mind.
At first he considered taking "My Seven Grand-
mothers" as a topic, but it did not fit the jumble of
jests. The title finally picked for the talk was taken
from that of a long and lugubrious ballad reciting the
woes of those unfortunate youngsters, "The Children
in the Wood," printed in *The Carpet Bag*, September
13, 1851, about the time of his arrival in Snow & Wilder's office, and which, very likely, he put into type
himself. It began:

> Now ponder well, you parents dear,
> The words which I shall write;
> A doleful story you shall hear,
> In time brought forth to light.

The lecture finally became "Babes in the Wood,"
but the début was as "Children." It was no casual
attempt he had in view, as some of his contemporaries
have written, but a real campaign had been planned
and dates made for several months ahead. They are
all listed in a note-book of the period. The first try-out

was at New London, Connecticut, on the evening of November 26, 1861. Frank Wood, his associate on *Vanity Fair*, kept him company during the ordeal. The "Children in the Wood" were duly advertised, and they were exhibited in Lawrence Hall. William Stuart, the Shakespearian critic, who was a resident of Ocean Beach, near New London, was a friend and may have encouraged his coming. The New London *Star* of the next day proclaimed "a decided success, full of funny and brilliant things, entirely characteristic. He kept the audience in a continual titter. . . . Wherever Artemus lectures the auditors may expect an unusually rich treat, and those who did not attend made a mistake."

After the lecture came the first of the long and exhausting aftermaths. Artemus was escorted to the rooms of the Nameaug Engine Company, in the City Hall, and entertained. He made an amusing address, for which the firemen showed their appreciation by electing him a member of the company.

The following evening, the 27th, the show moved up the Thames to Norwich. Here it also made an effective appeal. The Norwich *Bulletin* on the 28th said of it:

"Artemus Ward's lecture in Breed Hall last night was rich, rare, and racy. The audience was quite large, but many who would have been glad to be present were kept away by the inclemency of the weather."

Newark, New Jersey, was covered on the evening of Monday, December 2d. The Newark *Daily Advertiser* gave the show this advance mention:

"The well-known humorist 'Artemus Ward' will deliver a characteristic lecture on the 'Children in the

Wood,' at Library Hall, on Monday evening. Artemus, whose real name is Charles F. Browne, is a young man about twenty-five years old and a relative of Vice-President Hamlin. He has displayed an extraordinary degree of talent in one so young. His lectures are highly commended by the press throughout the country."

The material for this notice was furnished by the showman himself and gives what appears to be the first appearance of the added "e" to Brown. Thereafter he was Charles F. Browne, although *His Book*, issued later, does not use the "e." It was already in Carleton's hands and he was too busy or too careless to fix the trimming. That he was practising the new signature is to be inferred from a sample autograph written in his note-book on a page close to the list of the early dates, thus:

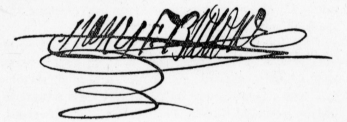

The relationship to Hannibal Hamlin was pretty remote, his father being a very distant cousin of that eminent gentleman. The Newark appearance would appear to have been successful. The New York *World* of the Wednesday following contained a press notice of the lecture, evidently encouraged by the lecturer, saying:

"Mr. Charles F. Browne, 'Artemus Ward,' delivered his humorous lecture, 'Children in the Wood,' in Newark on Monday evening last. The audience, we learn, became highly enthusiastic over Artemus's droll stories, so much so that he was obliged to stop his lecture and wait for them to recover."

From Newark he went to Salem, Massachusetts, speaking there Wednesday, December 4th. The following night, the 5th, he was in Concord, New Hampshire, and on the evening of the 6th amused Boston for the first time, lecturing to an appreciative audience in Tremont Temple. The Boston *Post* of December 7th gave this mention:

"The widely and greatly admired 'Artemus Ward,' alias Charles F. Browne, gave a lecture last evening at Tremont Temple. The reputation of the lecturer, or, rather, of the writer (editor of *Vanity Fair*), added to a natural curiosity to see one who penned so many funny things, attracted an audience nearly filling the spacious hall.

"Mr. Browne, we will state for the information of our readers, is a young man of some twenty-eight years, with a pleasant, genial face, a keen, humorous eye, and a countenance suggestive of close powers of observation, and a fresh, *live* intellect. Of a nervous, sanguine temperament, he has a type of body which may be classed among the 'thin.' His voice is clear, sweet, and pleasant, and his manner attractive and agreeable. To this imperfect description we may add a neatness of dress, and, altogether, that he is calculated to make a most favorable impression before a public audience."

[103]

The pleasant pathway now opened fast and wide. In Boston he made quick entrance to the inner circle of literary interest, that gathered around Mrs. Anne Adams Fields, wife of James T. Fields, the most distinguished of American publishers. On the morning after the lecture he breakfasted with Mrs. Fields at her home, No. 148 Charles Street, on the edge of Beacon Hill, overlooking the Back Bay, and had the great felicity of then meeting Dr. Oliver Wendell Holmes, who was present, with his son, now the distinguished Justice of the United States Supreme Court. Mrs. Fields's diary gives this glimpse of him:

"*Sunday, December 8, 1861.* Yesterday morning Artemus Ward, Mr. Browne, breakfasted with us: also Dr. Holmes and the Lieutenant, his son. We had a merry time because Jamie [Mr. Fields] was in a grand humor and represented people and incidents in the most incomparable manner. 'Why,' said Dr. Holmes to him afterward, 'you must excuse me that I did not talk, but the truth is there is nothing I enjoy so much as your anecdotes, and whenever I get a chance I can't help listening to them.' The Professor complimented Artemus upon his great success and told him the pleasure he had received. Artemus twinkled all over, but said little after the Professor arrived. He was evidently immensely possessed by him. The young lieutenant has mostly recovered from his wound and speaks as if duty would recall him soon to camp. He will go when the time comes, but home evidently never looked half so pleasant before."

The lecturer's note-book records a date at Portsmouth, New Hampshire, December 7th. Monday, the

9th, he is listed for Trenton, New Jersey; Tuesday, the 10th, for Hornellsville, New York; Monday, the 12th, Brooklyn; and Tuesday, the 13th, Paterson, New Jersey. There is a break until the 18th, when he is down to appear in Williamsburgh, a part of Brooklyn, with a close connection the next day at Lynn, Massachusetts. Manchester, New Hampshire, heard him on the 20th, according to the schedule; Roxbury on the 21st. South Danvers, Massachusetts, was named to be covered on the 22d, but this date is erased, and changed to the 25th. Clinton Hall, in Astor Place, New York, was engaged for the 23d, and the lecture first given to a metropolitan audience on that evening. "Artemus Ward will speak a piece," was the announcement. He liked to treat himself with as little seriousness as possible, and this advertisement was an echo of school-days in Waterford and Norway, when with other scholars he was called upon at the term end, or at the "literary" exercises, to "speak a piece." The night was snowy and but few people turned out. There was a net loss of thirty dollars. "Frank Wood was one babe and I was the other," he said afterward.

On the morning after the Clinton Hall venture, in its issue of December 24th, the New York *Times* printed this notice, which is found pasted in his note-book:

"THE CHILDREN IN THE WOOD

"A lecture, with the above title, was delivered last evening in the Clinton Hall lecture-room by Mr. Charles F. Browne, a gentleman widely known as a humorous writer, under the nom de plume of 'Artemus

Ward.' The night was a most inclement one, and, if the room was not quite filled, the wonder is that so large an audience could have been drawn together, under the circumstances. Naturally and justly, those who are acquainted with 'Artemus Ward, Showman,' through his writings only, pictured him, in fancy, as a burly, middle-aged person in somewhat seedy apparel, and with an address more or less suggestive of the 'side-show' type of character. On the contrary, Mr. Browne is a tall, slim, and gentlemanly-looking young man, rather careful in his dress than otherwise, and gifted with an imperturbable expression of face, which adds very materially to the effect of the droll philosophies that are propounded by him. 'The Children in the Wood' is a title skilfully made use of by the lecturer as a medium for saying a great many spicy and smart things upon the current topics of the day. Every now and then he alludes to the title, as having no immediate reference to something that has just been spun out by him, the effect of which, aided by the droll solemnity with which it is uttered, convulses the audience with laughter. By the gift of nature, Mr. Browne is a comedian. His delivery is provokingly deliberate, and there is a subdued humor visible in every expression of his face. The reading was a decided success, and will be repeated in the same room on the evening of the 2d of January."

He seems to have filled the engagement at South Danvers, Massachusetts, on the 25th. New Haven, Connecticut, and Gloucester, Massachusetts, were favored on the 26th and 27th, respectively. December 30th he lectured in Corning, New York, and on the

31st in Elmira. The lecture was given a second time in New York on the first day of the new year, and from that time on dates follow in thick order. The venture was fully launched. While the success was considerable, the early fees were low. Having no management, he worked through bureaus and with local committees for fixed pay. There are mentions of receipts in the note-book. Burlington, Vermont, paid him fifty dollars; North Adams, Massachusetts, twenty-five dollars, while an evening at Charlestown netted him but fifteen dollars. A return to Burlington gave him twenty-five dollars, which seems to have been the sum most often received, with an occasional drop to fifteen dollars. That even these returns rolled up into respectable sums is seen by a note-book memorandum of three-year Treasury notes, numbered 36994, 36995, 36996, 36998, 36989, 36990, evidently newly acquired. He was rich enough on January 2, 1862, to lend Frank Wood twenty-one dollars. There are frequent jottings of loans in the note-book.

The January engagements were routed across central New York, as far west as Milwaukee, concluding with a glorious return to Cleveland on the last day of the month. The Academy of Music, where he spoke, was packed with friends, who made the evening a gala one. The gawky, ill-dressed Local had become a polished man of the world and master of its ways. He wore a dress-suit with elegance, and, as James F. Ryder said, "looked sweet enough to eat." The *Plain Dealer* of February 1st chronicled the event in these terms:

"ARTEMUS WARD AT THE ACADEMY—Immense Jam—

Children in the Woods—Great Enthusiasm—The Kangaroo Quiet—Everybody Good-humored.—The Academy was crowded to its utmost capacity last evening to hear the great showman's (Mr. Charles F. Browne) account of the 'Babes in the Wood.' We do not recollect ever having seen a larger audience in Cleveland before. At fifteen minutes before eight Mr. Browne appeared in the back part of the stage and after considerable difficulty made his way to the front, amidst enthusiastic cheers. He was presented to the audience by Mr. G. A. Benedict, of the *Herald*. The latter alluded to Mr. Browne's happy faculty for making everybody good-humored, incidentally mentioning the far-famed 'waxwurx' and unmanageable kangaroo, after which he introduced him to the immense audience. The following synopsis of the lecture will hardly convey a correct idea of it, as to be appreciated you must see the speaker; the affected seriousness, pauses here and there to be followed by something immensely ridiculous and comical, all combined to make it irresistible.

"Mr. Browne said as his introduction: 'It is possible that I have not grouped my thoughts in a very attractive manner. I can only plead as an excuse that my ideas of a first-class lecture are in a rather confused and unsettled state. I never attend lectures myself—no, I should think not. I am not at all brilliant—I flatter myself I am too smart for that—but, having a taste for the pathetic, I have chosen the "Children in the Wood."'

"He went on to say that if the 'Children in the Wood' were not his subject, he would have talked of office-seekers, for instance, or crushed literary youths or modern reformers or the peace men of the North, or debt, or the suspension of specie payment. He attributed the flight at Bull Run to a rumor that there were three custom-house vacancies to be filled at Washington. He said that literary young men would not be crushed if they would write something useful, such as 'Thirty Days Hath September.' He ridiculed modern reformers by saying that some were opposed to razors, some to law, and all to work. Some of these reformers say tobacco will kill a dog. Well—let us not give it to our dogs and by that means we can save them. He knew of reformatory societies in the West whose tenets would make a gorilla to shudder or a negro minstrel to blush palpably through a double coating of cork. He spoke of debt as one of the greatest curses. When gorillas are particular about changing their linen —when the omnibus-horses on Broadway look contented and cheerful—when General Phelps, whose proclamation to the raccoons of Ship Island every one has read, is attacked with a rush of brains to the head— then, and not till then, will certain persons stop running in debt. 'In the midst of life we are in debt.' As intimately connected with the 'Babes in the Wood,' the suspension of specie payment was discussed by Mr. Ward. He trusted that banks would not claim originality for the movement, for some of his friends had suspended specie payment several years ago, while others took a broader view and suspended paper payment at the same time.

"In conclusion the lecturer said: 'But I suppose that you want to hear something about the children in the

wood. They were good children, they were unfortunate, and, as far as I have been able to ascertain,
entirely respectable, but I found the subject such a
difficult one to write about that I concluded that I
would not deliver a lecture on the children this evening.
I may do so some time, however, and so, in bidding
you good night, I will take the liberty of saying, "to
be continued."'"

One point the *Plain Dealer* missed. Ryder's brother-
in-law, Charles Park, occupied a front seat. Gazing
at him, Artemus told the tale of a lazy man who, rather
than walk five rods to a spring, took a cupful of hot
water from a tea-kettle and "blew" it cool enough to
drink. Then saying he did not like to spoil a story for
relation's sake, identified the idler as "Charley Park,
sitting right down there in the second seat." An
impromptu reception followed at the Elephant Club, of
which he had been a member. It was truly a night of
nights—such as has not since been duplicated in Cleveland. More than fifteen hundred people were in the
audience. The receipts were given to the Soldiers Aid
Society.

February was also a busy month. One of the trips
carried him to Maine, where he fell in with Charles A.
Shaw, a venturesome and agreeable young business
man residing in Biddeford, with whom he at once
struck a blood-brotherhood. Shaw undertook the
management of the show and contributed considerably
to its continued success. The two traveled together
as star and manager for a time and the tours were
prosperous. Autograph-hunting was at that period
a national misdemeanor. Every night an armful of

albums would be found in the lecturer's room. Often he would be so exhausted that he would throw himself on the bed, with his feet on the footboard, and refuse to see anybody, much less to write autographs. Being the right kind of an agent, Mr. Shaw would sit down and write up the autographs himself, that the community of collectors might feel good in the morning when they called for their books.

The success of the lecture soon led to dropping the regular connection with *Vanity Fair*. There are traces of his pen in the early winter of 1862, but the only signed "piece" was published April 26th. That he had left its employ before this is shown by the following paragraph, printed in the issue of April 19th, the only editorial reference ever made to him:

"TO FOUR HUNDRED CORRESPONDENTS

"We have been overwhelmed, of late, with communications from ladies and gentlemen expiring to know whether VANITY FAIR has ever been in control of the unctuous and urbane Mr. Brown, of Grace Church. Also, whether Mr. Brown, of Grace Church, is not known in literary circles as Artemus Ward. To these inquiries we answer in the negative. There are—or were—two Mr. Browns residing in New York, and by one of these, Mr. Charles F. Browne, alias Artemus Ward, this journal was for a while ably conducted. We do not in any way mean to disparage the unctuous and urbane Mr. Brown, of Grace Church, by this explanation. In special reply to one of our anxious inquirers—a fair one, we suppose, as she appends to her note the signature 'Blondula'—we have the honor to state that Artemus Ward is quite a good-looking young man and altogether unmarried."

The "unctuous and urbane" Mr. Brown in question was the fashionable sexton of Grace Church, without whose presence no wedding or funeral in that Gothic structure was complete. He, indeed, reached the dignity of an institution and held the position in New York society for many years. His dictum on the proprieties was law.

The publication of April 26th was "Artemus Ward in Washington," an echo of a lecture trip to the capital, containing a galaxy of good things and amusing allusions.

Mr. Lincoln's biographers have noted the keen delight with which the President turned from the torturing strain of public affairs to the jokes of Artemus Ward and the disgust of Secretary Stanton that he should be desirous of diverting himself with nonsense at critical times. But Mr. Lincoln, besides being what Mr. Stanton was also, a great patriot and statesman, was a Western American, and he saw in the showman's stories the real humor of the people whom he himself knew so well, and chuckled in the presence of defeat and disaster at the whimsicalities, to the comfort of his soul. Mr. Stanton had no sense of humor. His mind never seemed to require rest. Lincoln's did, and found it in jests and varied tales. Possibly Stanton's feeling may have had its rise in this paragraph, given in the sketch as a parting adjuration to the President:

"Tell E. Stanton that his boldness, honesty, and vigger merits all praise, but to keep his undergarments on. E. Stanton has apparently only one weakness, which it is, he can't allers keep his undergarments from flying up over his head."

Mr. Stanton lived to make humble acknowledgment of his mistake. It is a matter of curious record that at the Cabinet meeting held September 22, 1862, to consider the final form of the Emancipation Proclamation, President Lincoln read "A High-handed Outrage at Utica" before the solemn discussion began. This is Stanton's own version of the incident as once related by him to Judge Hamilton Ward, of New York:

"On the 22d of September, 1862, I had a sudden and peremptory call to a Cabinet meeting at the White House. They did not usually require me to attend those meetings, as my duties were so exacting I had to be constantly at my post, and it was only on rare and important occasions that I was asked to be present. I went immediately to the White House, entered the room, and found the historic War Cabinet of Abraham Lincoln assembled, every member being present. The President hardly noticed me as I came in. He was reading a book of some kind, which seemed to amuse him. It was a little book. He finally turned to us and said: 'Gentlemen, did you ever read anything from Artemus Ward? Let me read you a chapter that is very funny.' Not a member of the Cabinet smiled; as for myself, I was angry, and looked to see what the President meant. It seemed to me like buffoonery. He, however, concluded to read us a chapter from Artemus Ward, which he did with great deliberation, and, having finished, laughed heartily, without a member of the Cabinet joining in the laughter. 'Well,' he said, 'let's have another chapter,' and he read another chapter, to our great astonishment. I was considering whether I should rise and leave the meeting abruptly, when he threw his book down, heaved a sigh, and said: 'Gentlemen, why don't you laugh? With the fearful strain that is upon me night and day, if I did not laugh I should die, and you need this medicine as much as I do.'

"He then put his hand in his tall hat that sat upon the table, and pulled out a little paper. Turning to the members of the Cabinet, he said: 'Gentlemen, I have called you here on very important business. I have prepared a little paper of much significance. I have made up my mind that this paper is to issue; that the time has come when it should issue; that the people are ready for it to issue. It is due to my Cabinet that you should be the first to hear and know of it, and if any of you have any suggestions to make as to the form of this paper or its composition, I shall be glad to hear them; but the paper is to issue.' And, to my astonishment, he read the Emancipation Proclamation of that date, containing the vital provision that on January 1, 1863, 'all persons held as slaves within any state or designated part of a state, the people whereof shall be then in rebellion against the United States, shall be then henceforth and forever free.' I have always tried to be calm, but I think I lost my calmness for a moment, and with great enthusiasm I arose, approached the President, extended my hand, and said: 'Mr. President, if reading chapters of Artemus Ward is a prelude to such a deed as this, the book should be filed among the archives of the nation and the author should be canonized. Henceforth I see the light, and the country is saved'; and all said, 'Amen.' And Lincoln said to me in a droll way as I was leaving, 'Stanton, it would have been too early last spring.' And as I look back upon it I think the President was right."

In the worn and much-used pocket note-book before mentioned are to be found memoranda that afterward scintillated in this letter from Washington, including the mournful recollection of a man "who was so mean he took his wife's coffin out of the window for fear it would rub the paint off the doorway."

"Artemus Ward in Washington" pins this tale to an interview with President Lincoln, thus:

"I called on Abe. He received me kindly. Handed him my umbrella and told him I'd have a check for it if he pleased. 'That,' he said, 'puts me in mind of a little story. There was a man out in our parts who was so mean that he took his wife's coffin out of the back window for fear he would rub the paint off the doorway. Wall, about this time there was a man in an adjacent town who had a green-cotton umbreller.'

"'Did it fit him well? Was it customed made? Was he measured for it? The umbreller.'

"'Wall, as I was sayin',' continued the President, treatin the interruption with apparent contempt, 'this man sed he'd known that there umbreller ever since it was a parasol!'"

There is no record that Artemus ever met the President face to face, but their admirations were mutual. His habit of picking up odd sayings as he traveled and incorporating them in his writings was also in evidence in this letter. Just before his visit to Washington he had journeyed from Waterville to Portland, Maine, with his friend Charles A. Shaw, when his ears were tickled with the oft-repeated phrase used by a man behind him who was telling the story of a marital disappointment, "The reason why he couldn't have her was because he was a drunken sailor." In his account of his interview with Secretary Welles, in the Washington letter, he brings it in:

"I called on Secretary Welles of the Navy. You know he is quite a mariner himself, having once owned a Raft of logs on the Connecticut River. So I put on saler stile and hollered: 'Ahoy, shipmet! Tip us yer grapplin'-irons!'

"'Yes, yes!' he sed, nervously, 'but mercy on us, don't be so noisy.'

"'Aye, aye, my hearty. But let me sing about how Jack Stokes lost his gal:

> "'"The reason why he couldn't gain her
> Was becoz he's drunken saler!"'

"'That's very good, indeed,' said the Secky, 'but this is hardly the place to sing songs in, my friend.'

"'Let me write the songs of a nashun,' sed I, 'and I don't care a cuss who goes to the legislator! But I ax your pardon—how's things?'"

The first sentence of the last paragraph is embedded in the old note-book. Several other bits of penciled memory from the note-book recall this visit to Washington. One reads, "I hastily gathered up Treasury notes under the impression that I was a member of

Congress." Another is more mysterious: "Hearse, you have no idea of the extent of our bar business." The note has this explanation in the account of his adventures in the District of Columbia:

"Washington, D. C., is the capital of our once happy country, if I may be allowed to koin a frase. The D. C. stands for Desprit Cusses, a numerosity of which abounds here, the most of whom persess a Romantic pashun for gratitious drinks. And in this conjunction I will relate an incident. I notist for several days a large hearse standin in front of the principal tavern on Pennsylvany Evenoo. 'Can you tell me my fair Castillian,' sed I this morning, to a young Spaniard from Tipperary, who was blackin boots in the wash room—'can you tell me what those hearse is kept standin out there for?' 'Well, you see our bar bisness is great. You've no idea of the number of people who drink at our bar during a day. You see those hearse is necessary.' I saw."

Concerning his abandoned editorship he once said: "Comic copy is what they wanted for *Vanity Fair*. I wrote some and it killed it. The poor paper got to be a conundrum and so I gave it up."

This was not quite fair either to himself or to the paper. They remained friends as long as it lived, which was until the Fourth of July, 1863.

Derby & Jackson having discontinued business under the pressure of the times, *His Book* was bundled into a green-baize bag and taken to George W. Carleton. It was a mass of ill-gathered scribbling and clippings. The Hoyt drawings had been lost

"I remember that Artemus came to me and gave

me his manuscript and newspaper clippings and left them with me to decide whether I would publish them in a book," said Mr. Carleton, thirty years after, in recalling the incident.

"Two things struck me forcibly: Ward's appearance and the bad and almost illegible manuscript, blotted here and there, stuck with mucilage, and plastered with newspaper clippings. Artemus looked to me then somewhat like the caricature of Uncle Sam, only he never wore his trousers quite so short. His hair was long and rather unkempt, and he appeared at first a serious man. Looking at him at the time, I wondered if there could possibly be any humor in him. I told him that I would look over his stuff and decide what I could do, but not immediately. He said time was no object, and strode out. His manuscript came near giving me the nightmare, it was so mixed and written all over everything. It was months before I concluded to publish his book. I did not have so much faith in Artemus at that time, for he was comparatively unknown; Doesticks and John Phœnix were popular and their works were selling well. Before long his work on *Vanity Fair* began to show, and I soon saw that he was more than an ordinary humorist, and decided to publish his book. It was a job to get his manuscript straightened out and put together right. I had not only to edit, but to write a good deal; so much so that Artemus said to me one day, 'The next book I write, I'm going to get *you* to write.'"

Carleton seems to have accepted the book in the fall of 1861. There is mention of it in the following letter, written when plans for the lecture were being settled, answering an inquiry as to the chance of Ward's visiting Down East at an early date:

"NEW YORK, Nov. 19, 1861.

"DEAR MR. FLETCHER: I have an appointment at Portland, but none at Bangor or Portsmouth—unfortunately for those places, as I cannot but think they need some cheerful paragraphs down that way.

"I had not forgotten your introducing me to Gov. Raymond, but I have scarcely felt like bothering him about my lecture tour. He lectures himself and might be jealous of me!

"I shall try and reach you on the four-o'clock train.

"Many thanks for the letter to Prof. Angell—and many thanks for your kindness generally.

"Very truly yours,
C. F. BROWNE.

"P. S.—Rudd & Carleton are about to issue my 'stuff' in book form, illustrated by Stephens. The volume will be launched under very bright auspices, and I am consequently happy."

Notice was given that the book would be forthcoming, in the columns of *Vanity Fair*, which offered it as a premium to subscribers in the initial number of Volume IV, January 4, 1862, where it was described as "A copy of the Artemus Ward Letters, shortly to be published by Rudd & Carleton. Price, one dollar." Three dollars secured the book and paper combined for one year —a great bargain as it turned out. Mr. Rudd left the firm, and the real title was first given in the premium announcement for March 9th, *Artemus Ward: His Book*, to be published by "Carleton." It was finally issued May 17, 1862, dedicated to Charles W. Coe, of Cleveland, "a friend all the year round." The illustrations were pick-ups from *Vanity Fair*, supplemented by several new ones by Henry L. Stephens.

Forty thousand copies were sold outright, an enormous edition for the time. The author was paid fifteen cents royalty on each copy. "He was living in very cheap lodgings in St. John's Square," recalled Mr. Carleton in the interview quoted above, "when I called upon him to pay him six thousand dollars, his share of the profits. I found him in a small hall room, and paid him over the money that started him on his career now so well known."

The "small hall room" was in a house on Varick Street, the first to the right hand from Canal Street, between that thoroughfare and St. John's Park. In after-years Artemus paused in one of his sketches to note with emotion that the house in Varick Street in which he used to board was being torn down and that some of the timbers, converted into canes, were cheap at a dollar. They would have been, indeed, had they existed.

A week after the publication of the book *Vanity Fair* honored its ex-editor with a first-page cartoon showing "Artemus Ward as a Popular Lecturer," which he had become. The immediate success of the volume made it easy for him to pick his ground for platform work, which he did with such skill that there were few failures to draw.

He was his own press agent, and one of the best.

ARTEMUS WARD AS A PUBLIC LECTURER

(Cartoon from *Vanity Fair*, May 24, 1862)

His easy intimacy with the profession and liking for the printing trade made him steer for the newspaper-office as soon as he reached a town. That he sometimes called on others for aid is evidenced by this appeal sent to James R. Osgood, from Waterford, July 29, 1862:

"Carleton says the newspaper will print it quicker for the author than for the publisher—as they (you and I know him unjustly) regard publishers as pirates and bloodthirsty robbers. Can you get it into the *Post* and into the *Transcript*, which I suppose nobody in Boston can drink tea without. Am I asking too much? Am I a nuisance?"

Osgood was also an Oxford bear, as natives of that Maine County like to call themselves, having been born in Fryeburg, a few miles west of Waterford. He was then beginning a notable career as a publisher in Boston. Search of the *Transcript* files fails to reveal any result of the appeal, though it was a liberal user of jokes culled from *Vanity Fair*.

Artemus spent a pleasant summer at the homestead and found time to prepare three "pieces" for *Vanity Fair*, all superior: "The Draft in Baldwinsville," published September 20th; "The Showman at Home," October 11th, and "A. Ward in Canada," November 1st. He also concocted a new lecture, "Sixty Minutes in Africa."

The partnership with Shaw, though profitable, was subject to interruption, caused by the latter's other interests, which included the promotion of sewing-machine factories and a jewelry business in Biddeford. Artemus, feeling the need of more certain and expert management, kept Doctor Hingston in mind. By happy chance that gentleman turned up eighteen months after the trip to Louisville and found Artemus Ward on the platform in Philadelphia retailing jokes in "Sixty Minutes in Africa"—much the same ones that had lain in the cradle of "The Babes." The lecture was given in the Musical Fund Hall. A big map of Africa hung upon the wall back of the platform, to which he would occasionally refer, as, for instance, pointing to Ethiopia: "Here in the center of the African continent is what is called a 'howling wilderness,' but for my part I never heard it howl, nor met with any one who has. It abounds in various natural productions, such as reptiles and flowers. It produces the red rose, the white rose, and the neg-roes."

Then he wound up the hour's foolery with this word of dismissal to audience and title:

"Africa is my subject. You wish me to tell you something about Africa. Africa is on the map. It's on all the maps of Africa I have ever seen. You may buy a good map of Africa for a dollar. If you will study it well you will know more about Africa than I do. It is a comprehensive subject—too vast, I assure you, for me to enter upon to-night. You would not wish me to—I feel that—I feel it deeply and I am very sensitive. If you go home and go to bed—it will be better for you than to go with me to Africa!"

After the lecture he took Hingston with him to his room in the Continental, where they were soon joined by the stars from Carncross & Dixey's minstrels, just then becoming a Philadelphia institution. There was plenty of wit and refreshment, and the night wound up at a fashionable "colored" ball. His head was full of

plans for new lecture routes, which Hingston took under
consideration, and a new book. This was in early
1863. Concerning the book he wrote Carleton:

"DEAR CARL: You and I will get out a book next
spring that will knock spots out of all comic books in
ancient or modern history. And the fact that you are
going to take hold of it convinces me that you have
one of the most massive intellects in this or any other
epoch.

"Yours, my pretty gazelle,
ARTEMUS WARD."

"The next spring" promise made Carleton for a book
that was to "knock the spots out of all comic books"
was not kept, either then or the spring following. The
platform and the pleasures of life absorbed all his
energies—which were none too great. Success remained with him and life was easy, except when he
himself made it hard with too much companionship and
radiation, for which he got small return and physical
exhaustion. He recuperated at the homestead in
Waterford, or in idle trips about the country.

In the winter of 1863 the showman's wanderings
carried him as far south as Memphis, then safely in
Federal hands, where Gen. William Tecumseh Sherman had his headquarters in the campaign against
Vicksburg. The movement under his direct command
had failed and the field work had been turned over to
John A. McClernand, leaving Sherman to look after
the troubles of Tennessee. These were plentiful, including the complaints of the numerous citizens who

had suffered for their loyalty during the conflict, and expected special consideration, resenting any shown their Confederate neighbors. This reminded Artemus of folks in Waterford. "They howl very loud for the old flag," he told Sherman, "but when the wind blows a hole in it, there isn't any one in the town who would buy a piece of bunting to patch it."

One of the most persistent complainants was a Union woman, with a husband in the Confederate army, who protested against the stealing of her chickens by members of the Federal forces.

"Madam," replied the general after much patient listening, "the integrity of the Constitution and the unity of the Republic must be maintained if it takes every chicken in Tennessee."

Sherman had an austere repute in the public mind and a distinct dislike for newspaper folks, but he took kindly to Artemus and a great friendship resulted between them. They dined together at the Gayoso House and supped at a little Italian restaurant on Front Street, with plenty of pleasant company, including Dan Rice, of circus fame, and Melville D. Landon, who afterward made some minor name himself as a humorist and lecturer under the guise of "Eli Perkins." Landon was a major on the staff of Gen. A. L. Chetlain, and this army relationship brought in many dashing companions.

The summer of 1863 Artemus spent, as usual, at Waterford, where he astonished the natives by strolling about in a gorgeously figured damask dressing-gown, wearing a smoking-cap perched on the back of his head, with a big gilt tassel depending radiantly therefrom. He returned to New York with the idea of visiting California uppermost in his mind. Hingston had been there on one trip as an amusement manager and was sounded as to the possibilities, with the result that an agreement was reached by which they were to go together as manager and attraction. The desire was sharpened by a telegram, which found Mr. Ward lounging in Carleton's office, from Thomas Maguire, the enterprising manager of the San Francisco Opera House, reading, "What will you take for forty nights in California?"

Straightway the reply went back over the transcontinental wire, "Brandy and water."

This cryptic message puzzled Maguire, who at first thought it something in code. The joke at last penetrated, the reporters got hold of it, and the widely circulated despatch proved a good advance agent, when its writer at last reached the Coast, where plenty of the commingled fluids were in waiting.

Artemus was too speculative and too much of a Yankee to "hire out." This was his delicate way of saying so.

In making the California venture, the lure of the land of gold was, of course, the main influence, but he was moved not a little by the letters of John Phœnix, otherwise Lieut. George Horatio Derby, U.S.A. These productions, a source of national glee in the middle 'fifties and up to the decease of their author in 1861, had an undoubted share in inspiring Artemus Ward to enter the field of mirth. Derby struck the same note of exaggeration and whimsicality that Artemus sounded, but in a style quite his own and in the best of English.

His satires on the "Coast" were keen, and the hits, though local, broad enough to excite general interest. They were gathered into book form in 1856, about the time our humorist began to note the comic currents of life.

Besides all this, the lectures were palling a little on lecturer and audiences alike. Both were longing for something new. True, he had entertained his audiences under a new title, "Ghosts," taken at the suggestion of Thomas De Walden, a play-writing New-Yorker, and one of his intimates, who urged utilizing the stir made in the amusement world by the optical illusion known as "Pepper's Ghost," then very popular. The "Ghosts" were mainly those of the old jokes in "The Babes" and "Sixty Minutes in Africa." There was hope for fresh material as well as adventure in the Golden West.

The routing of the expedition provided for a steamer journey to San Francisco *via* the Isthmus of Panama and a return across the continent, then unspanned by rail. Hingston demurred to this. It was no light undertaking to ride over the great plains, at their best, teeming as they did with hostile Indians. A summer trip was bad enough, but the program required winter traveling. Artemus, however, was obdurate. He wanted to lecture in Salt Lake City and see Brigham Young, having, of course, a deeper purpose—that of turning the Mormons to account—in his mind.

"There was a man in the next street to me," he said, "who committed suicide because he could not get on with two wives. I want to see how a man can get along who has fifty."

So it was agreed that the overland route home should be used if practicable.

When Samuel Booth, the printer in Duane Street, was packing the posters, prepared for use on the Pacific slope, Artemus remarked to Hingston, who was overseeing the operation:

"I hope you have kept a couple of bills out loose."

Hingston replied that he had reserved a number for carriage in his trunk to be posted en route at Aspinwall, Panama, and Acapulco.

"That's all very well," remarked his employer, "but I want you to have two loose in your pocket, with a hammer and some nails."

"To use where?"

"When the steamer gets to San Francisco it will have to pass through the Golden Gate," Artemus replied, soberly. "Now I have never seen it myself, but as you go through I want you to stop the steamer and just nail up one of my bills on each side of the Gate."

Moved to outdo this suggestion, Hingston remarked that if this was not enough he would organize a torchlight procession to parade on the night of his arrival at San Francisco.

"Do it before I arrive," he responded, "and have a great wax figure of me in a chariot, with my babes on each side of me." The "Ghosts" had been tried out at Niblo's Salon, an annex to the famous Garden. The notices were favorable. "Take them with you," observed Artemus Ward to Hingston, "and have the notices copied. We shall want the ghost to walk in California."

10

V

CALIFORNIA, NEVADA, AND UTAH

IT was arranged that Hingston should precede his principal by a fortnight and prepare proper *éclat* for his reception at the Golden Gate. He therefore sailed from New York on the *North Star*, October 3, 1863, well provided with lithograph portraits, the bills "sculpt by Sammy Booth," and one hundred copies of *Artemus Ward: His Book*. He reached the Isthmus in due season, hung up a few posters and pictures at Aspinwall and Panama to show Artemus Ward he was "on his job," and then proceeded to San Francisco on the steamer *Golden Age*.

Artemus passed the interval preceding his own departure in making a visit to his mother at Waterford. He sailed from New York on the steamer *Ariel* on October 13, 1863. The ship was crowded and uncomfortable. In his notes on the voyage he remarks, "She is a miserable tub at the best," and expresses regret that Raphael Semmes, of the *Alabama*, who once captured the *Ariel*, had not made mincemeat of her. Nine disagreeable days were spent at sea before Aspinwall was reached. Crossing the Isthmus by rail, he paused briefly at the Howard House in Panama, and then on a "cheerful and well-appointed boat," the *St. Louis*, Captain Hudson, left for California. The vessel made landings at Acapulco and a few Pacific ports. After an uneventful trip San Francisco was reached on Sunday, November 1, 1863. Here he met with a warm welcome. The diligent Hingston had made good use of the time. All the newspapers were filled with points on the lecture, and open hospitality awaited his employer, who was driven to the Occidental Hotel, then lavishly run by Louis Leland, of the famous inn-keeping family. The hack-driver advised him that, as he was there to amuse folks, the fare would be only five dollars. A leading citizen was on hand to invite him to dinner. The trunk with Artemus Ward's best clothes had not been removed from the steamer. He pleaded this as an excuse for declining.

"Never mind," said the host, "it doesn't matter what you wear in California."

"That's fortunate. I never *was* much," retorted Artemus.

The joke traveled and did its share in the advertising. The telegraphic correspondence with Maguire had also served well. The latter was anxious to secure control of the tour, but Hingston concluded they would fare better independently, and his opinion was justified by the outcome. He selected Platt's Hall as the place for opening, and here, on the evening of November 13, 1863, "The Babes in the Wood" were "trotted out," according to promise. One dollar in gold was the admission price, and more than sixteen hundred persons paid it. So fast, indeed, did the dollars come that they baffled accounting and were tossed into a hat held out by the door-tender. Their weight broke the crown of the head-gear and many rolled away. Almost as many more could not get in. Thomas Starr King, the eminent Unitarian divine, welcomed the lecturer on the platform, and, to help with good-will, Maguire closed his opera-house for the night. Returning to the hotel after the lecture, a brass band gave a serenade, to which half the city listened. It was indeed a triumph, upon which Hingston lingers lovingly in his reminiscences.

San Francisco was, and perhaps always will be, a man's town. It was built for men, by men of the most adventurous type, to suit themselves and their kind. They were exiles who had made an old country new and their own. To such the humorist had a peculiar appeal. His thoughts were their thoughts, grimly amusing, incongruous, and tinctured with pathos. So his welcome was prodigious.

Naturally, such a city was strong on amusements and newspapers, both of which circumscribed most of Artemus Ward's interest in life. There were plenty of theaters; the California on Bush Street, then under the management of Lawrence Barrett and John McCullough, and backed by William C. Ralston, produced plays with prodigious splendor. Strange visitors included Adah Isaacs Menken, the famous "Mazeppa," traveling with Robert H. Newell, a very recently acquired husband, who had taken the place of John C. Heenan, the pugilist, in the lady's fervid affections. Newell had made a conspicuous name for himself as author of the "Orpheus C. Kerr" papers, published first in the New York *Sunday Mercury*, and then in several volumes by Carleton. These were very able and humorous letters from Washington and have a deserved place in the literature of the day. The pair were living in luxury at the Ross house. It was a tradition that when Newell first acquired the lady he did not know her previous ownership. At any rate, they were not long husband and wife. She died, not many years after, in Paris, after a memorable European career and an odd friendship with Charles Dickens and Algernon Charles Swinburne. He continued to be a literary figure for a decade and then faded out of sight, being found dead on the 12th of July, 1901, in the home of his sister-in-law, Mrs. C. B. Newell, 128 First Place, Brooklyn, where he lodged during the family's absence for the summer—a forlorn end to a brilliant life!

It was an era of good living at low prices. Artemus Ward paid two dollars and fifty cents per day at the Occidental, where, according to the gloating Hingston, the table groaned with good things—beef from Contra Costa, potatoes from Bodegas; richly tinted apples from Oregon, then and for long after unknown in the East; juicy grapes from Sonoma; strawberries from Oakland, and luscious peaches from Marysville. The milk was rich and the butter "magnificent." The bar, too, was a "commodious apartment, radiant with white marble, gilt, and glittering crystal," while Mr. Jerry Thomas, the keeper thereof, was a most accomplished artist who had written a book on the proper compounding of mixed drinks. He blazed with diamonds and received the palatial pay of one hundred dollars per week.

Several minstrel troupes were playing in the city. They greeted the lecturer as an old friend. Hingston shrewdly supplied the "end men" with copies of *His*

Book, and the jokes were freely interlarded by the interlocutors—all of which increased the advertising.

The show was shifted from Platt's Hall to the Metropolitan Theater, where it was successfully repeated on the 17th. Betweentimes Artemus took in the town. Maguire often acted as guide as well as an unselfish counselor and friend. He took the showman to Ralston's bank on Sansome Street, asking him if he would like to walk on gold. "I should like to dance on it," was the reply

This came duly to pass. The floor of the vault was paved with bricks of the precious metal. Here, after a bottle of champagne had been cracked, the showman gave a "breakdown" with much saltatorial success, while Maguire and the company furnished music by whistling the air of "Hop Light-Loo"—whatever that might have been.

Chinatown made a warm appeal to the visitor. The almond-eyed heathen gave him the novelty for which he always yearned. Here he enjoyed at the Celestial Theater what he afterward called "sixteen square yards of a Chinese comic song," and saw a people who were wholly new, but by no means devoid of humor or the capacity for appreciating a joke.

The first lecture outside of San Francisco was at the very Mexican town of San José. On the suggestion of the village editor, Hingston hired an orchestra to play in the outer balcony of the "Opera House" and built a big bonfire in the street before it. This, it seems, was the customary way of calling the citizens to that place of entertainment. These brought together a very scant audience. Artemus was disgusted and dismayed. He had been idling in the express-office, awaiting the opening hour, but could perceive no popular movement toward the theater.

"Confound that band!" he exclaimed to Hingston. "The whole thing is ridiculous. What do you want with a band at a comic lecture?"

The local custom was explained reassuringly; also, that the crowd would not go inside as long as the band remained outside. The musicians were accordingly sent within. Hingston then apprised his principal that the audience awaited his presence.

"What have you done with the artist of the drum?" he demanded.

Hingston replied that the drummer was bravely beating the sheepskin in the house.

"But I am not the Colleen Bawn nor Richard the Third," Artemus remonstrated, wrathfully. "What do I want with an orchestra? What will the people expect? Do stop them before I go in, or these musical idiots will start up 'See, the Conquering Hero' or some other nonsense, and turn out that drummer—he's abominable."

The drummer, be it said, had already knocked himself out. He had forgotten his whisky-bottle and, starting to regain it from the balcony, had fallen down the stairs and was badly damaged. The crowd laughed at the lecture, but plainly expected waxworks.

Pausing after the talk to admire some Mexican saddles in a shop, Artemus Ward tried to talk Spanish to a very lively young lady at the door of the establishment and narrowly escaped pistoling at the hands of a jealous admirer overloaded with mescal. With great presence of mind, he blew out the light in the saddlery, and the crack of the pistol that followed only heralded a shot astray.

"Comic lecturing has nothing to do with saddlery," observed Artemus, coolly, as they made a quick get-away. "Old fellow, just keep your comic lecturer to his business, or you'll lose him. That Mexican wanted to saddle the wrong horse."

Santa Clara extended an invitation to the show. "We are all warm-hearted people in Santa Clara," said the citizen who brought the request.

"Warm hearts always want free tickets," Artemus commented. "I once lectured at a place in Connecticut where a whole-souled manufacturer of sewing-machines asked me if I didn't feel a great wish to be introduced to his family. I told him my inclinations were that way. People said he was the warmest-hearted man in the whole place. In the evening he brought himself, his wife, and sixteen nephews and nieces. He introduced them all, and they said they would just take seats and listen. They filled all my front chairs. Next day I sent for the admission money. Answer came back that a mistake was made. They were all Mr. Ward's friends and couldn't think of paying. But their hearts were as warm to me as ever—bless them!"

On reaching Santa Clara, it was found that the sponsor for its warm-heartedness had made no arrangements for the show. He said he was then on his way to the Jesuit College in the hope that its priestly principal would provide room and audience. He had given the prelate a copy of *His Book* and expected that would fix it. It did! The pair went along and found a portly father with a copy of the immortal work in his hand and a puzzled look on his face.

"Do you propose to lecture on a philosophical subject?" he inquired.

"No—history," replied Artemus Ward. The good father said he had examined the book, but its purpose was not clear. It did not appear to be historical. What department of history did Mr. Ward propose to illuminate? "Early history," he answered: "'The Babes in the Wood.'"

"Do you mean Romulus and Remus?"

"No, little Billy Smith and his sister. It's a fairy-tale of the ancient Greeks in New England. Your college would like it, I am sure. All colleges do. Students howl over it."

The principal concluded the topic was not suited for his classes, so the party hunted for another hole. A dilapidated Methodist chapel was induced to open its doors. Handbills were hastily distributed. When the hour came only eight persons appeared at its doors, and but three of these put up their dollars. The other five were "warm-hearted" deadheads. The hall was illuminated by tallow candles. These were blown out and the three dollars returned. A sympathetic store-keeper invited the company across to his shop for a drink. It turned out that Santa Clara was suffering for the evening from an epidemic of "surprise"-parties, a group from one of which, including some very agreeable young ladies, invaded the store. Soon the situation was made plain. More people came in and at last an impromptu entertainment resulted, Artemus holding forth joyously from a perch on the counter by the light of a candle stuck on the head of a flour-barrel. The young folks were from New York, and nothing would do but to take Artemus Ward along to the next "surprise." Not to be outdone, he bought a half-dozen bottles of olives and carried them to the unsuspecting hosts—a newly married couple.

"I shall present them with these jars of olives," he said, "and a pot of honey. The honey they can eat, and keep the olives to grow and have branches."

It was daylight before the fun ended. He was used up and very dull on the ride to 'Frisco. Hingston, who had better powers of endurance, remarked that he did not look like a humorist.

"No. I am a headachist," was the mournful rejoinder.

These and other lecture excursions radiated out from San Francisco, where Artemus Ward found life very delightful. There was much going on and plenty of people to make things interesting. He pined for companionship and contact with the odd. San Francisco supplied both desires abundantly. Among other things, in conjunction with Samuel W. Wilder, one of his former Boston employers, now adventuring in California, Artemus and Hingston gave a new start to a wandering conjurer who turned up broke in 'Frisco, after many amazing adventures in the Orient—at least, the tales he told of them were amazing.

"That will do," said Artemus to Hingston. "He has that sweet respect for truth which noble conjurers have. If he can force a card as well as he can lie, he's a lovely artist."

He himself prepared the program for the magician. It paraded the performer as the "Renowned Basiliconthaumaturgist," and gave a burlesque list of Far Eastern notabilities before whom he had appeared, including the Selectmen of Waterford, Maine. The boost given the conjurer brought him moderate prosperity. He repaid his helpful friends by blanketing the show in the country towns with such persistency and bad effect that Artemus finally overhauled him and stopped the practice by remarking, firmly:

"Professor, two basiliconthaumaturgists cannot get on together in one town. If you don't keep off my track I shall turn blood-red wristist myself and do it in my lecture."

This last remark related to the conjurer's trick of making letters in blood appear on his bared arm— an old dodge with the spiritualist mediums, then much in vogue. The threat settled the opposition and the natives were thereafter treated to one show at a time. He followed at a respectful distance and, reaching Salt Lake, became magician in ordinary to Brigham Young.

The show finally moved to Sacramento en route for the Sierras, going by the steamer *Chrysopolis* to the capital of California. A joke of the trip was the misadventure of a temperance lecturer who made their acquaintance en route. The "dry" advocate fell overboard. It was late in the fall—indeed, early winter—and the water chilled him to the bone. His first words when fished out were:

"Whisky—get me some whisky!"

He was given a bottle and took a hearty nip.

"There'll be a third conversion—sure," remarked Artemus to Hingston.

He was warmly received in Sacramento, lectured at the Metropolitan Theater to a six - hundred - dollar house, and gave five hundred dollars of it the following day to the widow of an actor whose home had been destroyed by fire, for whom a local subscription was being raised.

"Don't put my name on the list," he told Hingston. "Let them say, 'Subscribed by a religious Indian.'"

The mining-towns were next invaded. Folsom was the first of these. Hingston went ahead to fix dates and hang out the handbills. He did not see Artemus Ward until some days after his Folsom début.

"The maniacs stopped me when I was orating sublimely," Artemus told the doctor, "and called upon me to sing. They howled for a song."

"Did you sing?"

"I had to, or they would have thrown cart-wheels at me."

Knowing that Artemus was a poor warbler, Hingston asked him what song he selected.

"The cheerful lunatics wanted 'Maggie by My Side.' They pitched the tune, and I joined in with them. It was a farce, altogether. Put at the bottom of the bills, 'No singing allowed'—that's a good fellow, or I shall have to be a walking opera-house before I get through many more mining-camps."

Marysville and Oroville were next uplifted. At the former point a decision was reached that settled the question of returning overland definitely. The impending winter was strong argument in favor of an easy return by sea. Artemus took a twenty-dollar gold piece out of his pocket. "We'll toss for it," he said. "If it comes down eagle we'll go to the Mormons."

The bird showed when the coin came down. They therefore routed a tour through the mining-camps *via* North San Juan, crossing the Yuba to Shelby Flat, where Mr. Ward met the famous Mr. Blazes, who appears in the *Travels.* Nevada City, Grass Valley, Placerville, Auburn, Drytown, Jackson, and Sonora furnished welcoming audiences. At Nevada City the theater and hotel had been consumed by a fire that swept the town. The Baptist church sheltered the show, after being emptied of a stock of apples kept in store. At Grass Valley Hingston found the house where Lola Montez had finished her burning career, to the ruin of the lucky miner whose "stake" she soon cleaned out. He killed himself, and the woman had returned to New York to die in poverty and distress: she who had consorted with a king and had been the toast of the gayest circles of Europe!

Most of the time Artemus traveled alone, following Hingston, whose work was always ahead, though they met at short intervals to exchange notes and arrange schedules. The showman picked up the material for his classic account of "Horace Greeley's Ride to Placerville," with Hank Monk's sententious order, "Git him there by seving"—a tale that annoyed Mr. Greeley very much, but which still refuses to die; also, the apothegm of the stage-driver who gloomily remarked that at the "next tip-over" he intended to go around and finish the mutilated passengers who survived with the king-bolt. "Dead folks don't sue. They ain't on it."

At San Juan Hingston interviewed Judge Stidger, editor of the *Press*, and received assurances that the show would receive a good reception. When the pair reunited at Auburn, Hingston found that the brick church at Oroville had been crowded. The result at San Juan had been different. Replying to Hingston's query, Artemus said, reluctantly:

"They had no lecture out of me."

"But why not? I paid fifteen dollars for the hall, and Judge Stidger was to write you up well in his paper."

"Write me up? I should think he did! He told the noble inhabitants that I was coming with a whole menagerie of snakes and animals, and a half a dozen wagon-loads of wax figures. When I got into the town and found what the people had been led to expect, I left by the next stage. Do you think I would have stopped? Why, I should have been steamboated first and lynched afterward."

"And the burned-out city, Nevada—did that pay?"

"Here's the money-taker's return. It's just half what I received. The people opened the windows and sat on the sills, while others stood in rows around the church. When I came out they all waited to see me, and paid up their dollars for standing-room. I like churches to lecture in, but if you take another one for me, set some footlights to the pulpit."

At Jackson there was trouble in leasing the hall. A friendly sheriff offered the use of a brand-new jail. "Let your comic man make his speech here," he said,

ARTEMUS WARD THE LECTURER

genially. "You can have the place for nothing. He can stand up on a table in the middle, we'll place forms for the people, and there's the place for your boxes."

The "boxes" were cells designed to accommodate murderers, none of whom had yet arrived!

Finally, California was covered, and after a brief return to San Francisco a direct departure was taken for Nevada. Hingston, as usual, went ahead. The first show in the silver territory was given to a rough crowd in Carson, which filled the Johnny Moore Theater. This was a rude playhouse with saloon and gambling-house attachment. Hingston credits its ownership to one "Doc" Schermerhorn, an exile from Baltimore. This is an error. "Schermerhorn" was a local celebrity who made the theater and its annex his lounging-place. His real name was Charles S. Lightle and he enjoyed a local reputation as a wit. The audience was unappreciative. Artemus did not relish the experience and hastened on to Virginia City. Here the brightness of life again asserted itself. Thomas Maguire's comfortable opera-house sheltered the show and a nine-hundred-dollar audience, taken at dollars and half-dollars. But, more to his delight, the holiday-time fell here, where he found a coterie of affinities. There were then twelve thousand people in Virginia City, with three daily newspapers. One of these, the Virginia City *Enterprise*, had for its proprietor a man of talent and taste much above the merits of a mining-camp, Joseph T. Goodman. He had picked the paper up for one thousand dollars in promises, and the coming of the Comstock boom made it a prosperous publication, employing five editors, twenty-three printers, and earning money at the rate of one hundred thousand dollars a year. He extended open house to the geniuses that blew in on the breeze of the Big Bonanza, and the galaxy included Stephen Gillis, Denis McCarthy, William Wright (better known as "Dan De Quille") and Samuel L. Clemens, then twenty-eight, a gaunt young adventurer, who had followed his brother Orion from Missouri to share the pickings of the office of Secretary to the territorial government of Nevada. James W. Nye was the Governor—afterward to be known as the famous "Bill Nye" of "The Heathen Chinee," then a sociable soul. With this company Artemus came at once into joyous contact. It is difficult to discover any coherent account of the stay. Hingston armed himself with a stout cane and, with a bottle of champagne for a companion, explored the hills. Artemus visited the mines and loafed with Mark Twain by day and at night held festivals with all hands. He had intended to stay but three days, but dallied as many weeks. There is a flash in Mark Twain's recollections of Artemus with blackened face, standing on a table at the Melodeon, a popular twenty-four-hour resort, reciting Thomas Bailey Aldrich's "Ballad of Baby Bell" to the admiring sinners with tearful results, concerning which Twain wrote in after-years to Mr. Aldrich: "Just at this moment [January 27, 1872] a picture flits before me. Scene: Private room in Barnum's restaurant, Virginia, Nevada; present, Artemus Ward, Joseph T. Goodman (editor and proprietor *Daily Enterprise*), and Dan De Quille and myself, reporters for the same; remnants of the feast, thin and scathing, but *such* tautology and repetition of empty bottles everywhere visible to be offensive to the sensitive eye; time, 2.30 A.M. Artemus thickly reciting a poem about a certain infant you wot of, and interrupting himself and being interrupted every few lines by poundings of the table and shouts of, 'Splendid, by Shorzhe!' Finally, a long, vociferous, poundiferous and vitreous jingling of applause announces the conclusion, and then Artemus: 'Let every man 'at loves his fellow-man and 'preciates a poet, 'at loves *his* fellow-man, stan' up—stan' up and drink health and long life to Thomas Bailey Aldrich—and drink it stan'ing!' (On all hands fervent, enthusiastic, and sincerely honest attempt to comply.) Then Artemus: 'Well, consider it stan'ing, and drink it just as ye are!' Which was done."

In a pocket of an Artemus Ward note-book I found an interesting relic of this gladsome sojourn in the Bonanza regions, a filled-out form under the seal of James W. Nye, Governor, whereby, "reposing special trust and confidence in the integrity and ability of Artemus Ward," he appointed the said Ward "for the term of his natural life" "Speaker of pieces" to the people of Nevada Territory. Orion Clemens had retired from the post and the certificate is signed by William King, then Secretary of the Territory.

He received another and more definite token of esteem. The admiring miners sent him a chain of gold so long that it could be worn about the neck, but its weight was so great that it was uncomfortable and was seldom carried by its owner. One of the bacchanalian banquets cost him two hundred and thirty-seven dollars! He seems to have escaped from his admirers by flight, and was next heard from at Austin, through this letter to Mark Twain:

"Austin, Jan. 1, '64.

"My dearest Love:

"I arrived here yesterday A.M. at two o'clock. It is a wild, untenable place, full of lion-hearted boys. I speak to-night. See small bills.

"Why did you not go with me and save me that night—I mean the night I left you after the dinner-party. I went and got drunker, beating, I may say, Alexander the Great in his most drunkenest days, and I blackened my face at the Melodeonard and made a gibbering, idiotic speech. . . . I suppose the *Union* will have it. But let it go. I shall always remember Virginia as a bright spot in my existence, as all others must, or rather, cannot be, as it were.

"Love to Jo Goodman and Dan. I shall write soon, a powerful, convincing note to my friends of the *Mercury*. Your notice, by the way, did much good here, as it doubtless will elsewhere. The miscreants of the *Union* will be batted on the snout if they ever dare pollute this rapidly rising city with their loathsome presence.

"Some of the finest intellects in the world have been flouted by liquor.

"Do not, sir, do not flatter yourself that you are the only chastely humorous writer onto the Pacific slopes.

"Good-by, old boy, and God bless you! The matter of which I spoke to you so earnestly shall be just as earnestly attended to, and again with my warm regards to Jo and Dan, and regards to the many good friends we met, I am faithfully yours,

ARTEMUS WARD."

The fact that Artemus had been captured by the staff of the *Enterprise* led to much hostility on the part of their strenuous brothers of the *Union*, the rival journal of Virginia City. Hence the allusion. Of the editor of the *Union* Artemus gave this account in his *Travels:*

"My arrival in Virginia City was signalized by the following incident: I had no sooner achieved my room in the garret of the International Hotel than I was called upon by an intoxicated man who said he was an editor. Knowing how rare it was for an editor to be under the blighting influence of either spirituous or malt liquors, I received this statement doubtfully. But I said:

"'What name?'

"'Wait!' he said. And went out.

"I heard him pacing unsteadily up and down the hall outside. In ten minutes he returned and said:

"'Pepper!'

"Pepper was indeed his name. He had been out to see if he could remember it and he was so flushed with his success that he repeated it joyously several times, and then, with a short laugh, he went away.

"I had often heard of a man being 'so drunk that he didn't know what town he lived in,' but here was a man so hideously intoxicated that he didn't know what his name was.

"I saw him no more, but I heard from him. For he

published a notice of my lecture, in which he said I had 'a dissipated air.'"

Writing to Bret Harte in San Francisco from Salt Lake City, January 26, 1864, Artemus gave these glimpses of his inner feelings respecting the *Union:*

"Thanks for the kindly manner in which you spoke of me in the *Era.* There seemed to be an unhappy impression among the editors in the interior that I was a highway robber, and they pursued me with unpleasant energy. But the respectable papers all treated me kindly except the *Bulletin,* which is a good paper, its chief weakness being that it mistakes itself for the New York *Evening Post.* My march through Nevada Territory was in the main a triumphant one. The Virginia *Union,* however, abused me in a long editorial in which it was said I was a mercenary clown."

The item in the *Golden Era* of December 27, 1863, to give the paper's full title, for which he thanks Bret Harte, follows:

"Artemus Ward is not the greatest American humorist, nor does he himself profess to be, but he deserves the credit of combining qualities which make him the representative of a kind of humor that has more of a national characteristic than the higher and more artistic standard. His strength does not lie simply in grotesque spelling—that is a mechanical trick suggested by his education as a printer—and those who have gone to hear him in this expectation have been properly punished—but it is the humor of audacious exaggeration—of perfect lawlessness; a humor that belongs to the country of boundless prairies, limitless rivers, and stupendous cataracts. In this respect Mr.

Ward is the American humorist par excellence, and *His Book* is the essence of that fun which overlies the surface of our national life, which is met in the stage, rail-car, canal- and flat-boat, which bursts out over camp-fires and around barroom stoves—a humor that has more or less local coloring, that takes kindly to, and half elevates, slang, that is of to-day and full of present application."

The *Mercury*, to which A. W. referred in his note to Clemens, was the famous New York Sunday newspaper of that name. Artemus evidently kept his promise. Several articles were sent and published. Vows made at their parting included promises from "Charley" to "Sam" to help him reach the light. Eventually he did it. Calling on Clemens for a Western skit to insert in his *Travels*, the latter forwarded that key-note to his fame, "The Celebrated Jumping Frog of Calaveras County." When the yarn reached New York the *Travels* had gone to press, and George W. Carleton, the publisher, did not think it worth while to disarrange the make-up. He therefore handed the MS. over to Henry Clapp, editor of the *Saturday Press*, with the remark:

"Here, Clapp, here's something you can use."

The story appeared in the issue of November 18, 1865, and the world had its first real laugh with "Mark Twain."

When the success of *The Innocents Abroad* had steered him to the lecture platform, Mr. Clemens concocted a monologue on "Artemus Ward." Writing to James Redpath, his manager, from Washington, on October 28, 1871, he says of this effort: "Dear Red,—I have come square out, thrown 'Reminiscences' overboard, and taken 'Artemus Ward, Humorist,' for my subject. Wrote it here on Friday and Saturday, and read it from MS. last night to an enormous house. It suits me and I'll never deliver the nasty, nauseous 'Reminiscences' any more."

This last was a reference to the title of the talk he had been giving. In full, it was "Reminiscences of Some Uncommonplace Characters That I Have Chanced to Meet." He was announced to give this in the Franklin Course, at Plymouth Church, Brooklyn, on the evening of Tuesday, November 21, 1871, but on the day of the lecture the advertisement in the *Eagle* was altered to read, "Artemus Ward, the Humorist." The *Eagle* gave no report; the *World* published a friendly notice of Twain as a lecturer, but gave no word of the talk. A fragment of it is given in Frederick Hudson's *History of Journalism in the United States*, as follows:

"Artemus Ward's real name, as most of you are probably aware, was Charles F. Browne. He was born in Waterford, Maine, in 1834. His personal appearance was not like that of most Maine men. He looked like a glove-stretcher; his hair, red, and brushed well forward at the sides, reminded one of a divided flame. His nose rambled on aggressively before him with all the strength and determination of a cow-catcher, while his red mustache, to follow out the simile, seemed not unlike the unfortunate cow.

"Ward never had any regular schooling; he was too poor to afford it, for one thing, and too lazy to care for it, for another. He had an intense, ingrained dislike for work of any kind; he even objected to see other people work, and on one occasion went so far as to submit to the authorities of a certain town an invention to run a treadmill by steam. Such a notion could not have originated with a hard-hearted man. Ward was a dutiful son, and his first act, when money began to come in on him from his lectures, was to free from incumbrance the old homestead in his native town and settle it upon his aged mother.

"His first literary venture was type-setting in the office of the old Boston *Carpet-Bagger*, and for that paper he wrote his first squib. He tried every branch of writing, even going so far as to send to the Smithsonian Institute—at least, so he himself said—an essay entitled, 'Is Cats to Be Trusted?' He soon tired of settled life and poor pay in Boston, and wandered off over the country to better his fortune, obtaining a position in Cleveland as a reporter at twelve dollars per week. It was while in Cleveland that he wrote his first badly spelled article, signing it 'Artemus Ward.' He did not think much of it at the time of writing it, but it gave him a start that speedily sent him to the top of the ladder without touching a single rung.

"He soon left Cleveland, and, going to New York, assumed the editorship of *Vanity Fair*. Settled employment, however, did not suit him, and he soon started out on his first lecture tour. The success of this new employment, although not great at first, soon exceeded his most sanguine expectations, and he adopted it as a permanent profession. When he went to England his reception was of the nature of an ovation. It is said that for each of his articles contributed

to *Punch* he received six hundred dollars. His pano-
ramic exhibitions in Egyptian Hall were a grand success, drawing, night after night, immense crowds to
witness them.

"The English climate of cold and fog seemed to
have the effect of eating away his life, and, although he
struggled hard, he had to relinquish his avocation.
When he knew that he must die, his only desire was
to get home, but this was denied him. He got as far
as Southampton, but his physician peremptorily for-
bade his attempting the sea voyage, and at Southampton, in the thirty-fourth year of his age, he died."

Despite his enthusiasm for the topic, Twain used it
but eleven times, reverting to selections from *Roughing
It* as an entertainment. The excerpt given above seems
ill-natured, as indeed are most of his references to his
first mentor, smacking somewhat of envy. Just why
he should have expressed himself slightingly toward the
friend who embraced him so unaffectedly and to whom
he owed his first sunrise in the East is hard to explain.
The errors of statement are left uncorrected.

Artemus found Austin to be a one-year-old mining-
camp with a court-house and a daily newspaper, the
Reveille. His fame had gone before and he was heartily
greeted by many adventurous souls. There was no
hall for the lecture, but choice lay between the court-
house, which Judge Brownson offered, and "Holbrook's
new granite store." The store was selected. The plaster
on the walls was still wet and there was no illumination.
Artemus led the way from the International Hotel to
the place of entertainment, carrying a lighted lamp in
his hand, followed by most of the audience to give

what had been announced in the *Reveille* as "The Pioneer Lecture in the Shoshone Nation," as indeed it was, the lecturer being the first platform speaker to brave the perils of the Sierras. Many of his hearers brought chairs from their homes on which to sit. The rest squatted on benches or stood. To end the hilarious night a dance was started that lasted far toward dawn.

The inhabitants of Big Creek, a mining-camp twelve miles from Austin, petitioned for the lecture. Hingston had armed himself with a big revolver against the perils of the plains and had been dubbed "Warrior" in consequence by his companion, who also bought a weapon but prudently kept it in the bottom of his trunk.

"Warrior, what do you say? Shall we go to Big Creek?" queried Artemus when the request came.

"Why not?" replied the agent, who recites the episode in "Artemus Ward among the Shoshones," contributed to the *Savage Club Papers* for 1868. "It must be a queer place to see, and to lecture there will be something droll to do. We will announce 'The Pioneer Lecture in the Shoshone Nation.'"

"We'll do it, Warrior," replied Artemus, with enthusiasm. "Only take care to have at the bottom of the bill, 'Admission, One Scalp; Front Seats, Two Scalps.'"

The lecture was given in the Young America saloon, with the bar in full action. One hundred and fifty miners paid three dollars each to sit on planks resting on kegs and roar approval at the jokes in "Babes in the Wood." The barkeeper assisted in the applause by yelling, "Bully, boys—bully!" at each successful jest, and whooping a peroration: "That's Artemus Ward from New England. Listen to him! Ain't he sweet? Ain't he hell!"

There were no fit lodgings in town and the pair drove back to Austin in the buggy by which they came. On the road they were waylaid by a band of their rough admirers led by one William Albaugh, made up as Shoshones, who captured them before Hingston could operate his shooting-iron and kept the pair on their knees half an hour under silent, menacing, savage guards. Then one of the "Shoshones," in bad English, asked Artemus his name:

"Artemus Ward," was the shivering reply. It was very cold and the scare added to the tremors.

"Wh-r-r-r-r-a-he! Uo! Uo! Uo! Americano talkee man!" whooped the questioner, joyously. Then he gave an imitation of scalp-taking on the lanky locks, while the crowd yelled:

"Talkee! Talkee!"

"My good Indian friends—" he began, to be interrupted by a "savage" pushing a bottle in his face, crying:

"Whisky—devite, devite! Drinkee, lecture, talkee!"

"Noble Shoshones," he began, "brave and heroic warriors of a mighty race! The Constitution of the United States was framed by the great and glorious George Washington. He wrote it out at tea-time over a bottle of bourbon and a hot corn-meal cake. He wrote in that glorious document that the Shoshone nation should ever be respected. He wrote, did that great and good man—"

"Bosh!" cried one of the Indians in a tone that

identified the jokers at once. Hot toddy and a cheery escort back to Austin followed—also a warning not to be careless in wild country.

At the end of five hilarious days Artemus and Doctor Hingston took passage from Austin on one of Ben Holladay's transcontinental stages for Salt Lake City. He had misgivings as to what his reception might be in view of the wide publicity given his "Visit to Brigham Young," printed in *Vanity Fair*, November 10, 1860, and based upon popular Eastern impressions, in which he had described Salt Lake as a "2nd Sodom and Gomorrer, inhabited by as theavin' and unprincipled a set of retchis es ever drew breth on eny spot on the globe."

The Gentiles in Nevada had been at great pains to warn him that this remark might bring unpleasant consequences in Utah, and he approached the borders of that territory with considerable misgiving. The country was full of weird tales of Mormon atrocities and the murderous deeds of "Destroying Angels." There were no adventures by the way, beyond an unjustified Indian scare and the shooting of a wolf who scented the supplies belonging to the party. The humorist kept his hand pretty steadily on the hilt of his revolver, but did not have to use it, though he scared Hingston by giving imitations of scalping and reciting tales of savage torture.

A glimpse of his entry into Mormondom is found in this excerpt copied from what was a bit of MS. of the *Travels*, evidently excised by the vigilant Carleton, in editing the work, for its offensive reference to Martin Harris, who had been one of the earliest of Joseph

Smith's followers at Palmyra, New York, and who mortgaged his farm to pay for the printing of the first edition of the *Book of Mormon:*

"We are now seven miles into Utah Territory, and for the first time in several days eat a tolerable dinner. The station is kept by a voluble Mormon who talks me into a sweet sleep about his Faith. I wake up as he is about closing and hear him ask, 'Was or was not Moses right?'

"'Moses who?'

"'Moses in the Bible.'

"Mr. Libby, the stage-driver, who is a scoffer, comes to my relief with the remark that Mose was all right. 'His head,' added Mr. Libby, 'was round'—which on the plains means that a man's head is unusually clear.

"At breakfast the next morning we met Mr. Walter Davis, the telegraph operator, and his young and pretty wife. They are Mormons, and the lady mentions that she came from Kirtland, Ohio. I had often been there; it was the first regular 'stake' the Mormons ever established, and I asked her if she knew a crazy old rascal there of the name of Martin Harris.

"'I did,' she said; 'he was my father!'

"This made the people at the table laugh as much as it did the children when Mary's little lamb went to school."

Another stop was at the home of Porter Rockwell, known as chief of Brigham's Destroying Angels. He was not at home, but Mrs. Rockwell took great satisfaction in showing the travelers a nine-hundred-pound hog. Hingston found comfort in a copy of the London *Times,* for which Rockwell was a subscriber.

At Salt Lake they were "put up" at the Salt Lake House and warmly welcomed by James Townsend, the landlord, and wife No. 2. Wife No. 1 was not in evidence, though existing elsewhere. No. 2 soon became "Townsend's better third" in A. W.'s vocabulary. He argued polygamy with her to small purpose, the lady having thoroughly accepted the situation.

"Why shouldn't a man be able to love two wives?" she asked.

Artemus replied that to his mind the heart had much to do with love—and he knew of no man with two hearts.

"God loves all," was her naïve response. "Man is a part of God, and when man belongs to the Church the image of God is in him; he loses his selfishness, becomes like God, and can love many."

Less than an hour after they were located at the hotel, Hingston relates, they were waited upon by a bland gentleman wearing a Scotch cap, a Mexican poncho, and a New England "comforter," who glided in with the pussy-footed step of one accustomed to going on delicate errands. He proved to be T. B. Stenhouse, a native of Scotland, once a reporter for James Gordon Bennett the elder, on the New York *Herald*, and then postmaster of Salt Lake City. He brought some letters for the humorist, and, what was more, a message of welcome, for, in addition to his postal responsibilities, he was an elder of the Church and official spokesman for Brigham Young. By skilfully leading the conversation, Stenhouse soon discovered Artemus's anxiety to ascertain his own status.

"The president has your book in his library," he

said. "He has all the books that have been written about him. You ought not to have made ridicule of our Church."

Artemus was properly contrite and explained his coming was due to a desire to lecture in the city and be free to see the Mormons as they really were. He was assured that his lecture would be heard and that all doors would be open to him. The next day Hiram B. Clawson, son-in-law of the Prophet, called with a sleigh to bear the travelers to his presence. They were driven to the official residence. The interview was brief but pleasant. Artemus was promised the use of the theater, after some consideration as to terms, Brigham preferring a share of the receipts to a fixed fee, though he intimated there might be no charge, presumably if he liked the show.

All being thus amicably arranged, preparations for the lecture were stopped by the sudden illness of the showman. An attack of mountain fever sent him to bed in the hotel, with considerable odds against his recovery. The vivid nights and long days in California and Nevada had taken heavy toll on his slender vitality. Hingston was distracted with anxiety. His own stock of remedies had been left behind in Nevada and there was no physician in the city, beyond a quack herbalist. The saints "cured" their ills by laying on hands. He therefore galloped on horseback to Camp Douglas, where he found Dr. Jonathan H. Williamson, of the Second California Volunteer Cavalry, the post surgeon, who at once responded to his call and took the patient under his care for the trying two weeks the fever ran. The good doctor did not believe his patient would recover. Hingston was warned to prepare for the worst and went so far as to see if the Overland Stage Company would transport his friend's body East. Nat Stein, the agent, said this would be impossible. "The last time we sent on the body of one of our people," he explained, "the wolves smelled it and attacked the mules. Our orders are never to send on another."

Artemus wrote himself in the *Travels:*

"My case is pronounced dangerous. I don't regard it so. In fact, I don't regard anything. I am all right myself. My poor Hingston shakes his head sadly, and Dr. Williamson . . . pours all kinds of bitter stuff down my throat. I drink his health in the cheerful beverage known as jalap, and thresh the sheets with my hot hands. I address large assemblages who have somehow got into my room, and I charge Dr. Williamson with the murder of Luce, and Mr. Irwin, the actor, with the murder of Shakespeare. I have a lucid spell now and then, in one of which James Townsend, the landlord, enters. He whispers, but I hear what he has to say far too distinctly: 'This man can have anything and everything he wants; but I am no hand for a sick-room. I never could see anybody die.'"

Mrs. Townsend had no such fears. She watched the patient with unremitting care and secured the services of Mrs. Battershall, an elderly Englishwoman, who was an experienced nurse. A Sacramento farmer, Jerome Davis, whose acquaintance had been picked up on the stage from Austin, volunteered, and his strong, tender hands came into play, lifting the fevered body of his friend. The city was full of interest and compassion. Brigham Young sent Stenhouse daily to inquire of the patient. At the end of a fortnight the fever left him, leaving him, as he said, "frightfully weak" and "fearfully thin," so much so that he put Hingston's overcoat on over his own when able to go out, and so "succeeded in making a shadow."

One of his first acts on recovering was to write this letter to Mark Twain at Virginia City:

"Salt Lake City, Jan. 21, '64.

"My dear Mark:—I have been dangerously ill for the past two weeks here of congestive fever. Very grave fears were for a time entertained of my recovery, but happily the malady is gone, though leaving me very, very weak. I hope to be able to resume my journey in a week or so. I think I shall speak in the theater here, which is one of the finest establishments of the kind in America.

"The saints have been wonderfully kind to me. I could not have been better or more tenderly nursed at home. God bless them all.

"I am still exceedingly weak—can't write any more. Love to Jo and Dan and all the rest. Write me at St. Louis.   Always yours,

Artemus Ward."

To Bret Harte, in San Francisco, he also expressed his gratitude: "I was taken very ill of fever on my arrival here. A Mormon woman—may God in heaven bless her—nursed me through as kindly and tenderly as my own mother could have done."

There were many callers, including, late one evening, a huge, strange-looking personage with a copper visage, wearing heavy jack-boots, with his hair plaited and worn like that of an Indian. It was Porter Rockwell, chief of the Destroying Angels, whom they had missed on the route. He sat beside the bed for half an hour, talking pleasantly. When he departed Artemus told Hingston who the visitor was.

"They say he has shot eighteen men," he exclaimed. "He's a cheerful angel to call on a sick man!"

As he convalesced attentions increased. General Connor sent him champagne from the officers' mess at Camp Douglas. Brigham Young added some fine-flavored native wine. The ladies of the Church contributed fresh eggs, jellies, dried fruits, and other domestic delicacies. All were enjoyed, but the food that lifted him from his couch was found by Jerome Davis in a local grocery—a dozen cans of Baltimore oysters—squares of block tin in which the bivalves then made long journeys.

"Get out the bills for the lecture," said Artemus, after his first stew. "See Mr. Clawson and arrange for the date. The show is safe enough, now we've got on an oyster basis."

February 8th was selected as the date. The theater was crowded, but the receipts were light—four hundred and ninety dollars. The price of admission was low, and most of the prominent saints were admitted free. Brigham Young sat in his rocking-chair and enjoyed the jokes in the "Babes," as did the more intelligent part of the audience, but Hingston noted many stolid women in the assemblage to whom the frivolity was Greek. Two days later, on the afternoon of Wednesday, February 10th, accompanied by Doctor Hingston,

12   [159]

Artemus departed by sleigh overland for the East, amid farewells from Mormon and Gentile, by way of Denver, Colorado.

Despite his good treatment he came away with a poor opinion of Brigham Young as a human being, but with high regard for his genius and ability. Exchanging views afterward with Hingston, the latter ventured the suggestion that Mormonism was a compound of Swedenborgianism and Mohammedanism.

"Petticoatism and plunder," was A. W.'s sententious reply.

At Denver, where the humorist was to lecture, this interesting episode occurred:

After the attack of mountain fever, his features became so attenuated that, to quote his own phrase, used in the lecture on the Mormons, "my nose was so sharp I didn't dare stick it into other people's business for fear it would stay there." His thin yellow locks added to the sharpness of his face, and he sought and found a remedy for his ill appearance. Reaching Denver, he hunted up a hardware-store and bought a pair of curling-tongs. Hingston, met him coming out of the shop with the package.

"I want you, old fellow," he said. "I have been all round the city for them, and I've got them at last."

"Got what?" asked the Doctor.

"A pair of curling-tongs. I am going to have my hair curled to lecture in to-night. I mean to cross the plains in curls. Come home with me and try to curl it for me. I don't want to go to any idiot of a barber to be laughed at."

Hingston successfully frizzled the lanky locks, and

CALIFORNIA, NEVADA, AND UTAH

ever after Artemus Ward wore curls, becoming, as he remarked, his own "curlist." In the Mormon lecture he would observe "a Mexican lady's hair never curls— it is straight as an Indian's. Some people's hair won't curl under any circumstances. My hair won't curl under two shillings"—meaning the barber's fee.

He was not alone in this gentle vanity. Captain Gronow, in his *Anecdotes of the Camp, Court, and Clubs*, relates that Scrope Davies, once entering Lord Byron's chamber, found the poet in bed with his hair in curl-papers, and cried out:

"Ha! Ha! Byron, I have at last caught you acting the part of the Sleeping Beauty!"

"No, Scrope," was the reply, "the part of a d—d fool, you should have said."

"Well, then, anything you please," said Davies. "But you have succeeded admirably in deceiving your friends, for it was our conviction that your hair curled naturally."

"Yes, naturally every night," replied Byron; "but do not, my dear Scrope, let the cat out of the bag, for I am as vain of my curls as a girl of sixteen."

Leaving Denver, the party pushed across the plains to reach the outpost of Eastern civilization at Atchison, Kansas, on a Sunday morning of the early spring. The trip had been a success in every respect. Plans were made for a rapid lecture tour, beginning at St. Louis, where a six-hundred-dollar house was gathered to hear "The Babes in the Wood" at the rooms of the Mercantile Library. Alton, Bloomington, Peoria, and Chicago responded nobly to the call. So did a series of Ohio towns. The expedition came back to New York with full pockets to prepare for a fresh campaign with "Artemus Ward among the Mormons."

Some idea of the financial success attained, despite extravagant outlay on top of a high legitimate expense, is found in this statement made by George W. Carleton:

"When Artemus returned from California I remember that he came into my office and, pulling out a long stocking filled with twenty-dollar gold pieces, he handed it over to me. It contained, I think, fifteen thousand dollars. Artemus put his money in bonds and securities, and for a while I kept them in my bank. One day I told him that the responsibility was great, and I would much prefer his taking care of his own money. He took it then, and deposited it in the Pacific Bank. A month afterward he went to England, where he died. When his executors went to the bank to draw his money they were confronted with a receipt. Artemus had drawn out every dollar before he left for England, and what he did with it is a mystery to this day. He was a careless man, and it would be difficult to tell where his money went. I think he purchased, or had purchased, a house in Yonkers before he deposited the money."

VI

THE MORMON LECTURE

LONG before the days of the "movies" there existed a popular form of entertainment called the "Panorama," a device by which vistas of famous scenes were painted on long strips of canvas, wound on rollers, and so slowly passed across a stage. The desert journey was to be thus depicted, accompanied by a patter of humorous talk.

The lecturer selected New York as a starting-point for the new venture. Much pains were taken to get the show into the public eye. While riding with Hingston one day across the plains on the homeward journey, Artemus, after a long silence, broke out, "I think I ought to go back to my B."

"Who is she?" Hingston asked.

"I mean the B in my proper name. Artemus Ward is a good name for newspaper work and books; but I must go back to my old 'Charles Browne' to be a showman. All good showmen begin with a 'B.' There's Barnum and Booth, Burton and Bateman."

"What about Sothern? You said the other day that you thought him to be a good showman."

"Well, he can't get on till he's got his B. That's why he's gone over to join Buckstone."

"Then make yours Brigham Young!"

The "B" stuck in his mind until the pair reached New York, where almost his first act was to send Hingston

[163]

down to Barnum's Museum at Broadway and Ann Street to consult the great P. T. on the merits of the proposition and the best place to produce.

This "B" notion, by the way, was one of Barnum's own foibles. It was known to the initiated in the circus business that to have a name that began with the second letter of the alphabet was a pretty certain passport to a job with the old man. A supporting tradition is that his most successful partner, James A. Bailey, was really born McGinnis, substituting Bailey as more certain to cement their relationship. Mr. Barnum gave a favorable opinion. Halls were few, and finally Dodworth's, a dancing-academy annex at 806 Broadway, was selected. It was small, badly arranged, and proved in the end a poor choice.

William Wheatley, lessee of Niblo's Garden, loaned the services of William Hilliard, his chief scene-painter, and Gus Maeder, while Charles R. Thorne aided with advice. A studio was set up next door to Wallack's Theater at the corner of Broadway and Eleventh Street, where the Panorama soon took shape. While this was going on Artemus went to Waterford.

His home-coming was saddened by the death of his brother Cyrus W. Brown, who died at the homestead on April 22, 1864, aged thirty-seven years. This bereavement made the summer somber and narrowed the world for mother and son. He spent the season quietly working up his lecture and putting his travel notes into shape.

Returning to New York in the early fall, the Panorama was set up in the hall and the lecture rehearsed. The perspective was not right, and to improve it the picture-frame was placed across the corner of the room. Artemus brought back from Waterford a boyhood friend, Horace Maxfield, a rosy-cheeked young man, son of the local stage-owner, who returned home after this adventure and took up the reins, to be ticket-taker. James F. Ryder was summoned from Cleveland to keep the lecturer company and hold his hand, so to speak. Copy without date went out to the newspapers, reading:

> Artemus Ward
> Which his number is 806
> Artemus Ward among the Mormons
> Dodworth Hall, 806 Broadway
> Just beyond Stewart's up-town store
> Opposite Eleventh Street
> Next to Grace Church
> And over the Spa.

His Entertainment,
  His Pictures,
    His Journey and
      His Jokes.

The 'Spa' was a famous soda-water dispensary in the days before the fountain was common. He cleverly annexed the best-advertised spots in town as neighbors. To add to the stir twelve Hibernians were hired, painted and befeathered to look like Indians, and each, carrying an umbrella announcing the show, solemnly paraded Broadway, reviewed incog. by their employer, who was deeply delighted by the interest aroused. Occasionally the procession paused to "whoop" and do a few steps of war-dance. October 17, 1864, was selected as the opening night. The house was well papered, invitations to the well-known going out in the form of a ticket admitting "the bearer and ˜ ·e Wife."

By no means the least meritorious part of the show was the program. Its four octavo pages teemed

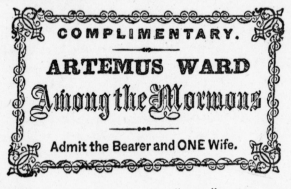

COMPLIMENTARY.

ARTEMUS WARD
Among the Mormons

Admit the Bearer and ONE Wife.

A TICKET TO THE "SHOW"

with wit and included this important bit of personal statistics:

"Traveler.—'How long was Artemus Ward in California?' 'Five feet ten and a half.'"

Finding that a small seating capacity and low prices could not work out successfully from a monetary point of view, Artemus increased the charge for admission. It was during war-time and prices were jumping. The Broadway stage line had just doubled its rate of fare from five to ten cents. The showman gravely used the same reason for his hoist, "The increase in the cost of oats."

Success was moderate but continuous. The hall when full could not hold a large-paying audience and had other drawbacks. The season lasted, however, for two months, then the show took to the road in New England, opening at the Boston Melodeum, on Washington Street, December 26th, and turning away crowds for a week. The Panorama was found too large and cumbersome for easy traveling and fitted badly in most of the halls. It had been painted by the best scenic artists and was really too good for the background of a jester's play. Artemus divined this and had another prepared in Boston of smaller size and with more of caricature in the execution. The big pictures were abandoned in Providence; the smaller served through the season and next, journeying at last to England.

The long season in New York caused it to be more and more "home," and here he enjoyed himself hugely with a plentiful supply of boon companions.

William Winter in his *Old Friends* gives a pleasant picture of Artemus at his best in New York: "His person was tall and thin; his face aquiline; his carriage buoyant; his demeanor joyous and eager. His features were irregular; his eyes of light-blue color, and in expression merry and gentle. His movements were rapid and inelegant. His voice was fresh and clear, and, though not sympathetic, distinctly communicative of a genial spirit. His attire was rich and gay—the attire of a man of fashion. He possessed to an extraordinary degree the faculty of maintaining a solemn composure of countenance while making comic or ridiculous statements—as when, in his first lecture in New York, he mentioned the phenomenal skill of his absent pianist, who, he said, 'always wore mittens when playing the piano,' and he could impart an irresistible effect of humor by means of a felicitous, unexpected inflection of tone. There is little in his published writings that fully explains the charm he exercised in conversation and in public speaking. . . . The charm . . . was that of a kindly, droll personality, compact of spontaneous mirth and winning sweetness. It is an attribute that words can but faintly suggest."

He lived at one time in the Jones House, at the southeast corner of Broadway and Great Jones Street. One night, Winter relates—or, rather, about 3 A.M.— he and other gay companions accompanied A. W. to his rooms. Here Artemus summoned a servant and, ordering copious refreshments, "earnestly inquired, with an imposing aspect of solemnity, an aspect by which I was completely deceived," whether it would be possible to arouse the landlord. The servant hesitated.

"It is late, sir," he said.

"I know it is late," replied Artemus, "but I have a message for him of the utmost importance. It is urgent and I am sure he will be glad to receive it. Do you think you could wake him?"

"Yes, sir, I could wake him, if you—"

"If you will, I will see that you are not blamed. Will you remember what I say, and be careful to deliver the message exactly as I tell you?"

"Yes, sir."

"Well, then, give him my compliments; be sure you mention my name; he's an old friend of mine; he'll be delighted to hear from me. Wake him, and tell him; speak distinctly, will you?"

"Yes, sir."

"Tell him, with my very kindest regards, that *the price of liberty is eternal vigilance.*"

ARTEMUS WARD
(From a portrait owned by the Lotos Club, New York)

THE MORMON LECTURE

The success of the jest filled him with glee. The appreciation of the landlord, aroused from his beauty sleep, is not on record.

The De Soto, a restaurant on Bleecker Street just east of Broadway, was his favorite dining-place. Here there was usually a coterie of choice spirits to aid in enjoyment of the meal. One of these survives in the person of George H. Story, the eminent artist, long curator of paintings in the Metropolitan Museum of Art, whose wife, Eunice Emerson Kimball, had been a fellow-member with A. W. in the Thespian Club at Norway, Maine, long before.

Dining here one day with Story, David Wambold, the minstrel, Dan Bryant, and some others, one of the unknown persisted in making some boresome, childish remarks in competition with the genuine wits. He became a nuisance, but was silenced at last by A. W., who took out his note-book and gravely inquired, "What is your age, sir?"

Mrs. Story was a relative of Ralph Waldo Emerson, who had been a familiar figure in Waterford, and was a sister of Charles P. and Hannibal I. Kimball, both men of note in Norway when young and who later in life had distinguished careers, the first as a great manufacturer in Chicago and the second as the recreator of Atlanta, Georgia.

One night the Storys went to the show, sitting well up front. Cracking a joke that elicited much applause, Artemus explained, much to the confusion of the lady, that it was an old one, first used in Norway, Maine, when he and "Eune Kimball played together in the Thespian Society!"

His Cleveland friends were always welcome. The Ryders were chief of these. One evening he took James F. Ryder and Susan, his wife, to a benefit for Agnes Robertson, an early wife of Dion Boucicault, at Wallack's Theater. As Oliver she headed the cast, which included, besides, Charlotte Cushman as Nancy Sykes; Lester Wallack as Bill Sykes; J. W. Wallack as Fagin; George W. Jamison, the Artful Dodger, and William Davidge, the Beadle. Surely a galaxy of stars to be looked back to in these modern days when we no longer go to see actors, but the play. Mrs. Ryder wept copiously over the rail of the balcony, until Artemus told her the people below were hoisting umbrellas to fend off her tears. His eyes were leaking, too, but the chance for a jest was too good to be lost.

Following the close of a very successful season with "The Mormons" in the summer of 1865, he betook himself to Waterford for a needed rest and to polish up the proofs of *His Travels* for issue in early fall. Pausing in Biddeford to visit his friend Shaw, he found that gentleman had been elected mayor at the spring election in addition to thriving in business. Out of his prosperity he had purchased a fine horse and beach-wagon and took comfort in the thought of long, easy drives along the hard, smooth beaches of York and Old Orchard. He exhibited the new outfit. It was a fatal error. The seaside season was not open and Artemus pleaded to be allowed to drive the team across country to Waterford. Mr. Shaw was not delighted at the proposal, but consented with a feeling that his summer's fun would go with the outfit. So it proved. A month went by, but no tidings of the team. The

summer advanced.   Then one day, looking over a copy
of the New York *Clipper*, which carried a department
chronicling the doings of the wandering country cir-
cuses, he saw a notice that some proud aggregation
had been exhibiting at Paris Hill, the county-seat
town, fifteen miles from Waterford, and that in the
audience was "the distinguished humorist," Mr.
Charles F. Browne, who exhibited with pride a
splendid equipage presented him by his old friend the
mayor of Biddeford.   He wrote a half-angry appeal
to Artemus to send his horse home, and got this reply:
"I don't see what you want to fuss so about your old
horse.   I'm *looking after* him every day."   September
came and with it the beach-wagon and its nag.   But
the rig looked as if it had summered with the gipsies.
It was entirely unfit for the use of a handsome and
dashing young mayor.

The summer brought him many visitors, including a
favorite friend, Daniel Setchell, the comedian.   The
two took long rides across country, indulging in
mystifying jokes by the way, on one occasion exhibiting
Setchell securely tied and giving a startling imitation
of a lunatic in charge of a keeper en route for the
asylum at Augusta.   Setchell was the master of
grimace, and his facial expressions were terrifying to
the rustics.   Artemus once suggested, when Washington was menaced by the Confederate army, that Dan
should stand at the end of the Long Bridge and make
faces at the advancing foe, certain that it would scare
them away.   "Old Setch can do it," was his concluding
comment.

Mr. Setchell was very stout and insisted while at

Waterford in doing all the chores to fend off a tendency to apoplexy, while the idle Artemus loafed and gibed him.

"Poor Mr. Setchell," said Aunt Caroline Brown once to the writer. "He was *so* afraid he would die of apoplexy, and when here he always insisted on drawing all of the water, splitting and bringing in the wood, in order to get thin. And to think that after all the trouble he took he should have been drowned at sea."

Such, indeed, was the fate of the merry gentleman. He embarked on board the *Trieste*, a sailing-ship bound for New Zealand, at San Francisco, January 1, 1866, and the vessel was never heard from again.

During this visit, a village damsel became deeply enamoured of Setchell, so much so that she would visit the homestead on small excuses and linger for hours. Perceiving the nature of the disease, and feeling that a disillusion was necessary to save much unhappiness, the pair stole an idea from Tom Robertson's "David Garrick," just then made popular by E. H. Sothern, using Setchell's greatest accomplishment as a means of breaking the spell. One morning when the lovelorn maiden called to inquire if she might see Mr. Setchell, Artemus assented, but expressed the fear that she had arrived just in time to see him have one of his "terrible fits." She was ushered into the parlor, where Dan at once gave his performance, writhing and contorting his features into horrible semblances. The poor girl fled in terror and never came back again.

Journeying from Waterford to Portland on the Grand Trunk, then and now a rather deliberate rail-

road, Artemus was annoyed at the slow progress, and, hailing the conductor, said:

"Dear friend, it is plain from the speed of this train that it could never catch a cow if one chanced to travel on the track in front of it. Therefore, the cow-catcher is a useless protection where it is. But there is nothing to prevent a cow from catching up with us in case she should choose to follow. I beseech you, therefore, to remove the cow-catcher from the locomotive and place it on the rear car and so save us from disaster!"

From Waterford he returned invariably to New York, where, besides the friends in Bohemia, the actors, minstrels, and showmen there rendezvoused were his intimates, and he was much in their company. Two special chums were Dan and Neil Bryant, whose theater was a center of joy. He always headed for the place when in town. The late Frederick Habirshaw, of Brooklyn, who spent much time during the war as an engineer taking monitors to Hampton Roads, once related to me that late in August, 1865, he was invited by one of the Bryants to occupy a box seat at the show. He found Artemus Ward, Charles Dawson Shanly, and a tall young stranger there before him. After the minstrel performance was over, Neil Bryant and some of the performers joined them and the crowd proceeded rather noisily along Broadway. They were stopped by a policeman, who sought to muffle the hilarity. At this, Artemus hurled himself against the broad bosom of the officer and with a sob proclaimed his belief that "a metropolitan policeman was the noblest work of God."

Mr. Habirshaw often wondered who the tall stranger was. Oddly enough, it was left for me to find out—quite by chance. Visiting the exposition held at Nashville, Tennessee, in October, 1899, with an excursion managed by the Brooklyn *Daily Eagle*, I went out to visit Gen. W. H. Jackson's famous Belle Meade farm. Sitting on the edge of the station platform, waiting for the return train, I happened to be next to Maj. John M. Keiley, of Brooklyn, brother of that A. M. Keiley whose appointment as minister to Austria made so much trouble for President Cleveland. He had been chief of Longstreet's staff, and told me how he had put all of the equipment of the Georgia Railroad in a row and pushed it off the wrecked bridge at Knoxville to prevent it from falling into Sherman's hands. He recalled that soon after the war he came North, hunting for a job and a food supply, and while looking about a friend gave him a box seat for Bryant's Minstrels. He had for companions in the box Artemus Ward, Charles Dawson Shanly, and a thick-set young man whose identity he did not discover. Then he told me the police incident almost in Habirshaw's words. So I had the pleasure of telling him who the stranger was—thirty-four years after. Habirshaw had departed this life a short time before.

One gay night Artemus induced Dan Bryant and Nelse Seymour, another famous minstrel, to invade the property-room at Bryant's theater and garb themselves in stage armor. Then, arming themselves with broadswords, the trio sallied forth and waylaid belated citizens, forcing some of them to sink on their knees in prayer by way of ransom. The sport was interrupted

DAN BRYANT AS "PAT MALLOY"

by a policeman, who escorted the mirthful three to the Tombs. The next morning his Honor let them off with a lecture. As a prelude to this performance they made a midnight call on Thomas Jackson, who brought the first Swiss bell-ringers to America. Violent pulls at the door-knob brought him to an upper window.

"Who are you and what do you want?" he demanded, angrily.

"We want an engagement," responded Artemus, sweetly. "We are the original bell-ringers!"

Once at a Turkish bath in Twelfth Street he saw two attendants diligently tugging away at the head and feet of a patron, and was moved to ask the reason for their unique exertions.

"He is half an inch too short to be a policeman," was the reply.

"Can you really stretch him out that much?" was his further interested query. He was informed that an inch could be added in a couple of weeks.

"If that's so," he said, softly, "I wish some one would stretch Bayard Taylor into a Humboldt."

His second season with "The Mormons" opened at Irving Hall, Fifteenth Street and Irving Place, New York, August 28, 1865. It was successful. An account-book found among the few relics at the Waterford homestead gives some of the figures, which are interesting. The receipts for the first two weeks were $2,117.50, of which the book notes that "Ward" got $961.85. Six nights in Washington earned $2,008.75. "Ward" received but $476 of this. Two nights in Baltimore lacked just 25 cents of tying, the receipts

being $551.25 and $551, respectively. He had fair
luck in Brooklyn. Three nights were spent there,
$373, $275, and $279.25 were collected. Philadelphia
did much better. Here the receipts for three nights
were $485, $629.50, and $564. Four nights in Mon-
treal netted $612.75, and four in Cincinnati $1,081.
All these accounts are kept in his own handwriting and
may be said to be the only orderly things he ever did.

The country success was very large, but called for a
wide range. Hingston went to Europe to attend to
some personal affairs, and Samuel W. Wilder, his
former employer, back from California, took the management under a contract and covered the Northern
states. Then, on his own hook, Artemus journeyed
South, late in the year.

This Southern trip was made by river from Pittsburgh, with pauses en route, including a very lively
stay at Cincinnati. The city was an important journalistic center then and housed at the time three strong
papers, the *Gazette*, *Times*, and *Commercial*. The last-
named journal was owned and edited by Murat Halstead,
robust in person and methods, and Henry Watterson
had a hand in making the *Times*. He was then a thin
youth of twenty-five, who had escaped from the Confederacy during its dying days and found his way,
after all was over, to Cincinnati in an effort to secure
something to eat, as he put it. C. W. Starbuck, publisher of the *Times*, gave him a job. He soon began
writing "pert paragraphs," assailing Halstead, who
was the lion of the local press. The latter stood the
prods for a brief spell and then emitted a roar to the
effect that if the little ragged Confederate who was

getting fresh in the columns of the *Times* did not cease his cavilings, the *Commercial* would turn some light on the personal past of his employer.

Halstead worked at a desk on the ground floor of the *Commercial* office, placed to face the street, so he could keep a handy eye on visitors. He also kept a revolver in a half-open top drawer to welcome any who chanced to come from Kentucky. One morning a slim young chap in worn butternut came in to face the battery. He soon made himself known as the little ragged Confederate, and said that Starbuck had told him to spike the *Commercial* or get out. As he had not had much food or any new raiment since the blood of Bishop and Lieut.-Gen. Leonidas Polk had spattered over him at Kenesaw Mountain, he wanted to hold his job. Halstead uttered a mighty whoop of welcome and took him to his bosom. They remained the warmest of friends ever after.

Not many days after this episode, the outside door burst open and, as Halstead once told me the story: "A tall, slim, impetuous, fierce, bright-eyed young man, evidently ostentatiously angry, dashed through the open door. He paused in a very alert attitude quite near me and glared down upon me, as I was seated, his fine nostrils quivering, with an expression of annoyance fixed upon his features, and slowly repeated my name, asking if I answered to it. I nodded assent and waited curiously to see what was up. The boys in the show business were always springing something on me, and I suspicioned a new one. Stepping back, he began a loud, incoherent harangue, out of which I gleaned he had some grievance and no hope of securing reparation. I was the kind of a person, he understood, to whom it was vain to make an appeal for justice. I tried to calm him and find out what it was all about, when I located the word 'show.' 'What show?' I asked. 'Hey? Why, my show!' he replied, hotly. The torrent of words went on until I began to think a crazy man had got in and that I had better do something. A sense of wrath was also rising in my soul. My visitor saw it and piled on the agony. To a curt protest of ignorance he replied, 'This is your regular way of treating those who call upon you good-naturedly for the least bit of justice—well, be it so—let it fall upon your own head!' Out of patience, I told him to go to the devil. At this he became more shrill in his denunciations. 'Oh yes, that's what I am told by everybody, no matter what I have been doing, and without reference to justice, human or divine. This is infernal! No man should be allowed to go on with his fellow-men as you are doing. I am not disappointed. Oh no, no, no! and you may go on forever, for all I care. I have now told you to your face what I think of you. I have known all the while there was no redress for me. Your outrageous conduct was witnessed by everybody. It is not a personal matter to me so much as a matter of principle. The people should be protected from this tyranny. In my case you have gone beyond all bounds. Not only have you assailed the show and maligned me, but *you have reviled the elephant!*' With this astounding declaration he made a quick turn and in a flash was out of the building. While I was wondering what it was all about, a boy came in with a note

from Fred Hunt, our dramatic critic, saying I was
wanted at the St. Nicholas Hotel across the street.
I went over and found a crowd of the fellows about
town, and was gravely introduced to my late visitor,
who was Mr. Artemus Ward."

To properly return numerous attentions Artemus
gave a dinner to the group of good fellows, which included Halstead and Colonel Watterson.

The trip was made partly to avoid the inclement
season in the North and partly to enjoy a visit to a
Southern plantation, owned by his friend Melville D.
Landon, who was trying to become a planter at Lake
Providence, a point on the river in East Carroll
County, Louisiana. He met Langdon at Memphis,
where the pair boarded the steamer for Lake Providence. Artemus had with him three trunks of personal baggage labeled thus:

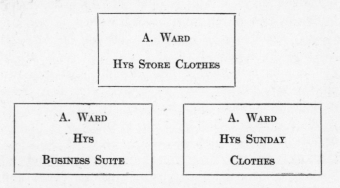

A. WARD

HYS STORE CLOTHES

A. WARD

HYS

BUSINESS SUITE

A. WARD

HYS SUNDAY

CLOTHES

Soon Landon discovered that he was the object of
much attention and at loss for an explanation. "Do I
look peculiar—am I not dressed properly?" he queried
of Artemus.

"Yes," he replied, "you are all right, my boy, but you have a deuced *distingué* look. You resemble General Forrest—that's what they are all looking at!"

Pretty soon a Christian Commission man came along with a request from the ladies in the cabin to "say some of your funny things," and thus Landon learned that A. W. had caused him to be pointed out as the owner of the trunks.

"Now you see what it is to be famous," he commented.

In forty hours Lake Providence was reached, and here Artemus loitered and laughed to his heart's content for a few pleasant days. The colored plantation hands were a source of never-ending entertainment. To one old darky, Uncle Jefferson, he was particularly attentive, holding forth to him one day in this fashion:

"Now, Uncle Jefferson, why do you thus pursue the habit of industry? Indolence is preferable. I prefer it. I am happier when I am idle. Why cannot you pursue a life of happy idleness, too? Why do you not break off this habit of working at once? Why, Jefferson, you could live for months without performing any kind of labor, and at the expiration of that time feel fresh and vigorous enough to commence it again. Idleness invigorates the system. It is a sweet boon. No one should work; they should get other people to do it for them."

"You is jest right," assented the receptive Jeff, whereat he was given a dollar and waved sadly away to the "quarters" to spread the satisfying doctrine where it would be further appreciated. One day, Landon relates, the negroes were grinding their hoes on a shaky old grindstone, which had been worn by much use into a wabbling ellipse. The contortions of the stone as it was turned moved Artemus to deep laughter. "There," he said, as he waved his arm in imitation of its eccentric movements, "is wit personified, or thingified. When you can express in an eccentric anticlimax instead of a rounded sentence, then you will have something funny."

Elaborating the point, he once said to Landon: "People laugh at me more on account of my eccentric sentences than on account of the subject-matter in them. There is no wit in the form of a well-rounded sentence. If I say Alexander the Great conquered the world and then sighed because *he could not do so some more*, there is a funny mixture."

An example in point is a phrase used in his lectures: "History is full of great men, but how few, alas! would we want to take home to supper with us!"

A considerable Northern colony centered about Lake Providence, tempting fortune in cotton-planting. They were young and agreeable men and got on well with their Southern neighbors, so A. W. met with much generous hospitality—too much, indeed, for his frail person. Leaving for New Orleans, he paused to give a lecture at Natchez, in the course of which he paid his compliments to his late hosts in these terms:

"I love my Southern brothers—and sisters. I think I shall marry a rich young Southern widow with a plantation of *free negroes*. Then I shall settle down and return the courtesies of that band of chivalric young Southern planters from New York who entertained me so well at Lake Providence."

Reaching New Orleans, then striving to rally from under the wreck of the war, he gave "The Mormons" to appreciative auditors at the Masonic Temple.

A. H. Williams, in his *With the Border Ruffians*, a book of wild Western adventure, mentions hearing the lecture early in January, 1866. "His humor," Williams writes, "certainly was of the driest, and his stories, told without the ghost of a smile, were most comical. I never heard an audience laugh so heartily as his did that night."

Here he gave a benefit for the relief of those who had suffered from the war—women and children. For this he was bitterly criticized on his return to the North—especially in Boston, which had forgotten that it once mobbed William Lloyd Garrison and sent a fugitive slave back South in chains. The criticism cut him deeply. The excessive hospitality and ener-vating climate of the lower Mississippi had exhausted him. He was worn and ill and took a needed and re-freshing holiday in Waterford. The long-nurtured determination to visit England here took shape and he devoted his time to fixing up his affairs for the journey.

In the course of a lecture trip to Canada he picked up a bright sixteen-year-old boy, George H. Stephens, whom he engaged as a page and valet. The lad trav-eled with him about the country and was retained for the European adventure, not that he was especially useful, but because his employer was lonely and liked to have somebody around.

At Montreal, during this visit, he fell in with Richard Worthington, then a venturesome young publisher, and John Lovell, an enterprising printer, whose son, John W. Lovell, later established a great enterprise in New York for the production of popular literature. The two undertook to issue an authorized edition of *His Book* for Canadian sale, and did so. It is a very rare volume, but one copy ever coming to my notice, that in the library of Mountville B. de la Bruère, of the Canadian Archives Bureau in Montreal. Mullen's pictures were used, and on the cover Mr. Ward stands wrapped in the American flag, his eyes lifted to the stars.

He had some misgiving that he might not return from Europe, and, among other preparations, had George H. Story paint his portrait as a gift to his mother.

"Of course," he said, at the first sitting with the artist, "I want as good a picture as possible, but please preserve the architectural characteristics of my nose."

VII

WITH fair warning to Hingston, the showman sailed from New York on Saturday, June 2, 1866, on the Inman liner, *City of Boston*, in company with E. H. House, a well-known journalist, and George H. Stephens, his valet. There seems to have been no stir over his departure. The *World* mentions it in the issue of Monday, June 4th, with a line and a half, reading, "Charles F. Browne (Artemus Ward) sailed for Europe Saturday."

The steamer made port on June 13th. Proceeding to London, he found instant welcome. A friend and schoolmate of his Waterford boyhood, Albion Chadbourne, was located in the city and bestirred himself to give him an agreeable introduction. Hingston had already been busy on his part. The summer season was spent in getting acquainted and in rest and enjoyment. With the magnetic instinct that always led him where he was most wanted and where he most wished to be, he was taken in body and soul by the members of the now- and long-famous Savage Club, then a very loosely constructed Bohemian organization, to which his coming gave great vogue, and he became its reigning attraction.

Like Pfaff's Bohemia, which formed itself around the staff of the *Saturday Press*, the Savage Club had its origin in a group of writers who contributed to the

[184]

making of *The Train—A First Class Magazine*, initially issued in London, January, 1856, meeting first at the White Hart Inn, at the corner of Exeter and Catherine streets, Strand. A room was later taken at the Crown Tavern in Vinegar Yard, opposite to the gallery entrance of Drury Lane Theater. It was a very informal and irresponsible body at the start and long afterward.

"I hear," said Edmund Yates to George Augustus Sala, one of the organizers, "that there is a new club started—The Savages. What is the subscription?"

"Just whatever the members choose to owe," was the response.

In reality, the "dues" consisted of five shillings yearly, paid to Landlord Lawson, of The Crown, by each member for the use of the room, mainly as an obolus given to obviate drinking "for the good of the house." The room was bare and whitewashed, but Robert Brough, Charles H. Bennett, and William McConnell, artist members, soon saw that the walls were brightly decorated. In April, 1858, the club shifted its quarters to the Nell Gwynne Tavern, in a courtyard off the Strand, where a regular rental of twenty pounds a year was paid and the membership put up dues, as they felt like it, in form of voluntary contributions. Indeed, there was no treasurer until 1864, when H. B. Chatterton, manager of Drury Lane, accepted the inconsiderable responsibility. The quarters were shifted several times and at the period of A. W.'s arrival had just been relocated in Ashley's Hotel in Henrietta Street, Covent Garden. Here Artemus found them when he reached London, and in the cheery surroundings he spent most of his idle time.

There were rare brushes of wit with Henry J. Byron; Thomas W. Robertson; the brothers Brough, John C., William, and Lionel; George Augustus Sala; Dr. G. L. M. Strauss ("The Old Bohemian"); H. B. Chatterton; Andrew Halliday; George Grossmith; James Hannay the younger; Tom Hood; J. E. Preston Muddock ("Dick Donovan"); Howard Paul; W. Jeffrey Prowse; George Rose ("Arthur Sketchley"); Barry Sullivan; W. B. Tegetmeier; John L. Toole, and Frank Vizetelly— while affording entertainment to scores of lesser lights in the Savage Bohemia.

He was "put up" for membership and duly elected on August 4, 1866. Charles Millward was his proposer. The seconds were Andrew Halliday, J. L. Toole, J. C. Brough, Henry S. Leigh, W. J. Prowse, Thomas Archer, Charles W. Quin, Charles Furtado, T. W. Robertson, and Howard Paul in the order named. Qualification: "Artemus Ward."

The life he led in London soon showed ill effects. The convivial nights at the Savage Club, supplemented by much private hospitality, were wearing in the extreme, not so much from the absorbing of liquids, though that was considerable, but from the mental strain growing out of being always drawn upon to provide amusement for the expectant company. His associations pumped him dry and the intellectual drain sapped his vitality. Mr. and Mrs. Charles Millward became devoted friends, and Mrs. Millward soon noted the fading physique of the laughter-loving guest, and felt moved to warn him to take better care of himself and live more quietly. "You must learn to say no," she urged, repeatedly.

Candidate for Election

(Savage Club.)

Charles F Browne

Qualification, - Artemus Ward.

Proposed by C Millward

Seconded by Andrew Halliday

J. W. Tooley

H Brough   Elected

Henry J. Leigh   Aug 14th 1866

Thomas J. Archer

W Phillips

Charles W Dunn

Charles Hurtado

J W Churton

Howard Paul

FACSIMILE OF A. WARD'S PROPOSAL TO MEMBERSHIP IN THE SAVAGE CLUB

LONDON

"One night," said Millward later to William Winter, "between midnight and morning, we were awakened by a loud knocking at our door; and on descending, I found Artemus there, in evening dress, unusually composed and serious. Of course I welcomed him, though at a loss to understand the cause of his untimely call. He urgently requested the presence of Mrs. Millward, and would take no denial—having, as he gravely declared, a most important communication to impart—that only she could appreciate. Yielding to his importunity, I persuaded Mrs. Millward to get up. The moment she appeared he greeted her with impressive solemnity.

"'It is done,' he said. 'I knew you would wish to hear it at once. I have been at the Savage Club all evening, and I have said no!'"

His particular intimate in all the talented throng was Thomas W. Robertson, then a fast-rising playwright, father of Madge Robertson Kendal, the famous actress of our time, and the first of English dramatists to concoct a comedy in the modern sense. Robertson had been rapidly making his way in the London theatrical world. He had adapted "David Garrick" to Sothern's talents and sold him the play for a small sum. Its success, when presented in 1864, was such that the actor sent him five hundred pounds as a bonus. "Society," produced at the Prince of Wales Theater in 1865, set him on the highroad. When the acquaintance with A. W. began in the summer of 1866 he was busy with the finishing touches on "Ours," to which his new-found friend contributed some of the fun. Indeed, its production in America was announced as an "Original Comic Drama by T. W. Robertson and Artemus Ward." Lester Wallack bought the American rights and its success here was the foundation of his fame and fortune. It was first presented at Wallack's Theater, New York, December 19, 1866, and met with a glorious reception from press and public. Artemus was very modest, indeed, as to his share in the merits of the comedy, as this undated letter to Robertson shows:

"*Saturday.* 57 PICCADILLY.

"MY DEAR ROBERTSON: I send some New York papers containing notices of 'Ours.' I regret not having the New York *Times* or the *Tribune* notices—that one for the latter journal having been written by my friend House, who came over with me, you remember, last spring. I am opined by private letters that your comedy is a very genuine success, and I hope by this time you are receiving substantial proofs of the fact.

"I think my friends of the press have given me as little prominence in connection with 'Ours' as was possible, under the circumstances. I wrote, sometime since, to House & Seymour to say just as little about me as possible. I mention this because two of the journals I send you will have it that my 'facile pen' was actually employed in the writing of the comedy. As you will see by these articles, dramatic criticism in America is in its infancy. It has been in its infancy over fifty years, I may add, and will continue in that highly juvenile state until the sordid-minded publishers of the New York journals can be induced to employ men who know what they are writing about. I do not refer, of course, to the New York *Tribune*, *Times*, *Albion*, or *Nation*. But the most of the 'Criticisms' I send are kindly in their tone—the writers mean well —and that is something.

"Always yours,

ARTEMUS WARD."

The American critics were quite sparing in their mention of Mr. Ward's share in the "piece," the *Times* failing to find much trace of his handiwork amid its sparkles.

The play was produced at the Prince of Wales Theater, September 15, 1866, and made Robertson king of his kind. It had the first "run" in history, lasting one hundred and fifty nights.

At one of Millward's "evenings," given in honor of the humorist, Robertson first met Marie Wilton, afterward Lady Squire Bancroft, an acquaintance that brought good fortune to them both and made the Prince of Wales Theater the home of artistic comedy.

The comic papers in London at once reached out for A. W., but *Punch*, the conservative and anti-American during the war, secured him as a contributor. He met Mark Lemon, then its editor, at a dinner-party given by Willart Beale and the engagement resulted. It was not the habit of *Punch* to publish signed articles, but of course this was no place for tradition, and "Artemus Ward" was blazoned not only in the columns of the paper, but in huge letters over the door of the publication office, to the infinite glee of the showman, who took delight in walking by the place and pointing out the unwonted decoration. He contributed eight

14

articles, all under the heading, "Artemus Ward in London." The first appeared in the issue of September 1, 1866, the last on November 3d. His honorarium was fifteen guineas per letter.

"This is the proudest moment of my life," he wrote to his friend Jack Ryder, in Cleveland. "To have been as well appreciated here as at home; to have written for the oldest comic journal in the English language, received mention with Hook, Jerrold and Hood, and to have my picture and my pseudonym as common in London as in New York, is enough for

Yours truly, A. WARD."

Lemon evidently had some difficulty in extracting the copy with the regularity required for a publication issued at stated intervals. Encountering Hingston one day when he had just returned from an interview with the editor, Artemus remarked: "Mr. Lemon tells me that I want discipline. I know I want discipline. I always did want it, and I always shall."

Then he added, serio-comically: "Can you get me a stock of discipline? You have more of it here than we have in the States. I should like some."

In addition to the letters to *Punch*, Artemus contributed "Converting the Nigger" to a volume edited by Andrew Halliday, *The Savage Club Papers*, published to aid the charity fund of the organization, and "Pyrotechny" to *The Five Alls*, a holiday publication issued by Frederick Warne & Co., and edited by the younger Hood. The frontispiece of the *Papers*, drawn by William Brunton and engraved by the Brothers Dalziel, shows the faces of the contributors,

A GROUP OF SAVAGES

Frontispiece of The Savage Club Papers for 1867, drawn by William
Brunton. Artemus Ward looking in from the right

grouped around Dr. G. L. M. Strauss, that of A. W.
looking into the picture from the right. Doctor Strauss,
in his *Reminiscences of an Old Bohemian*, records this incident of A. W.'s stay in London, showing his way of extracting and affording amusement along the pavement:

"Artemus Ward, the prince of humorists, positively
reveled in what I think he was the first to dub a 'goak.'
I remember, late one night in the fall of 1866, Artemus,
dear little Jeff Prowse, and my humble self were left
alone in the clubroom at Ashley's. Artemus proposed
an adjournment to the Alhambra. Prowse and self
joyfully assented. Artemus asked Jeff to charter a
cab. The vehicle soon drew up. It was a clear night,
and the hotel and street-lamps shed a bright light,
which gave us a full view of the driver's face. He was
grave and stolid-looking, and evidently self-possessed.
Artemus seemed to study the man's features for a brief
moment; then he intimated to me in a whisper that he
was going to have a lark with cabby. Assuming his
grave air, which sat so marvelously well on his face,
he addressed the man in slow, measured accents. 'My
friend,' he said, 'you look to me a man of thought and
experience, in fact, the very man likely to decide a
most important and most difficult question which has
arisen between me and my friend there,' pointing to
Jeff, who looked slightly puzzled. 'Do you take me?
Will you be arbiter between us?' Cabby looked so
dubious at first that I thought he was going to say,
'Gammon,' or, 'Shut up,' or something of the sort.
However, so wondrously intent did Artemus look, and
so supernally grave was his manner, that the man's
suspicions faded away from his face as snow will under

a hot sun. He gave a half-grunt, then said, briefly, 'Fire away, guv'nor, let's know w'at's all about.'

"'Well,' responded Artemus, with slow deliberateness, weighing every word apparently. 'Well, look ye here now, my friend; that gentleman there'—pointing again to Jeff Prowse, who, not knowing exactly how Charley might choose to compromise him with a mayhap irate Jehu, began to give slight signs of feeling rather uncomfortable—'maintains that it is the divergence of contradictory opinions, which in the natural logical sequence of reasoning, and in the inferential conclusions of argumentation, must in the final end inevitably lead to convergence, and concord, and harmony among people, and bring about that most devoutly to be wished for consummation when man to man the world all o'er shall brethren be and a' that. I trust you follow me, my friend?'

"'I follow you, guv'nor; fire away,' said cabby, briefly, who evidently was not quite clear yet what it all could possibly be about.

"'Now you see, my good fellow,' pursued Artemus, with increased intentness of face and graver ponderousness of manner and diction, 'I, on the other part, assert, and I mean to stick to it, too, let gainsay who may' —with a ferocious glare our way—'that it is contrariwise and opposite, the convergence of concurrent, concordant, and coincident opinions that must inevitably in its corollary and concomitant consequential train of its oncoming results lead to divergences, difficulties, and differences'—raising his voice to a higher pitch, and frantically sawing and beating the air with his outstretched right arm—'which will make one man jump at another man's throat and strive to strangle him to death!' Then he proceeded more quietly: 'Now, my friend, you cannot but admit that I have placed the case fairly before you. Now please give us your decision.'

"Cabby, who had apparently listened with much serious attention to this rigmarole, bent his head on one side, and, with one eye shut, gave Artemus the benefit of an inimitably droll look. Then he proceeded with gravity of manner equal to Ward's, and still more ponderous slowness of enunciation, to deliver himself of the following oracular decision, which would have done honor to great Bunsby himself: 'Well, guv'nor, it is a 'notty p'int and a 'ard nut to crack for the likes o' me, seein' as there is a great deal to be said on both sides; and don't ye think, now, guv'nor, it's rayther a dry question to settle? vich I know'd from the first, ye vos a gen'l'man hevery hinch o' you, guv'nor.' Having said which, he looked expectant.

"'Sold!' cried Artemus, laughing, and jumping into the vehicle, followed by us. 'You shall have your liquor, cabby. Drive on.'

"'Where to?' asked the man, cheerfully, evidently rejoicing in the anticipation of a drink.

"'To the boundless Prairie!' shouted Artemus.

"'Don't know no sich place about London,' said cabby. 'Maybe ye'll tell me vich vay.'

"'Alhambra way, then,' responded Artemus; and to the Alhambra we were driven accordingly, where cabby was liberally treated to gin-sling and dog's-nose, which seemed to be his special vanities."

The humorist's mother was not a very active correspondent, but his interest in her was constant and affectionate. Here is a letter to her, written when he was at his best in London:

> "54 PICCADILLY,
> "LONDON, Oct. 7, 66.

"DEAR MOTHER:

"It is a long time since I have had a letter from you. Now, answer this *at once*. Don't delay a moment. Tell me all about yourself. Give me all the news. Direct to 54 Piccadilly, London, England. I am all right. George sends love. Tell Horace to write. Regards to all who have an interest in me. I like England more and more the longer I stay here.

> "Ever yr. affectionate Son,
> CHARLES."

"George" was his young valet. "Horace" was Horace Maxfield, his Waterford friend and companion in the American "Mormon" tour. Of these happy days in London I have this reminder from Colonel Henry Watterson, written March 28, 1918: "A most affectionate intimacy existed between myself and Artemus Ward. We were in London together through the autumn and winter of 1866–67. He had his Christmas dinner with Mrs. Watterson and myself—only our three selves —for he was then a dying man. Our lodgings were adjacent, he over Kingsford's drug-store across the way from Egyptian Hall, where he lectured, and mine around the corner in Jermyn Street. We forgathered nightly at the old Savage Club, until he could go no longer, and, called unexpectedly home, I left him five or six weeks before he died at Southampton, where he had arranged to go. It was a kind of suicide for him to make an English *tour de force*."

The "show" was slow in getting under way. Egyptian Hall, which Albert Smith had popularized with his lectures on travel and George Rose, "Arthur Sketchley," further located in the public mind with his monologues, was selected as the place of trial. The Panorama was set up and tested and a pianist engaged to "tune up" the pathetic spots. The program was, like its predecessors in New York, a folder full of humor and included this invention, by way of a testimonial:

"TOTNES, Oct. 20, 1866.

"MR. ARTEMUS WARD.

"MY DEAR SIR,—My wife was dangerously unwell for over sixteen years. She was so weak that she could not lift a teaspoon to her mouth; but in a fortunate moment she commenced reading one of your lectures. She got better at once. She gained strength so rapidly that she lifted the cottage piano quite a distance from the floor, and then tipped it over on to her mother-in-law, with whom she had had some little trouble. We like your lectures very much. Please send me a barrel of them. If you should require any more recommendations, you can get any number of them in this place at two shillings each, the price I charge for this one, and I trust you may be ever happy. I am, Sir, Yours truly, and so is my wife, R. SPRINGERS."

The audience was also uplifted with the announcement that "during the vacation the Hall has been

ARTEMUS WARD

carefully swept out, and a new door-knob added to the
door." It was intimated that Mr. Ward would call on
the citizens of London at their residences and explain
any jokes in his narrative which they might not understand; further, that the audience might leave their
bonnets and cloaks at the usual place, but their money
with Mr. Ward, who would return it to them in a day
or two, or invest it for them in America, as they pleased,
and so forth; with the concluding assurance that the
Panorama was rather worse than panoramas usually
are, and that Mr. Ward would not be responsible for
any debts of his own contracting.

Other gibes on the program included the following:

"An American correspondent of a distinguished journal in Yorkshire thus speaks of Mr. Ward's power as
an orator: 'It was a grand scene, Mr. Artemus Ward
standing on the platform, talking; many of the audience
sleeping tranquilly in their seats; others leaving the
room and not returning; others crying like a child at
some of the jokes; all, all formed a most impressive
scene, and showed the powers of this remarkable orator.
And when he announced that he should never lecture
in that town again, the applause was positively deaf-
ening.'"

The lecture was carefully rehearsed. Mindful of
its rather mild first reception in New York, Artemus took painstaking care to be at his best. He
opened on the evening of November 13, 1866, to an
audience selected largely by himself and the prudent
Hingston from among the Londoners of the day whose
approval made things go. Hingston records that the
real cash in the house amounted to but eighteen

pounds. Instant success followed. In the whirl of interest *Punch* so far forgot itself as to puff the show, writing under the head of "A Ward That Deserves Watching," the following:

"Mr. Punch would recommend 'funny men,' on or off the stage, to hear Artemus Ward 'speak his piece' at the Egyptian Hall, and then, in so far as in them lies, to go and do likewise. Everybody who is liable to be afflicted by funny men, whether in his business —as dramatic author, say—or in his pleasure (so called), say as theater-goer or diner-out, must continually have felt how the dreariness of funny men is enhanced by the emphasis and effort with which they force their facetiousness into your face, or dig it into your ribs. The low comedian of the second-rate theater, the comic singer of the music-hall, is probably the most offensive organ of what is called 'amusement' ever allowed to outrage good taste, good sense, and good breeding, and to minister, unreproved, to coarseness, imbecility, and vulgarity. But nothing contributes so much to the irritating effect of an 'entertainer' of this deplorable kind as his way of emphasizing his own fatuousness, and writing himself down as ass in italics. Without this peculiarity, he would only make us sad; with it, he makes us savage.

"Oh, if these unhappy abusers of gag, grimace, and emphasis—these grating, grinding, grinning, over-doing obtruders of themselves in the wrong place— could take a leaf out of Artemus Ward's 'piece,' and learn to be as quiet, grave, and unconscious in their delivery of the words set down for them as he is in speaking his own! Unlike them, Artemus Ward has brains. That is, of course, beyond hope in their case. But if they could once be made to feel how immensely true humor is enhanced by the unforced way it drops out of A. W.'s mouth, they might learn to imitate what, probably, it is hopeless to expect they could understand.

"To be sure, Artemus Ward's delivery of fun is eminently 'un-English.' But there are a good many things English one would like to see un-Englished. Gagging, gross, overdone low comedy is one of them. Snobbishness is another. The two go hand in hand. One of the best of many good points of Artemus Ward's piece is that it is quite free from all trace of either of these English institutions. And it is worth noting that we owe to another native of the States, Joseph Jefferson, the best example lately set us of unforced and natural low comedy. His Rip Van Winkle was very un-English, too."

The *Queen* observed:

"The entertainment itself was a strange compound of truthful narrative with the most delightful fooling that it has ever been our good fortune to hear. During his extraordinary prologue the audience fairly laughed till they could laugh no more, for the strange, quaint, quiet, gentlemanly humor of the lecturer was irresistible."

The *Spectator*, in its issue of November 24th, described the lecture and its giver with such nicety as to merit reproduction in full:

"Artemus Ward is, as a true humorist should be, even better than his books. What his personal influence adds to the humor of his stories is not of course

always easy to analyze, but mainly, we think, this—
the impression which he contrives to produce that his
confusions of thought and speech are all inevitable on
his own part, that his mind drifts on hopelessly from
one of those grotesque ideas or expressions to the next,
as the creature or victim of some overruling power,
which chooses his thought and language for him, so
that he is not even a party to the transaction, though
he has an earnest and rather melancholy interest in
the result. When he first comes on to the platform,
with his long, hollow-cheeked face and his bright, sad,
interrogative eyes, we should expect from him, if we
knew nothing about the matter, almost anything
rather than cause for laughter. He might be, were
he not a little too quiet and polished in manner, an
eager philanthropist or religious preacher, who had
one sole passion left burning in his brain—to convince
the rest of the world of the duty of joining in some great
crusade. Yet he has the face of a humorist, nevertheless, the light in the eyes, the twitch about the mouth
which show, as soon as we know what he really is, that
the most opposite currents of association constantly
cross each and pull simultaneously at the most widely
separated chords of his mind. He never smiles, but
looks, on the contrary, pleading and entertaining, as
if he were above all things solicitous to get his thoughts
really disentangled this time, when he is approaching
one of his odd comparisons. When he first appears,
for instance, he says, with the greatest simplicity and
a pathetic kind of earnestness, that he does not himself think at all highly of his entertainment or expect
much from it, that he only hopes to obtain from it a

small sum of money sufficient to take him to New Zealand, for, he adds, 'if I could only go to New Zealand, I should feel that I had not wholly lived in vain,' and then as the audience laugh at this very new recipe for avoiding a completely vain life, he adds, with eagerness and a childlike sort of effusion to his audience, 'I don't *want* to live wholly in vain,' at which, of course, the laughter deepens into a hearty roar. That is a type of the whole character of his humor. He gets hold of two inconsistent and absurdly arbitrary ideas, connects them with a sort of simple fervor in his own mind, and presses them on his hearers with an air of plaintive good faith that is quite irresistible. So, a few sentences afterward, when he mentions that he would not allow a bust of himself to be taken because he could not bear the idea of people carrying him about everywhere, making him common, and hugging him in plaster of Paris, and his audience (rather prematurely) laugh, he assumes the laugh to be skeptical, and says, with a sharp, half-snappish air of innocent, argumentative irritation, 'Yes, they *would*'—and then those who saw nothing humorous before are fully carried away now and join in the universal chorus. All his best points are made by producing this impression— that his mind is floating inevitably along a natural current of ideas where his audiences see the most absurd combinations. In one of his *Punch* papers, Artemus Ward's best point was remarking quite simply that the Tower is a 'sweet boon,' but the humor of this criticism would have been immensely enhanced by his manner. He would have said it with such accidental pathos, as if the words were the only possible ones that

could have risen to his lips to describe the Tower, that
the humor, real enough in the printed letter, would have
convulsed his audience. All he says seems to be thought
aloud, as if it were just bubbling up new within him.
And when he hits on a deep thought, and says, for instance, with a sort of hesitating, perplexed candor, as
though he were getting a little beyond his own depth
and his audience's, too, 'Time passed on. You may
have noticed that it usually does, that that is a sort of
way Time has about it, it generally passes on,' a joke
of no absolute merit takes a very great humor from
his hesitating, anxious way of appearing to show the
analysis of his own embarrassed thoughts to the people
he is addressing. The character he best likes to fill
is that of a sort of intellectual Hans—the world simpleton of the old German stories—in the act of confiding
himself to the public. In the German stories Hans
only makes a practical fool of himself in all sorts of
impossible ways. But Artemus Ward intellectualizes
him, shows the inner absurdity of his own thoughts
with a pathetic earnestness and candor. His mind
seems to wander when he speaks of his own past with
winning simplicity. With the sunny days of youth,
he says many sweet forms are associated, 'especially
Maria—she married another—you may notice they
frequently do,' and he brings out all such for happy
generalizations with a real heave of intellectual travail
that convulses his hearers with good reason. Nothing
is better than his eager, ardent way of propounding
a truism. You cannot avoid the conviction for a moment that it has just struck him as a real truth. When
he points to the summit of one of the range of moun-

tains in Utah, and says, with an evident wish to be useful to his audience, 'the highest part of this mountain is
the top,' or pointing to one of the horses on the prairie,
'that beautiful and interesting animal is a horse, it was
a long time before I discovered it,' in spite of the ex-
ceeding simplicity and obviousness of the joke, which
any clown in a pantomime might have made as well,
he reaches the sense of humor simply by the engaging
earnestness and naïveté of his speech. Perhaps the
most humorous part of Artemus Ward's lecture, however, is the natural, unresisting way in which he drifts
about in search of words and phrases, often conveying
a sense of difficulty and of conscious error, and then
correcting himself by the use of a phrase still more
ludicrous, and on which yet he seems to have been
landed by an imperious necessity. Thus, when he says
that he used to sing, but not well, he stumbles in the
most natural way, and is a prey to melancholy that he
can't hit on the proper phrase. 'As a songer,' he said,
'I was not successful'; and then, in a depressed and
self-correcting way, conscious he had gone wrong, 'As
a singster I was a failure. I am always saddest when I
sing—and so are those who hear me.' The art with
which he gives the impression that he is floundering
along in his choice of words, the victim of the first
verbal association which strikes his memory, and yet
just familiar enough with language to feel uncertain
as to his ground, and to wish to get hold of some clearer
term, is beyond praise. When he lighted upon 'singster,' he evidently felt that he was near the mark, a
partial, but not complete satisfaction lit up his face,
and yet he did not pronounce it with confidence, but

with a modest sort of diffidence, as if the phrase was as near as he could get. A general effect of having to grope for his language before he can explain himself always hovers about his manner. When he says, with some pride, that he would not allow them 'to sculp' him, and that 'the clothes I now *occupy* produced a great sensation in America,' there is no glimmer of a smile on his face, and a marked absence of emphasis on the grotesque words, which he slips out exactly as if he were rather anxious to divert attention from points on which he feels his ground somewhat uncertain— just as an Englishman abroad hastily slurs over his doubtful grammar to get on to idioms of which he is more certain. Then occasionally he will fall in the most natural and helpless way into a language trap of his own setting, as when he says that in the hurry of embarking on board the steamer which took him from New York, some middle-aged ladies against whom he was hustled mistook his character wholly and said, 'Base man, leave us, oh, leave us!—and I left them, oh, I left them,' where he appears quite unable to help throwing the second half of the sentence into the form of an antistrophe to the first. It impresses one as a sheer inability to get out of the wake of the first half of the sentence, not as any wish to be amusing, that makes him interpolate the second 'oh!' He seems like a man who, having taken a good run, cannot stop himself at the right point, but must run beyond it; the rhythm of the elderly ladies' exhortation mastered him; he helplessly succumbs to it in explaining how he obeyed it. It is the fatalism of grammatical construction. So, again, when he finds the seventeen young

Mormon widows weeping, and asks them, 'Why is this thus?' he falls a victim to the perplexity and embarrassment with which the juxtaposition of 'this' and 'thus' has overpowered his weak brain; and goes on helplessly, 'What is the cause of this thusness?' He cannot evidently help developing at length those subtle suggestions of verbal confusion which so often strike everybody's ear with an idiotic jingle of fascination. This is closely analogous to his curious habit of floating feebly down the chain of intellectual association, however grotesque. When he tells us that the picture of the Nevada Mountains is by 'the ancient masters,' the mere idea of the ancient masters of course suggests at once that they are dead; so he goes on, 'This was the last picture they painted, and then they died.' So when he points out the lion on Brigham Young's gate, he says, pointing to a very ridiculous and elongated feature in it, 'Yonder lion, you will observe, has a tail. It will be continued *for a few evenings longer*.' The humor of all this is the humor of helplessness, the humor of letting your thoughts drift idly with the most absurd association that crosses them, and never rescuing yourself by any insurrection of common sense. Artemus Ward in all his best jokes—of course, like other professional jokers, he has some poor ones, at which it is wrong to smile—is, as we said before, an intellectualized form of the German village simpleton Hans. He yields a literal obedience to every absurd suggestion of thought and language, just as Hans does to the verbal directions of his wife or mother, and gets into intellectual absurdity just as Hans gets into a practical absurdity. This, with the melancholy earnest manner of a man completely unconscious that there is anything grotesque in what he says, conveys an effect of inimitable humor."

The *Times*, November 16th, contained this critique:

"Before a large audience, comprising an extraordinary number of literary celebrities, Mr. Artemus Ward, the noted American humorist, made his first appearance as a public lecturer on Tuesday evening, the place selected for the display of his quaint oratory being the room long tenanted by Mr. Arthur Sketchley. His first entrance on the platform was the signal for loud and continuous laughter and applause, denoting a degree of expectation which a nervous man might have feared to encounter. However, his first sentences and the way in which they were received amply sufficed to prove that his success was certain. The dialect of Artemus bears a less evident mark of the Western World than that of many American actors, who would fain merge their own peculiarities in the delineation of English character; but his jokes are of that true Transatlantic type to which no nation beyond the limits of the States can offer any parallel. These jokes he lets fall with an air of profound unsconsciousness, we may almost say melancholy, which is irresistibly droll, aided as it is by the effect of a figure singularly gaunt and lean and a face to match. And he has found an audience by whom his caustic humor is thoroughly appreciated. Not one of the old pleasantries slipped out with such imperturbable gravity misses its mark, and scarcely a minute elapses at the end of which the sedate Artemus is not forced to pause till the roar of mirth has subsided. There is certainly this foundation for an *entente cordiale* between the two countries calling themselves Anglo-Saxon, that the Englishman, puzzled by Yankee politics, thoroughly relishes Yankee jokes, though they are not in the least like his own. When two persons laugh together, they cannot hate each other much so long as the laugh continues.

"The subject of Artemus Ward's lecture is a visit to the Mormons, copiously illustrated by a series of moving pictures, not much to be commended as works of art, but, for the most part, well enough executed to give (fidelity granted) a notion of life as it is among the remarkable inhabitants of Utah. Nor let the connoisseur, who detects the shortcoming of some of these pictures, fancy that he has discovered a flaw in the armor of the doughty Artemus. That astute gentleman knows their worth as well as anybody else, and while he ostensibly extols them, as a showman is bound to do, he every now and then holds them up to ridicule in a vein of the deepest irony. In one case a palpable error of perspective, by which a man is made equal in size to a mountain, has been purposely committed, and the shout of laughter that arises as soon as the ridiculous picture appears is tremendous. But there is no mirth in the face of Artemus; he seems even deaf to the roar, and when he proceeds to the explanation of the landscape he touches on the ridiculous point in a slurring way that provokes a new explosion.

"The particulars of the lecture we need not describe. Many accounts of the Mormons, more or less credible, and all authenticated, have been given by serious historians, and Mr. W. H. Dixon, who has just returned from Utah to London, is said to have brought with him new stores of solid information. But to most of us Mormonism is still a mystery, and under those circumstances a lecturer who has professedly visited a country for the sake more of picking up fun than of sifting facts, and whose chief object it must be to make his narrative amusing, can scarcely be accepted as an authority. We will therefore content ourselves with stating that the lecture is entertaining to such a degree that to those who seek amusement its brevity is its only fault; that it is utterly free from offense, though the opportunities for offense given by the subject of Mormonism are obviously numerous; and that it is interspersed not only with irresistible jokes, but with shrewd remarks, proving that Artemus Ward is a man of reflection as well as a consummate humorist."

J. E. Preston-Muddock, "Dick Donovan," was present on the opening night of the lecture and thus describes the occasion in his *Pages from an Adventurous Life:*

"The opening night of the show Hingston introduced him in a neat little speech, and claimed the indulgence of those present for any nervousness the entertainer might display on this his first public appearance in London. He said it was a critical moment for Ward, and his fate trembled in the balance. Then Ward rose, came down to the footlights, and stood silent, casting his deep-set, brilliant eyes over the vast audience, and twiddling his thumbs in the most unconcerned way. A minute or two passed; under such circumstances it seemed much longer. The audience became fidgety. I heard one gentleman sitting near me exclaim to a lady at his side: 'What a fool! Why doesn't he say something?' Once more a silence fell upon the assembly, but the imperturbable man stood twiddling his thumbs. A murmur of disapproval swept like a wave over the audience, then a little more clapping, a little more stamping, followed by a silence during which a pin might almost have been heard to fall. At last, in his inimitable drawl, Ward spoke:

"'Ladies—and—gentlemen. When—you—have—finished this—unseemly interruption, I guess I'll begin my discourse.'

"It was as if an electric shock had passed through the people. They saw the humor of the situation. They rose to it. And seldom has a showman received such an ovation. The audience almost raised the roof with their cheers and applause, and it was fully five minutes before he could proceed. From that moment he became the idol of London."

For six weeks the lecture was given without interruption. On Friday, January 7th, he was compelled to abandon the platform from physical weakness and on two subsequent evenings it was necessary to close the house, to the great disappointment of the public. January 23, 1867, noted his last appearance. His vitality was gone. The *Times* of the 24th contained this rather frolicsome advertisement, the first with humor in it:

"Artemus Ward.—His Mormons. At the Egyptian Hall, Piccadilly, To-night. The seats should be secured. Box office open from 11 till 5.

"Artemus Ward.—His Jokes. This evening, Egyptian Hall, 8 o'clock.

"Artemus Ward.—For the Holidays—Egyptian Hall, Piccadilly.—Jokes recently imported from America, and merriments from the Mormon Region, every evening (Saturday excepted) 8 P.M. Doors open at half past 7. Saturday afternoon at 3. Reserved seats can be secured at the Egyptian Hall from 11 till 6; Mitchell's, 33 Old Bond Street; or Austin's, St. James's Hall. Stalls, 3s., area, 2s., balcony, 1s."

The announcement was not to be fulfilled, for in its place the next morning, January 25th, appeared this formal notice of the breakdown:

"Artemus Ward.—Medical Certificate: Mr. Artemus Ward is now laboring under so much irritation of the mucous membrane of the vocal and respiratory organs as to wholly unfit him for public speaking, and I have consequently urged him to suspend for a few weeks his entertainment at the Egyptian Hall, to afford him an opportunity of recovering his health, when he can again resume his lectures.—JOHN HASTINGS, M.D., Jan. 24, 1867, 2 P.M.

"Ladies and gentlemen who have secured seats will have their money returned on application at the hall."

Of the end, Moncure D. Conway wrote in his autobiography:

"'Artemus the delicious,' as Charles Reade called him, came to London in June, 1866, and gave his 'piece' in Egyptian Hall. The refined, delicate, intellectual countenance, the sweet, grave mouth, from which one might have expected philosophical lectures, retained their seriousness while listeners were convulsed with laughter. There was something magical about it.

Every sentence was a surprise. He played on his audience as Liszt did on a piano—most easily when most effectively. Who can ever forget his attempt to stop his Italian pianist—'a count in his own country, but not much account in this'—who went on playing loudly while he was trying to tell us an 'affecting incident' that occurred near a small clump of trees shown in his panorama of the far West. The music stormed on; we could see only lips and arms pathetically moving till the piano suddenly ceased, and we heard—it was all we heard—'and she fainted in Reginald's arms.' His tricks have been attempted in many theaters, but Artemus Ward was inimitable. And all the time the man was dying.

"Never was American in London so beloved. The Savage Club, founded in 1857, consisted of some half-dozen writers of plays who dined together every week in an old Covent Garden inn (Tom Robertson, then Chief, poked fun at them in one of his plays), until one evening some one brought Artemus there; then everybody wanted to belong, and the club entered upon its larger career. He was the life and soul of it. Yet all those brilliant articles in *Punch*, all those unforgetable dinners, lasted but six months, and the entertainments in Egyptian Hall only seven weeks. When it was learned that the most delightful of men was wasting away under rapid consumption even while he was charming us, the grief was inexpressible."

He fled from the chill and fog of the London winter to the more equable climate of the island of Jersey. This letter to Hingston tells the story of his stormy stay:

LONDON

"(*In bed*) BEAUCREST, MILBROOK, ST. HELEN'S, JERSEY.
Feby. 5, 1867.

"MY DEAR HINGSTON:

"I am so fearfully weak: I am so utterly 'gone' now the excitement is over and the reaction is come: that I think it very doubtful about me resuming my business in a month. But in a week from now I can tell better, and will let you know. I think I should be better off in London than here. I am very lonely. I am too weak to go out, and if I *could* go out I shouldn't see a familiar face. The sun shines now and then, but for the most part it rains in a wild and roaring manner, that I never saw equaled. But wait a week. Love to all, and believe me

"Yours Ever and Ever,

A. WARD.

"Tell Kingsford I *have* given up the rooms, and I tho't it was so understood when I left."

No benefits resulting, in company with George Stephens, his valet, he left Jersey after a short stay to make Radley's Hotel, at Southampton, his last stopping-place. Here he was surrounded by anxious friends. Bayard Taylor and other Americans, including Captain John Britton, our consul at Southampton, were in close attendance, and his English acquaintances were unremitting in their interest. All that medical skill could do was done, but without avail. The candle had burned too long at both ends.

Tom Robertson was one of those constantly present. One of the troubles of the nurses was to make the patient take his medicine. Among the prescriptions was

[211]

an iron tonic of extreme bitterness, to which he greatly objected. Filled with concern, Tom poured out a dose of the compound and held out the spoon.

"My dear Tom," said Artemus, protestingly, "I can't take that dreadful stuff."

"Come, come," said Robertson. "Take it, my dear fellow, just for my sake. You know I would do anything for you."

"Would you?" said Artemus, faintly, grasping Tom's hand.

"I would indeed."

"Then *you* take it."

Conscious that his life was ebbing, he called one day for pad and pencil and wrote this bit of biography:

"Some twelve years ago I occupied the position (or the position occupied me) of city editor of a journal in Cleveland, Ohio. This journal—The *Plain Dealer*— was issued afternoons, and I was kept very busy indeed from eight o'clock in the morning till half past three in the afternoon in collecting the police reports and other items that might be of local interest."

Wearied with this slight effort, he dropped the pencil and never took it up again.

The Savages were deeply concerned. A heartening message of hope and good-will was sent him in the name of the club, to which he replied by telegraph on February 13th:

"Sincere thanks for your sympathy and good wishes. Am too weak to get to London. God bless you all."

"In the fight between Youth and Death," wrote Robertson, "Death was to conquer."

Consumption, long latent in his slight physique,

JAMES RHOADES

now developed rapidly. He died at seven minutes past four o'clock on the afternoon of Ash Wednesday, March 6, 1867.

There was wide mourning in England at the departure of his blithe spirit, which found its best expression in the following lines, written by James Rhoades, and published in the issue of the *Spectator* for March 16th:

ARTEMUS WARD

I

Is he gone to a land of no laughter,
  This man who made mirth for us all?
Proves death but a silence hereafter
  From the sounds that delight or appal?
Once closed, have the lips no more duty,
  No more pleasure the exquisite ears,
Has the heart done o'erflowing with beauty
  As the eyes have with tears?

II

Nay, if aught be sure, what can be surer
  Than that Earth's good decays not with Earth?
And of all the heart's springs none are purer
  Than the springs of the fountains of Mirth?
He that sounds them has pierced the heart's hollows,
  The places where tears are and sleep;
For the foam-flakes that dance in life's shallows
  Are wrung from life's deep.

III

He came with a heart full of gladness
  From the glad-hearted world of the West—
Won our laughter, but not with mere madness,
  Spake and joked with us, not in mere jest;
For the Man in our heart lingered after,
  When the merriment died from our ears,
And those that are loudest in laughter
  Are silent in tears.

[213]

The *Spectator* itself made the verses and the public sorrow text for an essay on "Humor and Faith" full of deep feeling, over the place of humor in the fuller life "in which it would not displace the moral and spiritual nature, but serve as its framework and its foil."

The body of the gifted and lamented humorist was conveyed to London by his sorrowing friends, and taken to the house of Charles Millward, 9 Malden Crescent, Prince of Wales Road, Haverstock Hall, Kentish Town. Here it remained until a quarter past one on Saturday, March 9th, when it was borne to the chapel, Kensal Green, four mourning coaches and a number of carriages forming the cortège. Dr. E. P. Hingston, George H. Stephens, his valet, and Doctor Craft, his physician, were in the first carriage. The English pallbearers, Charles Millward, Andrew Halliday, Tom Hood, and J. L. Toole, were in the second, and the American pallbearers, Lawrence Barrett, Major Charles Temple Dix, Albion Chadbourne, of San Francisco, and Edward Curtis, of New York, in the third. Included among the mourners were Charles Francis Adams, the United States minister to England, and Benjamin Moran, secretary to the legation; Thomas Archer, Sells Martin, Charles Santes, Henry W. Chapman, dramatic editor of the *American;* Godfrey Turner, Henry C. Gallup, J. B. Browne, Jr., Henry S. Leigh, Charles D. Page, John Parks, J. C. Dalton, E. J. Williams, Alfred Wilkinson, J. F. Jacobson, Hiram C. Clark, of San Francisco; W. B. Tegetmeier, O. R. Chase, of Boston; W. Holland, P. Corri, J. B. O'Hara, Charles W. Denison, of Philadelphia; D. H. Wheeler, New York *Tribune;* Stephen Tucker, Edward Draper,

Walter Wood, Dr. Charles Mackay, LL.D., J. W. Anson, George Grossmith, William Moy Thomas, J. C. Hotten, Samuel A. Walker, W. Phillips, George Rose, Charles Williams, Louis Jullien, Arthur à Beckett, Henry D. Palmer, of New York; Colman Burroughs, Thomas Archer, Ashley Sterry, John Bellington, Charles Webb, E. C. Barnes, William Brunton, C. W. Quinn, John Adams Knight, C. C. Coffin, Boston *Journal;* J. F. Lockhart, of Nevada; A. H. Dixon, of San Francisco; Gen. John Lowe, of Indiana; John Clarke, Hain Friswell, Barry Sullivan, Charles Scott, W. S. Gilbert, J. W. Whitaker, John Hare, Frederick Young, W. Justyne, Mrs. Halliday, Mrs. Ballington, Mrs. Millward, Miss Clarke, Mrs. Hingston, and Mrs. Grossmith.

"I was requested by a committee of Americans," says Mr. Conway, "to conduct the funeral . . . and never had a more difficult or sorrowful task. For his unexpected death was a tragedy that almost unnerved me. The chapel in Kensal Green Cemetery was filled to its utmost capacity. All the chief actors and actresses, writers of plays, literary men and women, were present, and sorrow was on every face."

Mr. Conway read the service of the Unitarian Church in this melancholy meeting, after the chance contact in Cincinnati six years before. Following this the friends descended to the lower chapel, where he delivered a eulogy, thus summarized in the London *Observer* of March 10th:

"It had often been remarked that the fountain of laughter was close to that of tears. Comedy was closely followed by tragedy. In the ground where they were assembled lay many brilliant and fine wits, whose memories were intimately associated with our delights, and also with our tears for their loss, for their own sorrows, and, as too often happened, for their early deaths. How often did it happen that moralizing on the fate of the man of infinite jest and humor must be made, as in the play of 'Hamlet' on his skull. And how melancholy was the reflection in the present case that when they were sitting before the friend whom they had lost, convulsed with laughter at his brilliant sallies, and delighted with the fine touches of his humor, he was wasting away before them, and that the flashes of his eyes were mingled with the same fire that was consuming his life. There was something in all this; but the reflection was still more melancholy that he should die in a strange country, far away from his native land, far away from that mother in whose arms he had longed to expire. Still, he had been here surrounded by friends, and tended by them with feelings true and genuine, a fact that he [Mr. Conway] was sure the countrymen of deceased would never forget. That was not the place to dwell on any criticism upon his works. The verdict of the entire literary world had been given on the subject, and the verdict placed him in the ranks of the finest and most exquisite humorists of his time. They all knew how bright and how delicate were the sensibilities which were required to make a man of fine and genuine humor, and the verdict given in both countries in respect to him would, he was sure, be confirmed by posterity. In Artemus Ward there was no meanness, no coarseness, no vice. He had lived in the public eye from his youth upward. He had been known, while yet a boy, as an editor of a paper in

Ohio. He had also been known in the same capacity
in New York. Thus he was a man who had lived in
the public eye, and had been criticized during his whole
lifetime, and he [Mr. Conway] would venture to affirm
that he had never met with one whom he had not made
his friend, and never lost a friend that he had once made.
He has never used his great powers of humor for that
biting purpose which was implied in the word sarcasm,
but had all through touched with the most delicacy
the follies and the weaknesses of the age in which he
lived. He had been a man not only of humor, but of
good humor. He had never made an enemy, and there
was no man who did not feel that he was the better
for having known him. Affectionate and simple as a
child, a fine fancy and fine intellect, he possessed the
highest elevation of character, and all who knew him felt
that with him had passed away a genial spirit, as true
a gentleman as ever lived. Ever since his landing in
this country he had been taken by the hand in a feeling
of generosity and sympathy—sympathy so deep that it
was chiefly owing to it that he had not returned to
his native land when he felt that the climate of this
country did not agree with him. This was highly
creditable to the republic of letters and would tend to
cement a feeling of brotherhood between those of the
two countries."

Dr. Spencer Hall, of Bowness-on-Windermere, next
addressed the company. The coffin of English oak
was metal lined and carried an inscription given by
the dead:

"Charles F. Browne, aged 33 years. Known to the
world as Artemus Ward."

It was lowered to the grave amid a passion of tears.

By one of those strange perversions that often creep into history, the statement went the rounds that in his dying hours a Catholic priest had been admitted to the death-chamber by a zealous Romanist friend and that the humorist departed from life in that faith. It occurred in print as late as 1904 in the New York *Evening Mail*. If true, the tale was not important, but it was not true. What happened was briefly this: George Rose, "Arthur Sketchley," was an ardent Catholic and did express an anxious desire that the last hours of his friend should be comforted by a clergyman. To this end the Rev. Father Robert Mount called three times. The London *Tablet*, organ of the church, asserted that Father Mount "did under the circumstances what he was justified in doing for the safety of the dying man."

This reference raised a storm in the Savage Club which, J. E. Preston Muddock wrote in his recollections, *Pages from an Adventurous Life*, was "very nearly the cause of wrecking it." A newspaper controversy followed and the club was filled with bitterness. The commotion subsided on the publication in the *Tablet* of this letter from Doctor Hingston, under date of March 23, 1867:

"SIR,—As your brief obituary notice of the late lamented Artemus Ward almost implies that my late friend was a Roman Catholic, will you kindly permit me to state that Charles Farrar Browne lived and died in the Protestant faith? It is quite true that a Roman Catholic clergyman called upon him during the early stages of his last illness, and kindly tendered his spiritual offices, but those offices were respectfully and firmly declined. The same reverend gentleman also visited my poor friend on Sunday, the 3d instant; but Mr. Browne was then unconscious, and from that hour to the moment of his death existence to him was a blank, and he expired peacefully and painlessly in the presence of friends whom he loved to know, but whom he failed to recognize during the last sad days of his life. Mr. Browne had previously repeatedly assured me that he was not a Roman Catholic, and hence it was that his sorrowing friends interred his body at Kensal Green in strict accordance with the faith he always professed. The same friends would have followed his dust with equal reverence to a Roman Catholic burial if their much-lamented companion had been a follower of that faith; but Mr. Browne lived and died a Protestant, and as a Protestant he was buried."

Though more than fifty years have passed since the young American scintillated among the Savages, his memory is still held dear. His portrait, in colored crayon, by Walter Dubisson, and one of the best extant, hangs in the unique club-house on Adelphi Terrace, together with a fine drawing of his Waterford home, by Charles Upham, one of the artists of the old Frank Leslie staff, and the bust from life, by Geflowski, stands in the hall. Ten copies of Geflowski's bust were made. It remains a notable fact that no other American ever so impressed himself upon the life of London. The Authors Club, in its rooms in the Carnegie Building, New York, possesses a manuscript copy of James Rhoades's poem, "On the Death of Artemus Ward," preserved in a frame, together with

16

a letter accompanying it sent by Mr. Rhoades to Dr. Rossiter Johnson, who added it to the treasures of the organization in 1913. In this note Mr. Rhoades says: "How well I remember going to hear Artemus Ward lecture in the Egyptian Hall (London). Mr. Macmillan, with my old friend Henry S. Sidgwick, sat in the row in front of me, and Bishop Temple, our old headmaster, afterward Archbishop of Canterbury, was behind us and laughed louder than any one."

If the bishop laughed with others, there were occasional Britons who did not, among them the good and great John Bright, who remarked, after hearing the lecture, that "its information was meager, and presented in a desultory, disconnected manner."

In 1870 the "Panorama" turned up in Halifax, Nova Scotia, chaperoned by another "Brown," who attempted to repeat the Mormon lecture in imitation of the original. It was not successful and the pictures vanished in the junk-heap of time.

A. W.'s will was made at Southampton, February 23, 1867. It provided first that the library of books bequeathed him by his uncle, Calvin Farrar, should be given the Waterford boy or girl who passed the best school examination between the first day of January and that of April following his decease, giving Moses Mason Robinson, a New York lawyer, a native of Waterford, the power of appointing the examiners and attending to the details of the bequest. Second, that George H. Stephens, his personal attendant, should work as a printer's apprentice for two years in the Riverside Press at Cambridge, at the end of which time, if his record was good, he was to be sent to the Academy

BUST OF ARTEMUS WARD BY GEFLOWSKI

at North Bridgton, a school still existing, and near Waterford, the estate to pay the cost of his education. Horace Maxfield and Livingston Gain Robinson, both of Waterford, were made trustees. Thomas W. Robertson, author of "Fashion" and "Society," was named as literary executor for his books and manuscripts in England, and Richard Henry Stoddard and Charles Dawson Shanley were appointed to a similar trust in America. He directed that all revenue should go to the support of his mother, save the sum needed to educate Stephens, and upon her decease one thousand dollars each to the children of John C. Gerry, of Waterford Lower Village, who was husband of his aunt Nancy, the balance to be paid as his mother might devise, save in case her decease preceded his, when the estate was to go to such kin as might legally be entitled to share in it. James Sharp and John Neat Pocock, of Southampton, were witnesses, and the will was further attested by John Britton, the United States consul. The next day, February 24th, the will was considerably amended by a codicil, in which he gave one hundred pounds each to Doctor Hingston's sons, James and John Cincinnatus Hingston, and limited the stay of George H. Stephens at North Bridgton to two years. Doctor Hingston was made co-administrator with Robertson in England, and the revisionary power over his estate was taken from his mother, directing instead that the residue go toward the founding of "an asylum for worn-out printers in the United States," the same to be paid to Horace Greeley, "his receipt alone" to be accepted as a sufficient discharge for the trustees. Pocock and Charles Millward witnessed this codicil.

The will proper directed that his body should be buried at Waterford Upper Village. The codicil changed this to Waterford Lower Village. This instruction was soon carried out. In May his body was taken from Kensal Green and sent across the sea, reaching Waterford early in June, 1867. The funeral was held on June 6th, when the children of the village gathered the wild flowers to strew upon his grave. The metal lining of the casket was unsoldered so that his mother might look once more upon his face. Then, conveyed in a common beach-wagon from which the seats had been removed, it was borne to Elm Vale, to be laid at rest under a stone bearing this inscription:

Rest, loved one, rest.
CHARLES FARRAR BROWNE
Known to the world as
"Artemus Ward."
Died in Southampton, Eng.,
March 6, 1867,
Aet. 33 yrs.
His name will live as
A sweet and unfading recollection.

All his family lie with him—the sisters, first dead, his father, mother, and brother Cyrus. After the death of Mrs. Brown, Alfred S. Kimball, the family attorney, carrying out her request, built a modest monument to mark the lot. It is indeed a vale under the feathery elms that give it beauty and a name.

VIII

LETTERS AND FRAGMENTS

THE shortened life of the humorist and his busy public career told against any great volume of literary activity. In all, four volumes were created from his pen, *His Book, His Travels, Artemus Ward in London,* and *The Mormons,* the last two issued after his death, in 1867 and 1868, respectively, under the editorship of T. W. Robertson and Dr. E. P. Hingston. The irresponsible John Camden Hotten put together a "complete" volume, and sold it widely, but the executors dealt with Ward, Locke & Co., and their volume is the best, though lovers of the humorist will find much of value in Hotten, interspersed with considerable spurious material. G. W. Carleton, in 1868, issued in wrappers, *Sandwiches by Artemus Ward,* containing many of his best efforts. He left no mass of rubbish to sort through for posthumous printing. His own sense of values was nice, and, as he once said: "I wait until some fancy strikes me, which by and by is followed by another. When there are a half-dozen or so I put them on paper. I may write two letters the same week and then a month or more may go by without a paragraph."

He knew, as do the wise, that the best juice flowed from the first turn of the wine-press; when the screw began to strain the product became acrid and without sparkle.

In a battered pocket note-book carried during 1861–62

are many idle fancies, jotted down to await a fitting mortise in his mind, together with dates, routes, laundry lists, penciled as they tumbled through his brain on trains and stages as he journeyed from town to town "speaking the piece."

Here in its worn pages are to be found all the traces of his literary ways that survive. They show that he really had no methods at all beyond responding to the devil's call for copy in the office of *Vanity Fair*. Humor must be jostled to display itself. To chance and incident Artemus owed much that was mirthful. These dim lines were the threads upon which he strung the jewels of his wit. Often the ideas are found repeated and do not always reappear in his writings. But in almost every case the notion crops out somewhere, a better thought having popped into being at the moment of writing.

It is not possible, therefore, to make a transcript of these scribblings altogether intelligible. Only they do not need to be considered a meaningless jumble. Here rambling across a page is the earnest query, "What is home without a mother?" Common enough a question now, whether used humorously or pathetically. Artemus brought it to life during the war-time when the sacred word was very much abused. Indeed, so much was he surfeited with the constant desire to know "Who will care for mother now?" that he once plaintively asked if "it wasn't about time somebody cared for the old man?"

Here are the phrases of a page:

"What of the fight? Better be a coward than a corpse."

"I am not, as is generally supposed, the author of 'Procrastination is the Thief of Time.'"

Half-wits, of whom there were some queer specimens in the village of his birth, possessed a strange interest for him. The note-book says:

"I once knew an idiot of peculiar construction who used to gibber with enhanced hilarity whenever a funeral occurred in the town. The only gentlemanly thing he ever did was to cut his throat one day. He did it effectively."

Ward's essay on "Forts" was one of his ablest dissertations. The note-book contains hints of it that were not utilized. They have a patriotic flavor befitting the time: "Gen. Halleck's fort is Fort Donelson"—that historic earthwork having just been taken, but not by Halleck—and "Gen. Stone's fort is Fort Lafayette." Gen. C. P. Stone had been placed in Fort Lafayette to await the result of a court of inquiry. There was no merit in either play of the word, and Artemus did not mar his essay with them.

Some reflections on the war period appear:

"Floyd stole out: of course he did: he'd stole the fort Donelson if he could."

"No Pillow. Floyd, Buckner, Johnson."

"Nothing else could do, unless they went South as Zollicoffer did."

"Without money; without Price"—referring to Gen. Stirling Price, the Missouri Confederate.

"Mr. Beecher said England had given us Puritanism. We'll give benefits."

"Burnside's expedition; let it be recorded."

Queer, indistinct enterings are plenty, such as these:

"He is sumach of all he surveys."

"Bedevelled kidneys."

"Present company expected."

"Writing on Erie road. Very jiggly."

"Dutchman! What of the night?"

"Squirmishes."

"Whited Seppulker."

"Lean and slippery pantaloon."

"Mrs. L.—dinner hour."

"Nearly all men are mortal."

"A Patriot's heart is pried."

"Certainly not. By all means! Procession proceed to procesh!"

"The benefits of intemperance . . ."

"If you belong to Gideon's band, etc."

"Refused by the New York *Ledger* . . ."

"Saved a good deal of liquor by friends drinking it all up."

For the public the note-book records this single reproach:

"People who don't like my lecture won't come to a good end."

The same page records the opinion that Albany, New York, "is a way station."

New Haven pleased him little better: The note-book says, crossly: "New Haven depot—thought it was a dungeon."

The poverty of his editorial days no doubt created the condition that caused the appearance of the subjoined thought:

"In the midst of life we are in debt."

Two phrases, "His wife's mother on the female

side," and "Ten years' experience in the ring," keep each other suspicious company. Here is the jumble upon another page:

"They say: 'Look at our papers,' which nobody will do upon any terms."

"I should rather be the author of a poem than the president of a temperance society."

" . . . which is a kind of a way leaves have in autumn."

"Rat jump over a trunk."

"Accommodations for fifteen thousand more guests, baths, etc."

"The old black cat kicked a hole in the looking-glass."

"Shell with oyster."

"Betsey J. at the levee." The last evidently the title of a never written sketch.

"Gov. Buckingham's turkey."

"Why do Summer roses fade? Because it is their Biz."

Artemus once remarked that Shakespeare would not have succeeded as the Washington correspondent of a New York newspaper because "he lacked the rekesite fancy and imaginashun," and he evidently believed that Shakespeare had not done his best, for the note-book observes, critically:

"Shakespeare would have signalized himself if he had tried."

Now and then the sensational crops out: "Macbeth? Murder? Immediate attention of the Selectmen?"

But the note-book is not averse to sentiment. Witness this:

"If you love me as I love you, no knife can cut our love in two."

Remonstrance is at times visible. Here is a sample: "Ethereal Cuss—none of your ingrammaticisms."

Along with his curling-tongs Artemus carried a small coffee-mill on his travels, in which the pure berry was ground to insure a good brew of the cheering beverage, of which he wrote in his note-book:

"Coffee is a slow poison—the slowest poison known." The mill is still preserved in a Maine household.

He reveled in odd expressions. Edward L. Parris, of Paris Hill, Maine, long an eminent attorney in New York, who had known Artemus in his school-days at Norway and in the ripe hours in the metropolis, was standing on the platform at Danville Junction, when the Grand Trunk train, bearing Artemus on his journey toward England, came along. The yellow curls were poked out of the window and the gentle voice asked:

"Where goest thou?"

"Upwardest," was the reply.

Then the train rolled on. He had gotten the answer he enjoyed: one in kind.

He delighted in children and in the note-book he jotted names and addresses of little folks. Occasionally the children wrote their own autographs. One of these, ADA MILLS, printed in a childish hand, stands out in big capitals. This was penciled by the bright little daughter of Myron H. Mills, of Cortlandt, New York, whose address is written underneath by A. W. She was a child of exceptional wit and understanding who made a strong appeal to the humorist. The family removed to Binghamton, where late in life Miss Mills married Celora E. Martin, judge of the New York State Court of Appeals, who died September 10, 1909, surviving him until March 30, 1917.

Artemus had a tolerant mind. One of Waterford's characters was Washington Hale, who once kept a hotel frequented by doubtful characters and after A. W.'s time was known to have harbored Langdon W. Moore, a noted cracksman, preparatory to robbing the savings-bank in Norway. "Upon mature deliberation," said Artemus, "I have decided to call him 'honest old Wash.' In view of the fact that he has been twice in the penitentiary and ought to be kept there all the time, it seems to me this is as complimentary as the occasion requires."

His life on the road was hard. The lecturer had not only to entertain the audience, but after the show was over it was expected that he would beguile the "committee" and a few of the leading citizens, including the local editors, into the small hours. The late E. Prentiss Bailey, for half a century the head of the Utica *Observer*, used to relate that when A. W. came to Utica he was chairman of the "committee." A prominent personage in the little city of that day was Gen. James McQuade, a distiller who produced a brand of whisky called "Mountain Dew," of whose pervasive potency he was justly proud. After the lecture he became the host for the tail end of the evening. A tempting collation was set out in the dining-room of his mansion, with plenty of the "Dew" on the side. "Help yourselves," urged the host. "There isn't a headache in a hogshead of it." They "helped." Mr. Bailey left at midnight. About noon the next day

Artemus, faded and ill-looking, dropped into the newspaper shop. Mr. Bailey looked at him inquiringly:

"I wish I'd taken a hogshead," said the depressed lecturer. "He said there wasn't a headache in one."

He had his own opinion of the hard-faced Maine farmer and liked to tell tales of crude characteristics. Indeed, he regarded farming in the state as a species of bad luck. In one of his skits he refers to a young man who jeered his baldness, remarking "the good head of hair" on the back of the showman's neck, for which ribaldry he was soon punished. "What happened?" observed Mr. Ward, in discussing retribution. "In less than a month that young man's aunt died and left him a farm in Oxford County, Maine. The human mind can picter no greater misfortin than this."

One of his pet yarns told of the farmer who set a jealous value on time, so much so that when his wife died a neighbor calling to extend sympathy found him in the well. He explained that his wife's death had sort o' broken up the day so he thought he'd make the best of it by cleaning the well. During the funeral services, called for 2 P.M., he was observed to snap his watch frequently until the coffin was lowered into the grave, when he announced, exultantly, "It was just two twenty when we got her in!"

Some of the few letters surviving from his considerable correspondence are cryptic now. Witness the following written in London, the point of which has vanished, but evidently concealed a crack at the person addressed:

LETTERS AND FRAGMENTS

"54 PICCADILLY,
Monday, Sept. 17 (1866).

"MY DEAR SIR:

"If you continue to be Ward, I shall feel compelled to tell you to be-Ware.

"Is not the point of the joke obvious?—is it not—but come and see me.

"A. WARD."

"I should think we came from Jerusalem," he once replied to Hingston when questioned about his ancestry, "for my father's name was Levi, and we had a Nathan and a Moses in the family. But my poor brother's name was Cyrus, so perhaps that makes us Persians."

"They are very rough," he once said to Hingston, of his neighbors in Waterford, "but they are a lot of good old souls. They don't understand me. Some of them—bless their kind hearts—think I ought to be sent to the state prison for having changed my name. More of them pity me for a poor idiot. Some of them want to make me good. They would give up all their time in trying to make me so, and be self-forgetful enough to let themselves run to the bad."

Even beyond the minstrels the circus appealed to his yearning for entertainment. All the clowns in America were on his list of acquaintances, and he never missed a show when one was near. He had also a close kinship for the stage and had tried his hand as an amateur actor, but with poor success. He was too original to be an imitation. He once tried to play Romeo at a local affair, but forgot his lines and had to ask Juliet for the prompt-book which she carried in her bosom in order that he might read the responses to her burning words!

Just as prophets are notoriously without honor in their own country, so, it would appear, are humorists. In Waterford, even little more than a decade after his death, there was scant knowledge of or interest in Artemus Ward. The village memory was only that of a careless, curious boy, not altogether bright in Down East parlance, an idler in school and of no importance in industry, while of his grown-up years they remembered the very queer gentleman with equally queer friends who spent summers in town enjoying their own inexplicable antics. Gen. George L. Beal, of Norway, once recalled that when he was colonel of the First Maine Regiment, quartered at City Point, one of his men remarked, disgustedly, to him:

"Colonel, I was up to Baltimore last night and saw a lot of posters advertising 'A. Ward will speak a Piece.' I went up to the hall, and there were several thousand people there who laughed and shouted fit to split. And who do you suppose the fellow was who spoke?"

"I can't imagine," was the colonel's reply.

"Why, it was none other than that gol-darned cuss of a Charles Browne we used to know up to Norway."

He was confirmed in his bachelorhood, though by no means averse to feminine society. "I fall in love," he wrote Charles E. Wilson, soon after reaching New York, "with a rapidity that would be appalling if I wasn't so well acquainted with myself." In the same note he avers that he is "straight as a string" in his female friendships.

Writing to another Charles Brown, of Fort Plain,

52 Piccadilly:

Monday. Sept. 17.

My Dear Sir,

If you continue to be
Ward I shall feel
compelled to tell you
to be = Ware.

Is not the point of
this joke obvious? — is it
not — but come &
see me. —

Yours truly
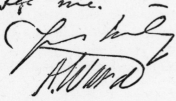
A. Ward

FACSIMILE OF AN "A. WARD" LETTER

New York, who had evidently been seeking kinship, under the date of June 5, 1864, while at Waterford, he said this of himself:

"There is really nothing very remarkable in my history. I was born in this quiet little town about twenty-eight years ago. My father died when I was twelve years old, and at the age of thirteen I entered a printing-office at Lancaster, New Hampshire. My father was a magistrate and lumber merchant—a clear-headed and thoroughly honest man, so competent in his business as to be consulted on all kinds of law questions, and so honest that he invariably had his hands full of business involving large sums of money. I fear he was a little too honest, for he died poor, after all. I ran away from the office at Lancaster, and entered a similar establishment at Norway, this state. This establishment failed, and I roamed through the state, setting type a short time in one place, and quietly running away to another. Running away appears to have been my chief weakness at that time. I finally landed in Boston, and worked at my trade until I was declared a tolerably good printer. I then went West and South, and for two years led a peripatetic kind of life. I commenced writing for a paper in Toledo, Ohio, about ten years ago. I succeeded as a paragraphist well enough to achieve a very good reputation, and moved to Cleveland and took charge of the *Plain Dealer* newspaper. I here commenced the Artemus Ward papers. The selection of that *nom de plume* was purely accidental. I wrote the first Ward sketch on a purely local subject, not supposing I should ever write another. Somehow the name Ward entered my head and I used it. Five years ago I moved to New York and assumed the editorial conduct of *Vanity Fair*, succeeding Charles G. Leland. For the past four years I have lectured almost constantly, and with a success that is perhaps unequaled, considering what a startling innovation I have made on a long-established institution. My writings and lecturing have given me a competency. I have a liberal offer to go to England this fall on a lecturing tour, and I may accept. I am writing now a book of travels, giving my experiences among the Mormons. I live in New York City, although I spend a portion of my summers here with my mother. That is about all. I have only drifted with the current, which has carried me gaily on of its own accord. As I am frank enough to say this, I hope I have a right to say that I have always meant the creatures of my burlesques should stab Error and give Right a friendly push. You are at liberty to use these facts, although my letter is necessarily written in a great hurry, for I am very busy. I am popularly supposed to be rusticating here, but it is a ghastly mockery. I am working very hard. The sketch in *Leslie* was pleasantly written by my friend, Frank Wood, who died just as we all were predicting a brilliant future for him. I thank you for your friendly letter and kindly intention, and am faithfully yours,

"CHARLES F. BROWNE,
(Artemus Ward)."

The temptation to tease his practical-minded mother was seldom resisted. She once visited Boston under

MRS. CAROLINE E. BROWN, MOTHER OF ARTEMUS WARD

the escort of Horace Maxfield. Artemus was to lecture and she was to hear him for the first time. The old lady had a favorite uncle by the name of Ransford Bates, and when she wished to give especial weight to some statement she would add, "My Uncle Ransford Bates said so." Before the lecture began Artemus said to Maxfield: "I am going to bring in 'Uncle Ransford' this evening. You watch mother and see her jump." Sure enough, at the end of some shocking absurdity he added, "I know it's true, for my Uncle Ransford said so." She "jumped" and never quite forgave him for his irreverent use of such an important authority.

Toward her he always maintained the closest, tenderest relationship. Her welfare was always uppermost in his mind and he greatly enjoyed her company. So intimate were they that he never spoke of her as mother. She was always "Caroline" and he "Charles." This was an oddity that came partly from his whimsical way of conversing and partly because the pair were really more brotherly and sisterly in their attitude toward each other rather than that of son and mother. She was sternly practical in all things, keen and shrewd, and yet very humorous without knowing it. Her speech was rapid, and she talked a great deal. Nothing escaped her observation, and her knowledge of local gossip was astonishingly copious. She was in her seventy-fourth year when I first came to know her at Waterford, and brisk as most ladies of fifty. She loved to recite her experiences at length, with minute details of dress and entertainment, and these her son seized upon with intense enjoyment and made her the model for Mrs. Betsey Jane Ward. She never comprehended the performances of the showman and his friends who indulged in high jinks when they visited Waterford. To me she once described Artemus and Dan Setchell as the "two fools."

Mrs. Brown made her son an extended visit while he lived in Cleveland, and this, with an occasional trip to Boston, marked her journeys into the outer world. For the rest she lived and died in the house where she was born—all alone up to the last, active, independent, and clear-minded to the end. The portrait given with this volume was taken when she was entering her seventy-fifth year.

His education had been short and desultory. He always felt the lack of better training in school, though it would probably have spoiled him. He once remarked that he had "about enough education for a sign-board." His employment in printing-offices had more than replaced the deficiency. This he well knew, and when instructing the attorney called to draw up his will, in which he provided that George H. Stephens, his boy valet, should be sent to a printing-office first and to college later, he said: "In the printing-office he will find the value of an education and want to learn when he gets the chance. I lost the chance before I felt the want."

The books of his uncle's library, which he directed in his will should go to the best scholar in the Waterford school, were awarded by the examiners to Florence Brown, daughter of his cousin Daniel. She became the wife of the Rev. O. A. Rounds, a Universalist clergyman of high standing, and in an early widowhood returned with her children to Waterford, living there at the present (1919) time.

George H. Stephens, the young valet, was educated under the terms of the will. He later came to Waterford, but the dull little village did not suit him after the lively life he had led, and he finally drifted out of sight. My old friend Charles O. Stickney, local editor of the *Bridgton News*, printed in a near-by town, once asked George what was the first thing Artemus ever said to him.

"Well, sir," was the reply, "the first thing Mr. Browne ever said to me was, 'George, bring me a gin cocktail.'"

Despite his considerable earnings, the gleanings from his estate were small. Besides taking care of Stephens, the Gerry bequests were paid. The gold chain given him by the Nevada miners vanished after his death, so did much jewelry, of which he was fond. A modest house at Yonkers, his only real estate, was rather heavily mortgaged. There was no trace of the large sum mentioned by Carleton as having been in his possession before leaving for Liverpool. His writings were liberally pirated abroad and in Canada. Fortunately, his mother owned the homestead and had some means of her own—perhaps enhanced without record by her son, so that all her years were comfortable.

One of the little boys who won the regard of Artemus in Waterford was Horace Porter. His father, Oliver Porter, kept the old-fashioned yellow "general store" adjacent to the Brown homestead and facing the village green.

Mr. Porter grew up to become a factor in the develop-

ment of Lakewood, New Jersey, in company with his
kinsman, David Porter. To the boy, the "grown-up"
neighbor in exile wrote a characteristic letter from the
office of *Vanity Fair*, April 9, 1861, a contribution long
treasured by its possessor which is reproduced herewith in facsimile.

Of his own place in life he wrote thus soberly:

"Humorous writers have always done the most
toward helping virtue on its pilgrimage, and the truth
has found more aid from them than from all the grave
polemists and solid writers that have ever spoken or
written. It was always so, and men have borne battle
for the right, with its grave truth fully in mind, with
an artillery of wit, that has silenced the heavy batteries
of formal discussion. They have helped the truth
along without encumbering it with themselves. They
have put it boldly forward and stood behind it and
hurled their fiery javelins at their opponents till they
have either fled ingloriously or been entirely silenced.
Rabelais—vile fellow as he was and revolting to
modern propriety and taste—did immense work for
the reform that began contemporaneously with him,
and from Rabelais down the shaft of ridicule has done
more than the cloth-yard arrows of solid argument in
defending the truth. Those who bolster up error and
hate the truth are still men and slow; men with no warm
blood; men who hate levity and the ebullitions of wit;
who deprecate a joke of any kind, and run mad at a pun.
Like Dominie Sampson, they can fire pointblank charges,
but the warfare of flying artillery annoys them. They
can't wheel and charge and fire, and the attack in flank
and rear by the light troops drives them to cover."

Office of Vanity Fair,

No. 113 Nassau Street.

LOUIS H. STEPHENS, PUBLISHER FOR PROPRIETORS.

New-York, April 9 1861.

My dear Friend Horace:

You know
I promised to write you
after I got to New York.

I had a very pleasant
journey indeed. From
Boston I went to "Allen's
Point," six miles beyond
Norwich, Connecticut, where
I took the steamboat for
New York. It was a stormy
night and the waves
ran very high, causing
the steamer to pitch
and toss like sleighs
going through those pitch=
poles in Waterford, only
much worse. Many of the
passengers were very
sick and were glad to

go to'bed. But I am never
sick on the water, and the
waves may run as high
as the Mountains in Wat-
erford for aught I care,
if the boat don't tip over.

New York is the largest
City in America and
one of the largest cities
in the world. People from
all nations live here, and
New York ships go to all
parts of the world, while
ships from all parts of
the world come to New
York. It would take forty
such villages as Waterford
Flat to make one com-
mon street here. Of course
there are many strange
Sights in so large a place.

I am sorry we didn't
find time to go "pickereling."

But we will go sometime.
I may come to Water=
ford this Summer and
make another visit; but
can't say. If I do come
we will go trouting.

You must be a good boy
and always mind your
father. Good boys make
good men, while bad boys
grow up into lazy, good=
for=nothing fellows and
are never respected
or loved by anybody.
I know you will be a
good boy. When you go
to school always get
your lessons THOROUGH=
LY and try to be at
the Head of your class.
Be pleasant to all
and polite so that
all who know you may say

"what a fine little fellow Horace Porter is!" Tell the Truth always, and when any boy asks you to do anything you know is wrong, firmly tell him "No Sir! I will never do a mean thing to please anybody!"

You must write me a letter and tell all about what is going on in Waterford. Give my regards to your father and brother.

Your True Friend,

Charles F. Brown.

THE FAIR INEZ
OR, THE LONE LADY OF THE CRIMSON CLIFFS
A Tale of the Sea
Edited by Artemus Ward

CHAPTER I.—THE "JANE GRAY"

MY story opens off the coast of Spain, in the month of April, 18—.

The staunch brig *Jane Gray*, Capt. George Wright, was riding lazily on the summer sea, just enough air filling her sails to keep her in motion. She was a three-master, clipper-built and sloop-rigged, with the exception that she carried cross-lashings and stump top-gallants in place of head guys and sheer jiggers. Her heel tackles were drawn tautly athwartship, but this did not in the least crowd her triatics and mizzen stays, or in any way interfere with the workings of her bowsprit toggles and starboard catheads, while her lee scuppers and gunwales were thoroughly slushed, giving the vessel immense advantage over craft carrying simply a bulwark bowse and jigger jibboom, as must be perfectly apparent to all navigators who have sailed in vessels rigged with foretop bowlines and capstan after-chocks. Another advantage possessed by the *Jane Gray* over similar craft was the admirable manner in which her dockyard sheers were guyed to her sling-fenders, thus giving full sway to her bulk-head toplights, no matter how cantankerously the gale might shriek.

Captain Wright was a thorough seaman, but a man of few words. Born when quite small, he had immediately commenced a seafaring life, and although several times shipwrecked and twice captured by the Onondaga County Indians, his health was very good.

As evening approached there were cheering indications of a smacking breeze to the N. W. E., observing which Captain Wright advanced to the middle of the deck and in a calm and dispassionate voice spoke as follows:

"General Order 510. Luff her! D—n your eyes, luff her! Avast!" He then went up-stairs to bed.

Chapter II.—Inez

It becomes necessary for us to go back three years. It was a wild night upon the coast of Spain.

A clipper ship, laden with staves and white beans, bound from Oxford County, Maine, to Madrid, had gone down near the Isle of Loneliness, and all on board had perished save the captain's daughter Inez— a sweet girl of seventeen summers and a like number of springs. Throwing herself upon a piece of sheet iron, she had floated to the lonely island, upon whose ocean-washed shore she wandered drearily up and down, all forlorn.

The night was fearful. It needed only the thunder's

crash and the lightning's flash to make the effect immense; but the maiden's quick ingenuity overcame these drawbacks, for by beating the sheet iron which had borne her to the shore, and burning blue-and-red fire in a small earthen bowl, fine thunder and middling lightning were made to lend their thrilling grandeur to the solemn scene.

Placing her hand upon her throbbing temples, the maiden said: "Ah, how these-er rer-ocks and cler-iffs

and this furious stor-rum remind me of My Happy Village Home"; and the maiden sang the popular ballad of that name—

"My village home, my village home,
My happy village home,"

[241]

rendering the last line of each stanza with operatic trills, thus:

"Me hap-ap ap-hap-er 'ap-er-veel 'eel-er-age ho-o-ro-o rum!"

"Ah, how sleepy I am!" she said, pressing her hands to her soft, dreamy blue eyes. "Methinks I will take a little slum." So, carefully adjusting her dress, she laid down gracefully upon a green baize rock and slept, while slow, sweet music filled the air.

Sleep had no sooner closed her eyelids than a young fairy in a short gauze dress and silk tights came up through a trap-door and, waving a magic wand over the slumbering maiden, asseverated thus:

"Maiden, maiden! feel no alarm,
    You'll see trouble, but you shall not come to no harm!"

Uttering which noble sentiments, the fairy whirled round several times for the purpose of permitting the dolphins and sharks to see how nicely her dress fitted her, and then vanished to appropriate music.

CHAPTER III.—AFLOAT AGAIN

WE will now return to the *Jane Gray*. That gallant craft was gliding gaily o'er the waters of the dark-blue sea, her squilgee toggles securely spliced to her back-stair bobstays, in true sailor style.

The officers had all retired to the extreme end of the deck to allow Will Somers, a gallant jacktar, sufficient room to dance the sailor's hornpipe.

The happy mariners, as is usual on board our merchantmen, were dressed in pure white trousers, bright morocco shoes, and white shirts, the bosoms of which were neatly embroidered with blue. Wide rolling collars, black flowing neckerchiefs, and tarpaulin hats completed their toilet.

"Well done, bold Will!" cried old Jack Ryder, an ancient seafaring man. "Shiver my timbers, my

hearty, but you're lively on your pins. Bile my lights and liver! Stuff my gizzard with salt junk! Avast!"

"Spin us a yarn, old Jack," cried Charlie Wilson, giving his trousers a hitch and taking a fresh chaw of tobacco.

"Wall, my hearties," said the old tar, allowing his tobacco to gently slosh round his mouth, "I've seen salt water in my day, and d—n all landlubbers, say I. I'd rather be a bootblack to Davy Jones than the biggest swab on shore. But tip us your ears, my hearties, and I'll tell you how the salt junk s'arved us on board the *Pretty Nell*, in 1842. You see, my lads, we were goin' up the Mediterranean, and had been out about three months. We thought the junk tasted rather queer, but old salts l'arn to stow away what's put afore 'em without axin' no questions. But when we all began to whinner; and found our ears growin' long and floppy; and bushy manes sprang out on our necks; and our feet commenced turnin' into hoofs; and we all hankered for hay and oats; and we couldn't be happy onless we had pieces of chain in our mouths like bits, and our heads didn't feel nat'ral onless we had bridles on—why, then, my hearties, we concluded we'd been eatin' hoss. The surgeon, Doctor Briggs, said we'd eventooally have to git our livin' by pullin' go-carts and fish-wagons if we didn't have beef right away. Beef was introduced and we got over it to a certain extent, tho' when I get on shore I allus steer for a stable, hitch myself in a stall, and fall to on the hay. Such is the force of education."

"Wall, pass the grog, old Jack," said Tom Clewline, "and I'll sing you two verses of 'Three Times Round,' and all bear a hand for the chorus:

"I have a mother in fair London town,
    And this night she is weeping for me,
Tho' little does she think this wessel it will sink,
    And go down to the bottom of the sea,
            Brave boys!"

Chorus: "Then three times round went our gallant ship,
　　　And three times round went she,
　　Three times round went our gallant ship
　　　And she sank to the bottom of the sea,
　　　　　　　　Brave boys!

"Then up steps this gallant Captain, O,
　And a well-spoken man was he,
　Says he, my boys, we ain't playin' at toys,
　We're bound for the bottom of the sea,
　　　　　　　　Brave boys!"

　　Chorus: "Three times round," etc.

"Bust my heart and gizzard," said old Jack, "but that's a good song!"

The crew then called for candles and were shown to their rooms.

Chapter IV.—The Corsair Chief

When Inez awoke the storm had ceased, the wild night had passed, and the morning was bright and beautiful.

The maiden looked around her. The scene was passing strange.

She was lying upon a fine twelve-dollar lounge, in an apartment of sumptuous elegance. "Where am I?" she murmured.

"Safe, dear lady!" said a soft, flutelike voice. "Safe from all harm!"

Inez looked up. A chivalrous-looking young man, arrayed in garments of red silken velvet, thick-studded with diamonds of incalculable value, stood over her— a genial smile irradiating his fascinating though swarthy

18　　　　　　　[245]

features. "Safe, lady!" he repeated. "You shall be the corsair's bride!"

"I don't see it!" said the gentle Inez.

"Ha!" cried the pirate, "longest thou, then, for the

laughing hillocks and bellowing bullocks of thy own chilly clime?"

"I have no hesitancy in asserting that I do," she replied.

"If gold be your desire," said the pirate chief, taking out his pocketbook and brandishing a ten-dollar bill on the Waukegan Bank of Illinois, "here it is!"

"Miscreant! I spurn the vile dross. Besides, there's ten per cent. discount on it." Thus spoke the noble Inez.

CONTRIBUTIONS

"You'll think better of it, ere many wanes have waxed and mooned, sweet lady," the pirate observed. "Listen! I am a Spaniard. My name is O'Mulligan! The world calls me a pirate, but no matter. Let that pass. And now the banquet. Ho! slaves, bring in the victuals."

Six contraband negroes, arrayed in bright yellow, immediately entered, bringing fishballs for one on salvers of solid gold. For the pirate they brought rum and molasses in a golden goblet.

"Have you a bill of fare?" asked Inez.

"No printed ones," said the pirate. "They are too expensive. But wherefore?"

"I was thinking whether or no you had any beans?"

"Pork, but nary a bean!" said the corsair, sententiously.

With an aching heart and a tear-suffused cheek, Inez restricted herself to the fishballs.

"We corsairs," said the Spaniard, "are not so bad as the World would make out."

"It's lately been merged with the *Courier and Enquirer*," said Inez, still intently placing herself outside the minced fish. [NOTE.—Meaning the New York *World*.]

The Spaniard, with a puzzled expression upon his face, continued: "We are loved by those who know us, and hold many positions of trust and influence. For instance, I am Street Contractor and Member of the Common Council, while a brother of mine is an army contractor. How does that strike you?" But the fair Inez had not yet recuperated her exhausted

[247]

energies, and a series of seraphic snores told the Spaniard that she slept. Gently throwing some buffalo robes over her fragile form, the Spaniard withdrew.

CHAPTER V.—THE PIRATES' REVEL

O'MULLIGAN and his merry men were passing the evening in a hilarious manner at the chief's cave, which was eligibly located among the cliffs, and fitted up with gas, baths, and all the modern improvements, including the comforts of a home, and within five minutes' walk of the depot.

The corsair chief was in a festive frame of mind, and absorbed his rum and molasses with no little industry and tenacity of purpose. In compliance with a highly enthusiastic call, he arose and addressed his men in a masterly speech. We regret that we only have space for a synopsis of the eminent speaker's remarks. After alluding to the rise and growth of affairs, and administering a withering rebuke to the opposition, he said: "Comrades! I am a Secessionist, and am for Peace and two Governments. I am the friend of virtue. Comrades! I am wholly your own!" (Cries of "Hi! hi! hi!" and the chief was instantly presented with a gold-headed cane by his brave followers as a slight evidence of their esteem. The presentation was wholly unexpected, and he could find no language in which to fittingly express his emotions.)

"François," said the pirate, "what special branch of industry didst pursue wherewithal to acquire thy hash and griddle-cakes ere joining our noble band?"

" I was a minstrel, my liege," said the young pirate. "I was an end man."

"Well, how do you feel this evening, Ginger?" said the chief.

"Sillubrius!"

"Oh no, Ginger, you mean salubrious. Wilt shake up a gleesome refrain, my fragile comrade?"

"I will, most noble duke; but first I should like to tell some new gags. I want to tell you about the ice-cream balloon, and I also wish to spell stovepipe—"

"No, no!" said the chief, excitedly, a gleam of horror passing over his face. "Sing the song!" and the ex-minstrel sang as follows:

> "When Jefferson Davis seseshed and went,
>   And wrote his name as President,
>   Quoth a Yankee who the act did see,
>   You've signed your epitaph, Jefferson D.,
>   With your quill so fine, tra-la!
>
> "Look on this picture, my bucaneer,
>   A crowd of people have come here
>   To see you swing on the gallows tree,
>   The traitor's fate, bold Jefferson D.!
>   With your quill so fine, tra-la!
>
> "A thousand seseshers bad and bold
>   Shall rattle their chains in dungeons old,
>   Of all that number none shall 'scape
>   Who led us into this wretched scrape,
>   With their quills so fine, tra-la!"

"Ha!" cried the chief, and his sword leaped from its scabbard and flashed fiercely in the gaslight. "A traitor-r-r-r to the Confederate Flag! So, so! Hast prayed to-night, François?" said the chief, gloomily manipulating the point of his gleaming blade.

"A few, my lord!" replied the trembling corsair.

"If you bethink yourself of any crime, unreconciled as yet to heaven and grace, solicit for it to onct."

"Alas, my lord, what may you mean?"

"I would not kill thy unprepared spirit."

"Talk you of killing?"

"I have said!"

"Well, I must be allowed to say that you are pretty rough."

The unfortunate young pirate was dragged from the cave, but, placing his mouth to the keyhole, he executed the following, in a disdainful, sardonic voice:

"To Miss Yancey in Paris

"Miss Yancey she is handsome,
Miss Yancey she is tall,
And when she blows her bugle,
Lord, how the Southrons bawl!
Oh, blow your bugle, Yancey,
Oh, go it while you may!
You won't last long, I fancy,
So throw yourself away.

"Miss Yancey blows a mellow horn,
She's a dashing, oily wench,
But just as sure as you are born
She cannot fool the French,
Oh, blow your bugle, Yancey, etc.

"So come home now, Miss Yancey,
Before you're kicked down-stairs.
Your little horn, I fancy,
Ain't adapted to French airs!
Oh, blow your bugle, Yancey," etc.

"That young man," said the pirate chief, sternly, "is a disgrace to his sex and is devoid of all kinds of noble sentiments. Let's all take a drink."

"He is a young man," said a sagacious pirate in a solemn voice and with a look of intense meaning, "he is a young man, that young man is, who is a young man —leastways he is younger than my old aunt Sally! I should say he was some young man, or at any rate he is some mens—"

"What the d—l is the matter with you?" cried the chief in a voice of horror. "Hang it, man, you are no more lucid than an editorial in *The New York Express!*"

"I want some rum wizzout any war-rer into it!" exclaimed the pirate. "D'ye hear? rum wizzout war-rer. An' now I'll tell you 'bout the young man—"

"No, you won't!" said the chief, hastily. "Put him to bed. Lift him up tenderly, handle him with care, fashioned so slenderly, young and so fair! He's been drinking. In short, he's drunk."

"Did you ever know, sir," said the inebriated corsair, in a subdued, mysterious voice—"were you ever acquainted with a red-headed gal, who sold mutton pies on a big tin pan, and they called her One-eyed Sal? Where is she now, sir? She sleeps 'neath the willow!"

"Away with him!" shrieked the chief. "Zounds, men, are we fallen to a state of gibbering idiocy?"

Rosy rum, however, mollified the incensed corsair, and ere the revel closed he sang, in the mellifluous tongue of his own sunny Spain, an ardent song of love, accompanying himself on the Shillalah.

CHAPTER VI.—THE ATTEMPTED ESCAPE

To remain with the pirates was repugnant to the feelings of Inez. They were not men of much moral principle, and she resolved to return to her native jungle in Maine. All right-minded persons will say, Good for her.

And so, one day when the corsair chief was absent on official business, the heroic girl determined to escape.

She wisely resolved to take as little baggage as possible—half a dozen bandboxes, an umbrella, a bottle of hair-oil, a dressing-case, a gauze nubia and some doughnuts, a poplin skirt, and a pair of point-lace gaiters, a tortoise-shell basque, and a few back numbers of *Godey's Lady's Book*—that was all. But even these trifles were found too cumbersome and she resolved to leave with no other clothing than her umbrella and a straw flat.

Her room was in the fifth story of the cave, which was built of Milwaukee brick, and all the doors were double-locked. She had no alternative, then, but to make her escape through the window. She was forced to use the bed-cord, but as she was a young lady of high moral principle, she resolved to send the corsair its full value by Adams' Express, if she in the least damaged it. Carefully fastening one end of the cord to the window-sill, she commenced letting herself down. But unfortunately the cord broke, shortly after the intrepid maiden had commenced her perilous descent —broke when she was high in the air, at a distance of over four hundred feet from the ground! Oh, it was frightful!

We cannot here too strongly urge upon manufacturers of rope the necessity of making it strong. It may cost more, but is it fair, is it manly, to sell rope knowing it to be of flimsy texture? Some may argue that it is owing to the poor quality of hemp, but we maintain that manufacturers should give their personal attention to the business and make good rope.

But to return to Inez.

Chapter VII.—The Crash

There was a crash and a stifled shriek.

But Inez lived.

Some agricultural pirates, returning from the pleasant meadows, whither they had been to gather the sweet new-mown hay, with a yoke of speckled oxen and a hayrick, were her preservers.

They had paused upon a smiling hillock to enjoy the splendors of an able and efficient sunset and to let the oxen rest.

They heard a sound as though something was whizzing—and on looking toward the cave they saw Inez falling.

Not a moment was to be lost. Putting spurs to the oxen, the pirates careered to the spot at a mad pace and backed the cart, which contained about a ton of hay, immediately under the windows of the cave. Inez lit upon the hay, where she lay unhurt, although trembling like the aspen leaf.

Thinking herself fatally injured, however, she raised herself upon her right arm, and requesting the orchestra to play up an appropriate dying air, she let her under-jaw fall and permitted her eyes to roll wildly. Then in a graceful, theatrical manner, she said: "How cold it is! A strange mist is before me eyes. I am dying! Come hither, Armand! Light—light— Me mother!"

But on discovering that she was only slightly injured she got off the cart and went into the house.

CHAPTER VIII.—THE CORSAIRS

O'MULLIGAN, weary of life on shore, resolved to put to sea again. He had recently received an encouraging note from another eminent pirate chief, Captain Crocketto Scovillo, who proposed to co-operate with O'Mulligan in any honorable enterprise which promised to yield large quantities of gold plate, bankable funds, and spoons. Scovillo awaited O'Mulligan at the mouth of the Maumee River with a brigade of negro chambermaids and a brass band, commonly known as the Black Horse Cavalry. He had also a chaplain with him named Coe, who was a high-toned man and a pleasing conversationalist. The Emperor of Rahway, Nicoli Speerini I, had tendered a platoon of two-horse coaches and a barrel of apple-jack. There were also good reasons to suppose that the Camden and Amboy Railroad would carry the pirates at half-price. Everything seemed auspicious.

"Do you regard it as safe to resume our noble profession upon the high seas at this particular period, my lord?" inquired a cautious corsair named Hoganni.

"Perfectly safe," replied the chief. "No danger as long as Connecticut continues to furnish Secretaries of the Navy."

"Ah, true," said the pensive pirate. "All I want is to get an honest living. So long as I get my hot dishes I shall be happy."

"Thou shalt return some day to the bogs of thy own

sunny Italy, my faithful Hoganni, with much gold plate and many ducats," said the chief, smiling approvingly upon the dark-eyed Italian.

"I'll make it lively for the boys in Cork!" joyfully exclaimed Hoganni. This talented and noble-hearted pirate then retired for the purpose of showing some relatives from the country how to play marbles, three-card monte, and other pleasing games.

A pirate now entered hastily.

"Ha! pampered menial, what bringest thou?" cried O'Mulligan, rising suddenly and breaking a clay pipe in his emotion.

"On yonder hill among the pine-trees we have surprised an Abolitionist. Escape by flight he could not, and so we nab'd him!"

"Drag him before me. But stay—didst tar and feather the Northern schoolmistress, and hang the white-chokered miscreant who had a *New York Tribune* in his pocket?"

"My lord, we didn't do nothing shorter."

"'Tis well. Away!"

The Abolitionist was ushered in. He stood before the chief with an erect form, a flashing eye, and an unblanched cheek. He said his name was Tell.

"What! William Tell? No! How are you, Bill? Whence comest thou?"

"From Ashtabula County, in Ohio. Our voices are for war, but we don't care about fighting ourselves. Our folks don't think it's no laughing matter."

"'Tis well!" said O'Mulligan, with a scornful laugh; "I'd have them as their hills that never smile, though wanton summer tempt them e'er so much."

"But we do sometimes smile!"

"Aye! When is that?"

"When whisky is three cents a glass."

A feeble smile lit up the noble features of O'Mulligan as this subtle witticism fell from the finely curved mouth of Tell, and some pirates commenced applauding, but desisted upon being told that the galleries would be cleared if the offense were repeated.

"They say, fellow, that you are deeply skilled in the use of firearms, and that as Captain of the Home Guards you have astonished people by the surpassing excellence of your shots."

"I can hit a barn door with buckshot at a distance of three yards!" proudly replied the bold mountaineer.

"Why don't they make a brigadier-general of you?" inquired O'Mulligan; but Tell essayed no reply.

Mr. Tell's boy, we should have stated, was with him at the time of his capture, and at the suggestion of Mr. O'Mulligan Mr. Tell placed a pumpkin on that interesting juvenile's head and fired at it with a bow and arrow, at a distance of three paces—the understanding being that if he didn't hit the pumpkin he was to be killed. This, as O'Mulligan aptly observed, was justice tempered with mercy.

Mr. Tell felt very bad at the idea of shooting at his young child, but he was compelled to do so, however much against his inclination. Who can describe a father's feelings who is forced to shoot at a pumpkin onto his young boy's head?

Mr. Tell fired—the pumpkin rolled off the child's head—the child lived!

CONTRIBUTIONS

"You may return to Ashtabula County, William,"
said the chief, deeply affected; but wherefore didst
hide that sled-stake under thy shirt-bosom?"

"To smash you in the snout, tyrant, had I slew'd
my young boy!"

"You don't say so!" said the astonished O'Mulligan.
"Well, it's a lucky go for me that you didn't hit him.
isn't it? Let me kiss him for his mother!"

"Little boy," said the sagacious pirate, whose eccentric and disreputable conduct we noticed in our last—
"little boy, give my love to your uncle Timothy.
Likewise to your aunt Betsy! Your aunt Betsy is
older than you be, but do not let that fact weigh you
down or interrupt your glorious career."

"Have you or have you not become a driveling idiot?" angrily inquired the chief.

"Sir," said the sagacious pirate, "figgers won't lie, and I consider you a dam' rascal!"

"Remove him at once," said O'Mulligan, "and don't let him get at the whisky again."

"You shall be super-super-se-(hic)-ded! Can you tell me why this lizzle boy is like—"

"Away with him!" shrieked the chief; "load him with chains!"

Mr. Tell and his son left for home on the first train; and O'Mulligan, sending for the last number of *The New York News*, put on his spectacles and sat down to the rich mental banquet which is always spread before the readers of that able South Carolina journal.

"This is a good paper," said the chief; "we must get up a club for this paper!"

Chapter IX.—Afloat Again

WE will now return to the ocean again.

The fine brig *Jane Gray* was gallantly breasting the waves, with her porpoise bobstays well holystoned and her mizzen marlinspikes tautly lashed to the poop-deck. Those of my readers who have seen active service on shipboard need not be told that all well-regulated vessels carry bulkhead jiggers as well as halyard toggles, and rest assured the *Jane Gray* was not deficient in these respects. Indeed, she not only carried the above, but taffrail scuppers and dockyard toplights, although she was not what is technically termed a gobline jib-boomer.

CONTRIBUTIONS

Will Somers, the gallant young tar of whom we have before spoken, was leaning gracefully against the topgallant skysail, evidently rapt in deep meditation.

"Avast, there, shipmet," said old Jack Ryder, who was holystoning some grummets near by; "all in the downs again, my hearty?

> "I wish I was old Stormy's son,
> Storm along, Stormy!
> I'd take my jacket and pawn it for rum,
> Storm along, Stormy!"

sang the old tar. "Come, come, Will, think of old Stormy's son and cheer up."

A tear glistened in William's eye. He was thinking of the fair Inez to whom he was betrothed, although her parents, who were wealthy, did not approve of the match. They thought he simply wanted to marry her so as to get the property. But they did William great injustice. He was above such things. His father had been a selectman in Stoneham for several years, and William was determined to keep up the reputation of the family. He was not aware of Inez's captivity, but supposed that she was home in Maine.

> "All in the downs the fleet was moored,
> The streamers waving in the wind,
> When black-eyed Susan came on board,
> Saying where shall I my true-love find,"

sang poor Will, still sadly leaning against the topgallant skysail.

"Sail ho!" cried the man at the wheel.

"Where away?" asked Captain Wright, seizing an opera-glass and bringing it to his eye.

"Two knots N. W. E. She flies the Secession flag!"

"'Tis the O'Mulligan's fleet!" said the captain.

"We shall be cut to pieces!" cried the first mate, in a voice of terror.

"I reckon not," said Captain Wright, taking a grown person's dose of tobacco; "I reckon not. There are no Congressmen, teamsters, or other old women on board to create a panic, and I guess we'll flax 'em."

"Sail ho! Three knots to the starboard!"

"'Tis the Black Horse Cavalry!" cried Captain Wright. "Gentlemen," he instantly added, in a cool voice, "there may have been a Bull's Run on shore, but there shall be no Calves' Run on the sea! To your guns!"

O'Mulligan stood upon the poopdeck of his flagship, his countenance lit up with the lurid glare of corn whisky and impending battle!

There was every prospect of an altercation.

CHAPTER X.—THE ENGAGEMENT

THE piratical fleet gradually surrounded the *Jane Gray*.

O'Mulligan's object was to deal gently with the erring Unionists.

He simply desired to confiscate their ship and its cargo and kill the crew with masked batteries. If in the enthusiasm of the moment some of his chivalric followers should mangle and cut up a few of the dead

Unionists and rob them of their clothes and watches, it was something that he could not avert. All O'Mulligan wanted was to be let alone.

His men were all high-toned gentlemen, with original ideas about statesmanship and honor; whereas the Unionists were greasy mechanics, low-lived, sniveling farmers, base laborers, gibbering and puling lovers of the aromatic African, d—d mercantile persons.

The idea of coming in contact with these disgusting creatures was so repugnant to O'Mulligan's magnificent mind that he conceived the ingenious expedient of fighting them with masked batteries, where he could not smell them or have his garments soiled by them, or breathe an atmosphere made putrid by their pestilential breaths.

O'Mulligan believed that if the admission to heaven was reduced to twenty-five cents per head, the people of New England would want to pay in tinware or produce.

It was very clear to the minds of O'Mulligan's men that William Lloyd Garrison was King of Boston, and that his subjects secreted fugitive niggers in Bunker Hill Monument, and went to the Museum arrayed in white chokers; while it was notorious that Greeley's sole object in hurling the grand Federal army upon Richmond was to free all the slaves, and put all the whites to death by sticking red-hot iron things into them.

Their newspaper organs teemed with intelligence of this pleasing and probable character, which the bucaneers swallowed as readily as they did their juleps and cocktails. And newspapers cannot lie, as those of my readers who can read print very well know.

"Pro bono cui bono et id omne verbatim ad captandum ad libitum ipse dixit nolle prosequi!" shouted O'Mulligan, in Latin, to the *Jane Gray*.

"Never!" replied Captain Wright in a voice of thunder. "Never, sir, while there's a drop of blood in these veins! I'm no such a character."

"Bully boy with the wax nose!" exclaimed a seaman, delighted at this unmistakable evidence of stamina.

"N'importe blasé eau d'vie qui vie recherché!" cried O'Mulligan in pure Canadian French.

"No, sir, I won't do that, neither!" replied Captain Wright, drawing himself up to his full height.

"Swei ine Guttenberg pong-bom-bum!" said O'Mulligan, this time in the sweet and dreamy German tongue.

"You lie!" cried Captain Wright; "and I favor you in that remark, for I think you'll steal."

O'Mulligan, desiring to awe the base plebeian with his scholastic attainments, then addressed him in Spanish—the stately language in which he had sworn at his grandmother in boyhood's sunny hours. "Won't yez be afther surrinderin' the bo-at, yer dirthy spalpane?"

"Not if I can help it," was the graceful reply.

"Let me talk to that man," said the sagacious pirate, whose disorderly and reprehensible conduct it has been our painful duty to notice before.

"I think I can fix him. I will dazzle him with a magnificent burst of wit—my last great conundrum. My Northern seafaring friend, with an uncontrollable passion for trading in apple-sass and tin pots, ahoy!" shrieked the sagacious pirate, mounting the hencoop; "can you tell me why—"

"Down, slave!" cried O'Mulligan, black with rage. "Is this ship a floating asylum for idiots?"

"Let him speak!" said all the men; and the chief, fearing mutiny if he proceeded farther, relapsed into a state of scowling silence.

"You can't browbeat me, sir, if your sister is cross-eyed!" said the sagacious pirate, with an air of triumph.

The chief recoiled before this splendid sarcasm, crushed utterly for the time being. The sagacious pirate then proceeded with his great original conundrum: "Why is Jeff Davis when he rides to Bull Run in an open four white horse barouche from Richmond, and pauses on the hillside to wipe the perspiration from his brow, and sees the epidemic—I mean the panic—and laughs in a sardonic manner, and thinks he will soon have Honest Old Abe in his clutches where he can't tell people any more little stories—why is he like a young girl who attends a fancy-dress funeral in the character of a sylph, and floats hither and thither like some light gondola in a sea of liquid silver? Answer: Because, The rose that all are praising is not the rose for me!"

Flushed with triumph, the sagacious pirate descended from the hencoop, but only to gaze upon a ghastly, a terrible spectacle. The entire ship's crew had fainted long ere he finished the great but subtle conundrum, and were lying stretched upon the deck as though they were dead.

"This it is to be a humorist!" cried the sagacious pirate in tones of fearful agony, wringing his hands and sobbing wildly. "Let the writers for the comic monthlies and Sunday papers take warning by my fate!"

The entire fleet—for the crews of the other pirate ships had also swooned—thus became an easy prize to the *Jane Gray*.

"We must board you," said Captain Wright, as he approached the flagship.

"All right," replied the sagacious pirate, "but you must find lights."

"I tell you I shall board you!" said Captain Wright, sternly, standing in the stern of the boat.

"I understand you. You will board me for $3.50 a week, and do my washing? I generally have about two pieces in the wash per week, to wit: a shirt and a drawer."

Captain Wright staggered wildly—he pressed his hands to his burning temples—his eyes glared frenziedly—white froth stood upon his lips!

"This it is to be a humorist!" cried the sagacious pirate, weeping afresh.

Captain Wright soon recovered and boarded the vessel. The pirates were put in chains, and the fleet was headed for the United States.

The next day the pirates waited upon Captain Wright in a body.

"What is all this?" asked that officer.

"We hear you are going to New York!" said O'Mulligan.

"Well, sir!"

"We are come to respectfully but most earnestly to ask you not to go to New York."

"Why?"

"Barnum is in New York, sir. We don't want to be exhibited with William Tillman, who killed three pirates, sir."

"If he kills old Barnum, as I rather suspect he will,"

said the sagacious pirate, "that will make four he's killed!"

This happy conceit pleased the sagacious pirate and he smiled sweetly. Captain Wright, however, regarded the pirate's remark as a piece of hideous levity, and reprimanded him severely; but he could

[265]

not be deaf to O'Mulligan's touching appeal, and the fleet was ordered to be headed for New Jersey.

The author of "The Fair Inez" has received several letters, complaining of what the writers are pleased to term inconsistencies in the plot and incidents of this romance. (One of these correspondents, who mailed his letter in Mississippi, mentions having inclosed a three-cent piece. The letter reached me safely, but I regret to say that the three-cent piece was absent. A sad commentary on the postal system of the Southern Confederacy.) I treat these letters with the contempt they so richly deserve. These correspondents doubt-lessly think they could write a better story than this. Perhaps they could. I know I could, if I wanted to. One correspondent—a fellow of very indifferent char-acter, I imagine—says that he could write a better story than "The Fair Inez" with his hands and ankles securely manacled, and have his meals sent to him from a cheap eating-house at that. Another fellow, who is evidently grossly ignorant of Scandinavian literature, remarks that he could dip a molasses-colored tom-cat in a pan of ink, and by "snaking" him over a few sheets of foolscap, produce a much better story than "The Fair Inez." Another fellow, of brutish instincts, no doubt, wants to know if the author of this romance wouldn't do better in his regu-lar avocation of shoemaking than in writing romances. Another low-minded person begs me to return to Poughkeepsie, where, he says, I was doing well white-washing barn doors, and not seek to gain a name by writing stories. He also ventures the assertion that

Inez is "shaky." These things do not disturb me. Oh, not at all. It is ever thus with genius. Twenty cities claimed Homer dead through which the living Homer could not get trusted for a drink. Nor do I forget that Tasso was refused admittance at the free lunches.

But I have set these men who sneer at my talents down as sympathizers with the South, if not Secessionists outright, and I want them to leave the country, as an outraged people will not stand this sort of thing, but, on the contrary, will arise in its majesty and put down this sort of thing.

Chapter XI.—The Oath of Allegiance

At half-past three o'clock on the day of the naval engagement so graphically described in our last, the battle clearly belonged to O'Mulligan. At fifteen minutes to four o'clock, however, the battle didn't belong to him as much as it did, so I suppose he was essentially defeated. The understanding had been that Scovillo would arrive at a certain period of the engagement with a brigade of negro chambermaids, but that distinguished corsair had become so deeply engrossed with a game of draw poker that he forgot all about the battle until long after the eagles of victory had perched upon the glittering banners of the Unionists. He was strongly censured for his conduct, although he endeavored to explain by stating that his brigade had only enlisted for three months, and that if they had gone into battle some of them might have been killed. Some people, however, thought he ought to be hurled from the Tarpeian Rock. As we shall not have occasion to mention this pirate again, we may here state that he was killed a short time ago by accidentally falling over a barrel of whisky while acting as floor-manager of a leap-year ball, given by some unmarried squaws of the Mackinaw tribe, of which association he was an Indian at the time of his premature demise.

The pirates were landed at Rahway, and took rooms at De Graw's Hotel. The emperor of that town made a few feeling remarks on the occasion, and the Bard of Union County recited some ingenious verses, bringing in all their names. They were ordered to bed promptly at twelve o'clock every night, that being the rule of the jail, and were otherwise carefully cared for and taken care of.

The pirates all said if they had known what fine people they had been killing and confiscating, they would never have gone and done it, adding that it was impossible to subjugate such a government. O'Mulligan was stricken with horror at the idea of having imbrued his hands in fraternal blood, and remorse and pip preyed upon his vitals. The sagacious pirate was affected in the same way. "Why, boys," said he, "we've been fighting our brothers! How sing'lar! Lor' bless me!"

The pirates united in representing the rebels as being in a frightful condition, with no resources, provisions, arms, or anything. Besides, there was a great Union sentiment in the South, particularly in the Everglades of Florida, which only wanted developing to exhibit itself. O'Mulligan thought that if the

government would go kind of easy with the rebels for
a spell, giving them time to consider how wrong it was
to imbrue their hands in fraternal blood, they would
ultimately rally round the Federal flag. He was
especially gratified to witness the efforts of those pure
patriots who were endeavoring to establish a Peace
Party in the North. Nothing, he said, could be finer
than a Peace Party in the North.

The corsairs manifested such sincere repentance that
they were finally released on taking the Oath of Allegiance, and O'Mulligan was appointed a quarter-
master in the Federal army. Others of the pirates
became army contractors, the army overcoat and
pantaloons business affording ample scope for their
peculiar line of genius. One pirate, with a diplomatic
turn of mind, was despatched to Portugal to keep
Harvey straight; another joined the Young Men's
Christian Association at Baltimore; and several others
received clerkships in the various departments at
Washington.

Thus the mists are rapidly rising from the marshes
of this Romance, for this Romance has mists and
marshes as well as that other story which is now attract-
ing some attention in literary circles—I allude to "Great
Fluctuations" by my friend and fellow-companion in
the rosy walks of first-class literature, C. D. of Gad's
Hill. While I would institute no invidious compari-
son, I may still be permitted to submit that my story
is Mistier and Marshier than his. I will bet five dollars it is, anyhow.

It may not be generally known that all of us—
Dickens, Bulwer, Old Thack, and the rest of us—have

no idea of what we are going to write about when we commence our novels, and it frequently occurs that we don't know what we are writing about after we have commenced them. These are peculiarities of eminent authorship, and should excite no astonishment in any well-regulated mind.

Chapter XII.—Inez

WE will now return to Inez. As soon as O'Mulligan had got well to sea, that fair young creature resolved to make her escape. She accordingly raised a window on the ground floor and got out. Then walking quietly to the depot she bought a ticket and went home in the cars. Her escape was consummately managed and reflected great credit upon her shrewdness and intrepidity. She did not get out with other passengers at the railway eating-houses for her meals, preferring to die a natural death.

Majestic scenery abounded along the route she had wisely chosen, and she could not but notice how assiduously the gentlemanly conductor, the indefatigable brakesman, the efficient engineer, and the urbane switchman performed their respective duties. It was the Broad Gauge route, and connected with steamboats for Slinkersville.

Her mother was glad to see her (her father, it will be remembered, met a watery grave by being drowned in the first chapter of this story), and the neighbors wanted to know "how much money she had laid up for a rainy day."

"Dear mother," said the fair Inez, "I know your

heart must bleed to see me come home without father!"

"Well, yes! rather. But he was awful on slapjacks? He'd eat forty on 'em at a single meal. But, poor man! he's eaten his last slapjack! Not another solitary slapjack will that poor drowned man never eat!" A tear glistened in the worthy widow's eye as she spoke.

"Pity he could not have died at home," said Inez, "in his bed, surrounded by kind friends."

"If he had," replied the affectionate widow, "we would have got up a gay old funeral for him, I tell you!"

Weeks and months went by on leaden wings. Where was Will Somers, the gallant sailor-boy? "Is my William true?" she asked herself one day.

"He is! he is!" cried a voice, and the young tar stood before her.

"Weelyum!" cried she.

"Inez!" cried he.

And they were locked in each other's arms, which it is a fine thing to do, my young readers.

"Well, if this ain't the crowner!" said the maiden's maternal parent, entering the room. "I was never so struck up in a heap in my nat'ral born days— faithful! Got any property, William? Got a thousand dollars?"

"There is the sum twice told!" cried William, casting a hefty purse of gold upon the floor. "Blush not to take it. There's not a coin that is not bought and hallow'd in the merchant marine service, reefing forecastles, splicing bulkhead jib-booms, and in the performance of other labor incident to a maritime pursuit!"

"All right," replied the maternal parent. "You may get married right away. Quicker the better."

The wedding-day came. The village bells pealed merrily. The white-haired old clergyman and the invited guests had all congregated, when a chariot, drawn by four faithful trotting-horses and driven by an honest horseman from the Union Course, Long Island, stopped suddenly at the door. The chariot contained O'Mulligan and the sagacious pirate! It did, upon my honor.

"Good people, make way!" said the sagacious pirate, brandishing a gold-headed club. "Room for his Imperial Highness Patricko O'Mulligan, Lord of the Swell-heads, King of Canal Street, Grand Fiduciary of the Bankrupt Soap-boilers! Lo! a great man cometh. Stag his nibs!"

"Silence, fool!" cried O'Mulligan. "My brave young sailor," he said, in a sweet voice, "I give her to you! Take her and be happy! Go to your William, Inez!" Then placing his hands upon their heads, he said, in a voice choked with deep emotion and whisky straight, "Bless you, my children! bless you!"

It was very affecting, though William and Inez were at a loss to precisely see what the reformed pirate had to do about it.

"And now," cried the sagacious pirate, running his fingers wildly through his hair and throwing his coat far back upon his shoulders—"now comes the touch-ingest scene of all! Inez! Inez! I now throw off the mask, worn so many years! I now reveal myself." Then seizing her frantically by the hand, he said, in a hoarse whisper, "You had a grandfather?"

"I did, I did! But he is dead."

"No, no! not dead, but lives—lives, Inez, to enliven this festive scene with his brilliant presence, and to bless you on this auspicious day! I am he! I am your long lost grandfather! Come to my arms!"

She wept upon his bosom.

"Stop!" said the maiden's maternal parent. "How old be you, sir?"

"Eighteen," replied the sagacious pirate.

"Ah, ha! ho, ho!" said the maternal parent, "now I've got you! Inez is nineteen herself! You can't come no grandfather dodge over on us. You are a impostuier!"

"Well," said the sagacious pirate, going up to third

discount he secured a large trade and ultimately ran the regular post-office out of town. He sells three-cent stamps for two cents, making a still greater reduction where people buy by the wholesale.

Doctor Briggs is a dentist at Moosup, Connecticut, and is a fine operator upon human gums.

Mr. Coe unintentionally dislocated his neck, a few years since, by falling from a scaffold in Illinois, a rope being twined about his neck at the time. There was a large crowd present, including the Sheriff of the County.

Charles Wilson is publishing a paper in Waterford, Maine, having more subscribers than he knows what to do with.

Old Jack Ryder renounced the sea and accepted a professorship in Oberlin College. He also conducts a concert-hall in that place, refreshments being handed round by beautiful Moorish maidens.

All the other characters of this romance are doing well, and so I leave them in the sunshine of their prosperity.

Gentle reader, has not my story a moral? Do you not see that honesty is the best policy, and that pro-crastination is the thief of time? Is not virtue its own reward, and should we despise a man who wears a ragged coat? Dress does not make the man, and try and lay up something for a rainy day. Live within your means! Pay your debts, and remember that the race is not to the swift. If you would thrive rise at five. Subscribe for your county paper!

Gentle reader, my story is done. It is hard to part, but try and bear up under it. Farewell, farewell!

CONTRIBUTIONS

WOSHY-BOSHY

OR

THE PRESTIDIGITATING SQUAW OF THE SNAKEHEADS

CHAPTER I

THERE once existed a powerful nation of Indians, and they were known as the Silvertoes and Snakeheads.

They lived in a vast and beautiful land, which abounded in the most delicious game. The lakes and rivers likewise teemed with the daintiest fish; and the rich skins of the deer and gray-fox were plenty in almost every wigwam.

These Indians thrived apace. They grew so powerful, indeed, that other nations thought it quite judicious to treat them with considerable urbanity. Their flag was respected everywhere, and in whatever clime one of them might be, he had only to announce his nationality and he could obtain all the fire-water he wanted on time, if he were hard up.

But after basking many years in the warm sunshine of prosperity these Indians became uneasy and began to indicate a sad but unmistakable desire to fly off the handle. The Snakeheads, who had labored unceasingly to erect this row, being considerably aided and abetted by a few incendiary Silvertoes, finally made a bold attempt to dissolve the nation and go to keeping house on their own hook. Personally the Silvertoes didn't care the impious expletive of a peripatetic repairer of damaged tin about the simple secession

20   [277]

of the Snakeheads, as those savages had been an extensive nuisance for many moons; but when those savages not only insisted upon going to housekeeping upon their own hook, but on stocking their pantry with fine plate belonging to the Silvertoes, and filling their cellar with much fat bear meat, also belonging to the Silvertoes, and then had the inflated cheek to ask to be let alone, the Silvertoes ventured to remonstrate. A struggle ensued. It is of the time in which that struggle occurred that we write.

Chapter II

In the heart of the trackless wilderness stood the wigwam of Woshy-Boshy, a chief in high repute among the Snakeheads.

On the evening we introduce him to our readers he lay stretched upon a dried buffalo-skin, smoking one of Shanly's brierwood pipes, and conversing with a brave from across the blue waters of the Shaggonana River, named Boozywoozy.

Boozywoozy was an orator of rare power, and his remarks were always able and appropriate.

He also played policy, his favorite numbers being 4, 11, 44. An adept at this pleasing game, he won many ducats, liards, pistoles, francs, and slums.

He inclined favorably to fire-water, but had never been attacked with delirium tremens. The complaint had broken out in his family, but the family was a large one, and there were not tremens enough to go round.

So he drank with impunity—or with anybody else who would treat.

CONTRIBUTIONS

"Will the warrior of many a wordy victory, whose voice is sweeter far than the pellucid waters of the fast-rolling Shaggonana, join Woshy-Boshy in a light bowl?" Thus spoke the Chief Woshy-Boshy.

"The words of the mighty chief fall pleasantly upon

the ears of Boozywoozy. He will moisten his diaphragm. Is it whisky?"

"Brother, it is."

"Did the great chief obtain it at any of the barrooms of any of the leading hotels on Broadway?"

"No, no!" howled the chief, a shade of horror creeping over his face. "Does my brother of the sweet voice and winsome eye take me for an aboriginal Borgia? Ugh! When Woshy-Boshy kills thee it shall be with the tomahawk! No gentlemanly Indian will give a friend poison."

"Woshy-Boshy speaks well. Here's luck!"

And they clinked the canakin.

During the evening they performed the Green Corn Dance, procuring the corn for that purpose from the shrill-voiced Ethiopian Females who perambulated the forest, shrieking, "Hot cor-run! 'Ere's yer nice hot cor-run!"

After dancing a good deal and clinking the canakin many times, Woshy-Boshy and the orator put on their yellow blankets and bright-beaded moccasins, preparatory for a stroll.

Previous to leaving the wigwam, however, Woshy-Boshy turned off the gas, as a matter of economy, and arranged the chairs in an orderly manner, so that in case his legs were ill on his return, he would have clear sailing to his bed.

Relighting their brierwoods. the Indians then went forth, arm in arm, singing:

"Then let the wide world wag as it will,
I'll be gay and happy still;
Gay and happy—gay and happy,
I'll be gay and happy still!"

Chapter III

Woshy-Boshy was about two hundred and forty years old, but his mind was unimpaired. He was as vigorous mentally as he had been a hundred and seventy-six years before.

There was a touching pathos about many of this savage's speeches.

CONTRIBUTIONS

Meeting a party of white emigrants on the plains one day, he said: "Brothers! the red man welcomes you to the wild hunting-grounds of the West. The pale face will some day drive us from here. How is our Great Father at Washington? I belong to a race that is fast becoming extinct. Is there any whisky or red pocket handkerchiefs in the party?"

Bursting into tears, Woshy-Boshy then scalped the emigrants, took their money and handkerchiefs, and fled to the primeval forest to conceal his emotion.

He was of good blood. His father had been a red man of gorilla proclivities, and had attained considerable local celebrity as a strangler of estray Mokes.

Woshy-Boshy, however, rather inclined to cannibalism.

He had in his childhood slain and eaten his grandmother, and he ever after alluded to her, with a depth of feeling which did credit alike to his head and heart, as "a sweet woman," a tear glistening in his sorrel eye the while he spoke.

"I wish there had been more of her," he one day said, while in a playful mood. "Grandmother on the half-shell is good."

He had a keen appreciation of humor.

His temperament was atrabilious, with a marked tendency to etherealosity, but he was a hearty eater, and rose at five; and although sometimes exhibiting flippancy in his converse, he was not knock-kneed or cross-eyed.

In battle he shone with marvelous luster—like a coal-oil lamp, I may say.

Mounted in a trotting-sulky and driving a pair of

somber mules tandem, he would drive furiously around in the rear of his warriors, and order them on, and then he would drive home and have his mules put up, leaving his warriors to on.

One night as he sat in his wigwam, smoking another of Shanly's brierwood pipes and discussing the Morrill tariff with Mullen the artist, he heard a horse-railroad car stop in front of his wigwam; and directly there entered, in hot haste, a youthful Snakehead.

"How now, good Wo-no-she? Comes the eagle-eyed brave with good tidings?"

"Woshy-Boshy! listen to Wo-no-she. My eye ain't so eagle as it was! The Silvertoes have beat us in a fight and captured sixteen of our braves. They are now in Fort Lafayette."

"Ha!" cried the chief, a sweet smile lighting up his bay countenance, "that's good! They'll take the oath of allegiance in a few days and get out, possibly bringing away some of the spoons with them. If they don't escape in this way we must smuggle some wash-tubs into their cells. The wash-tub business has only been done once, and I regard it as a rather large thing."

"They shall be free!" cried Wo-no-she, his knife leaping from his belt as he spoke; "Wo-no-she swears it!"

"Hunky boy!" said Woshy-Boshy.

"When will you have a battle?" inquired a gentleman named Etynge, artist of an illustrated paper.

"Well, I don't exactly know," said Woshy-Boshy, placing his forefinger thoughtfully upon his forehead. "When does your next paper come out?"

"In about two days."

"Well, we'll get you up a gallant skirmish this evening, and perhaps a total rout of the enemy. But a gallant skirmish sure. The pictorial papers must be encouraged."

"Then I will go to work on my sketches at once," remarked the artist.

"All right. But in whatever position you sculp me, be sure and give me a fierce nostril!"

"A picture of a battle, with red blood, would be a fine thing," remarked a savage with a dapple-gray countenance.

"It would indeed!" said Woshy-Boshy. "But we cannot force Art. Art must take her time. And indeed Art has made rapid progress. Already it enables the skilful draftsman to vividly sketch a battle several days before it occurs! Bully for Art, says Woshy-Boshy!"

"Bully for all!" cried the dapple-gray savage.

"Which reminds me of my new ballad," said Woshy-Boshy. "I will sing it. You have a great treat before you.

"I'll sing to you a bully good song,
        Bully aborigines, bully aborigines!
    Join in the chorus and help it along,
        Stewed peas, stewed peas!"

"Isn't 'stewed peas' rather far-fetched?" inquired a tall-complexioned savage. "Don't you think it mars the rhythm?"

"Not at all, sir. I wrote it in the iambic measure. Don't rouse me to anger, if you please, sir!" returned the chief, sternly. He, however, composed himself and proceeded with his composition:

"We're bully boys with copper skins,
    Bully for all, bully for all!
And we'll knock the Silvertoes off their pins,
    Previous to next fall, previous to next fall!"

At the conclusion of the ballad the savages joined in an Ethiopian walk-round and dance, Woshy-Boshy "patting" with all the vigor of a young man of ninety. Nobody who saw him "pat" would for a moment think that his mind was impaired.

Chapter IV

WINONA was the daughter of Boozywoozy, and she was young, fair, and frisky.

Her beauty was of the Andalusian, or South Amboy, type.

She was a coquette, and derived much pleasure in stringing the susceptible young braves of the tribe.

If a young Snakehead refused bear meat or declined joining in the exhilarating and genial pleasures of the chase, his parents knew too well that it was all owing to Winona.

She was marvelously fascinating, and could make the most obdurate aborigine love her distractedly by simply fastening her brilliant black eyes upon him. Hence she was called the Prestidigitating Squaw of the Snakesheads.

All parents told their sons to keep away from the Prestidigitateuress, and therefore they of course didn't.

Her tastes were sumptuous. She always wanted something new and nice. In this respect she was different from most young ladies. She was an incessant and most discouraging drain upon the money-pouch of her father, the sweet-voiced Boozywoozy.

Sometimes he would "put his foot down" and say she should not have another single dress.

"Do you think I am a United States mint, girl?" he would say, angrily casting her from him. But she would go behind his chair and softly caress his horse-tail locks. Then placing her fair, fresh face against his, she would say, "Don't be a cross Injin, papa, be a good Injin!" And the old man's face would soften and he would say, "Well, well, girl, go and buy what you want, but don't be extravagant."

There is some human nature in fathers, after all; and when a fair young girl presses her face to that of the author of her being, the effect is most always soothing. And it is a singular fact that when she acts in this way toward a young man, even though he be not related to her at all, the effect is more soothing. We cannot undertake to explain why this is so.

One afternoon as Boozywoozy and Winona sat in their wigwam the door-bell rang, and Woshy-Boshy was announced.

"Hail, great chief!" cried Boozywoozy, rising and blowing his nose.

"Woshy-Boshy salutes you; likewise the Lily of the primeval forest! Got any licker?" Thus spoke the illustrious chief.

"Great person! there's whisky in the jug! Winona, bring hither the Mountain Dew."

"Father! I fly," said Winona, and in a moment she reappeared with a comfortably sized keg ingeniously balanced upon her fair right shoulder.

[285]

"Prettiest waiter-girl in the city!" said Woshy-Boshy, placing the keg to his expressive lips.

"Been to the capital, I understand?" said Boozy-woozy.

"I have. I went to introduce my new cannon, which, as you are aware, can shoot a double-breasted columbiad into the middle of next week, and snuff a gas-jet at four hundred paces."

"Well!"

"The head of the Ordnance Department wrote me briefly thus, 'Hain't no time!' and I came away. The Ordnance Department is in the hands of young, roistering fellows, who only came in in 1808, and until they get some old, experienced men there I'm afraid things will go wrong. They want a man who is about two hundred and sixty-seven years of age. A gifted dotard, for instance, who has experience in driveling."

"You have thirty wives, you are a kind husband, a numerous father, and an exemplary citizen. I am surprised that they repulsed you. I am grieved, too. Listen to these tears!" said Boozywoozy, as his sobs rattled upon the wigwam floor.

"I doth! I doth!" cried the chief; "not a solitary sob escapes me—not a sob. By the way," he added, "Lynch ran well for Sheriff in New York, didn't he?"

"Lynch always runs well," said Boozywoozy. "He's used to it."

The savages went out, and hailing an omnibus, they drove to the camp.

"Advance and give the countersign and I'll shoot you!" said the sentry.

CONTRIBUTIONS

"The d—l you will!" replied Boozywoozy, starting back. "Here's a sentry for you! You'd better desert and join the Silvertoes. They'd make a brigadier of you!" Then withering the ignorant subordinate with a frown, Woshy-Boshy and Boozywoozy walked within the lines. Passing the guard-house they could not help overhearing the following song, which was executed in a riotous sort of voice, by an insubordinate private named Smiggy McGural, to the air of "Pretty Katy Ryan, O!"

"It was whin grate Gineral Price led his ahrrmy in Missouri,
  With his dhrums, an' his bayonets, an' pistils bright an'
    handy, O!
Sez he, 'Come on, brave followers widh fire an' sword an' fury,
  An' we'll lick the greasy Yankees, for it's I that am the
    dandy, O!'

"Och, they marched and they countermarched widh fifes an'
    bangin' cymbals,
  The soldiers they was bound to whip an' cut us all to pieces, O!
The Gineral was as lively as the game of peas an' thimbles.
  Sez he, 'We'll rob a bankin'-house an' all be as rich as
    Crœsus, O!'

"Thin off they went at double-quick, an' nothin' stood against 'em;
  With cavalry an' cannon, ivery gun in place to limber, O!
Till on a suddent there they saw the Yankee boys fernenst 'em,
  In solemn solid columns pourin' through the open timber, O!

"Thin the Gineral's ahrrmy stopped, for it was more than they
    expected;
  An' it ran about the lines, 'O wirra, now we're larruped
    surely, O!'
An' Price sez to an adjutant, in manner quite dejected,
  'Here, take my place a little while; I'm feelin' very poorly, O!'
[287]

"Thin back he rode to camp, an' niver drawed his feet from stirrup,
   . . . Though he had ridden like the wind o'er swamp and hill
      and hummock, O! . . .
Until he'd got a smashin' dose of peppermint an' syrup,
   For sez he, 'I've got an awful pain an' sinkin' in my
      stummock, O!'

"Meanwhile, the Yankee boys put in with valor quite undoubted.
   They fought till all the field was piled widh heaps of dead
      an' dyin', O!
The Rebels was repulsed widh loss, an' thin complately routed,
   An' them as wasn't took jist barely saved themselves by
      flyin', O!

"So Gineral Price left camp, as the papers all has told yez,
   For the line of Arkansas, where the ground don't lay so level, O!
An' nothin' has been heerd of the Gineral or his soldiers,
   Except he still was sick, an' they was runnin' like the devil, O!"

Chapter V

It became daily more evident that a battle was imminent. The Silvertoes, having encountered several reverses, were now nerving themselves for a grand effort. They were coming with fire and sword and that sort of thing.

Woshy-Boshy knew this, and yet he was calm. His cheek did not blanch. He was even cheerful, and laughed perhaps more heartily than ever over the jokes and sparkling paragraphs in *The National Intelligencer*. Yet the Snakeheads did not question his ability to lead them in this crisis. They well knew that when aroused he was as terrible as an army with banners, or a speckled jackass while in the act of kicking over a peanut-stand.

He chawed more tobacco, however, than usual.

One day he took a large chaw, and handing it to Boozywoozy, he said:

"Will you sustain me?"

"I will," replied the gentle savage, biting off a large piece.

"Take a pound of the best store tobacker," said Woshy-Boshy, "and soak it in molasses and rum,

and it makes as good tobacker as I want to use—that is, if it is chemically examined by Professor Chitton and warranted to contain no deleterious substances."

After enjoying themselves chawing tobacco for some time they commenced planning for the approaching engagement. "As we don't wish to become idiots and gibber, with straw in our hair, we won't look at those maps in *The New York Herald* any more. Let us souse a tom-cat in a pan of ink, draw him across a sheet of paper, and have a more intelligible map of our own." So said Woshy-Boshy, and Boozywoozy was agreeable thereto.

Woshy-Boshy had appointed the next day for the foe to advance. The plans were all made. Already the Snakehead troops were on their way to the field, three hundred masses and twenty-four barrels of them having gone round by Lake Superior, on board the steamer *Iron City*, Capt. Ed. Turner. Woshy-Boshy purposed going by way of Portland, and had engaged passage on Maxfield's stage. He was expecting Horace round every moment for his baggage. It was an effecting scene, the parting of Woshy-Boshy and Boozywoozy. (The latter had conscientious scruples about engaging in a war where they fired real bullets, and hence he was to stay at home.) They had known each other from childhood, and now they were about to part —perhaps forever. "Do you remember," said Woshy-Boshy, in a voice trembling with emotion, "how we used to throw stones at an old blind man and scalp apple-women, in the halcyon days of youth's spring-time? Innocent prattlers! Them days is past! Do you remember, too, how in after-years, as we were about blossoming into manhood, I used to borrow money of you!"

"I do," said Boozywoozy, tears standing in his eyes in chunks—"I do, distinctually!"

"Perhaps I sha'n't never borrow any more money off you no more!" continued the chief.

"You make me miserable! See! These tears are

real, and these poignant moans are nat'ral. Big thing!" So spoke Boozywoozy.

"Here is my photograph. It is by one of the old masters."

"Thank you—oh, thank you!" said Boozywoozy. "I'll wear it next to my heart," and he placed it in his left coat-tail pocket.

"If I fall," said Woshy-Boshy, clutching his friend by the coat-collar—"if I fall, promise me that you will break the news gently to my creditors? Prepare them gradually for the dreadful shock."

"Consider it already done!" said Boozywoozy, ever anxious to accommodate his old and tried friend.

"Our friendship reminds me of that of Damon and Pythias," said Woshy-Boshy.

"I think we are somewhat on that lay," replied his trusty friend. "But what are you putting that junk-bottle of peppermint in your pocket for?"

"To have it by me in case of emergency."

"Ah, indeed! I remember General Price had it pretty bad."

"Had what?"

"The emergency."

"And do you remember likewise, my good Boozy-woozy, how I one day, in the exuberance of my childish heart, tied a cooking-stove to the neck of my decrepit grandfather and shoved him into the river? Ah! the happy days of my childhood! Rock me to sleep, mother, rock me to sleep!"

There was profound silence in the wigwam for a moment, save the sound of the tears of the savages, which pattered, pattered, upon the floor.

"Will childhood's days," said Woshy-Boshy, at length, buckling on his armor, also his coat of mail—"will childhood's days ever come back to us again?"

"I'll bet the coffee and cakes at Meschutt's that they won't!" exclaimed Boozywoozy. "Is it a go?"

They conversed a few moments more, when Woshy-Boshy arose to depart. "You will see me mother," he said, in a soft voice, "will you not? Hush! If I fall ask her, 'Oh, why should the spirit of mortal be proud?'"

"I will interrogate that elderly female upon that important matter the moment I hear you have been scooped in!"

"'Tis well!' said the chief. "And now farewell! I fain would have thy blessing upon my head ere I go; and if you can also lend me your umbrella, I shall esteem it a particular favor."

They wept upon each other's bosom. They stood up to their waists in their own sobs. The floor of the wigwam was literally a lake of tears, and the chairs and tables were floating around like ships. Their sighs were heard ten miles off.

Agreeable to expectation, the battle occurred the next day. Woshy-Boshy was kicked in the stomach by an ambulance horse, and fell fatally wounded at the first fire. Previous to expiring, however, he handed Nicholson a five-dollar bill to give him a favorable notice in his report of the battle, in *The World*, and requested that Frank Wood should put him in his "Pulpit Pictures."

The battle was a decisive one, not only breaking the

back, but caving in the stomach of the rebellion. The Silvertoes never had any more trouble with the Snakeheads. Those savages, after considerable rehearsing, learned to behave decently. Reunited, the nations became stronger than ever and marched on resistlessly to greatness and grandeur.

Winona, the Prestidigitating Squaw of the Snakeheads, married a young Silvertoe of rich but respectable parents, and has lots of new dresses and things. She is very happy.

Woshy-Boshy's sons all went to farming except one —Minky-Winky. He is attached to all the various circus companies, and appears as the North American savage of the far-Western prairies. He contemplates getting up an entirely new act, which will involve the use of banners.

Boozywoozy left off being an Indian and assumed the duties of a chaplain on board the steamer *Western Metropolis*, and is now at work on a man named Morris, with some hope of converting him, but not much.

Thus closes a romance which was written with one arm tied behind me, and under other equally adverse circumstances. Gentle reader, however glad you may be that it is done, you cannot be more so than I am. Hurrah! Embrace me!

21

ARTEMUS WARD

MAINE IN MARCH

"Remember the ides of March."
—*W. Shakspeare.*

No need, oh, W. Shakspeare, of telling me to remember those ides. I shall not forget them—not a solitary ide—while I live.

The Prodigal Sun shone brightly and warmly the afternoon on which I tore myself from my weeping friends in Madison Square and started for Maine. Broadway was warm almost to sweatiness, and the classic Bowery lay in a cloud of dust. The dove-eyed maiden Spring was apparently here again, and methought I would have nice times among the squirrels and bluebirds and dandelions down in Maine.

I remembered a stately oak on the banks of a beautiful brook. I will recline under the oak, methought, and read *The New York Ledger*. But the dove-eyed maiden Spring, like several other dove-eyed maidens who have had the pleasure of my acquaintance, had no hesitation in repudiating her promises, and sent a big snow-storm after us.

It came roaring upon us just as the night was setting in, beating fearfully against the car windows and clogging up the wheels.

I am warranted in stating that it was one of the storms, leaving us in no doubt as to the drift of its meaning, for we soon found ourselves fast in a snow-drift. The "iron horse," as I think I have seen the locomotive called, made a few desperate plunges forward, and then seceded from us entirely, tearing down the track like the little bay beauty Flora Temple, with

[294]

her tail done up in pepper-corns of an extraordinarily persuasive character. We were in the woods and the storm was raging with all the fury of a woman "corned." The black night, like the black knights of our popular bloodthirsty literature, laughed in a sardonic manner at our "snow of troubles," and then frowned fiercely upon us—the innocent and helpless. We denounced the railroad company in withering terms. If I used stronger language than the rest—if I more thoroughly and convincingly laid bare the arrogant villainy of rail-road monopolies, it must not be attributed to a desire to make myself conspicuous, but rather to the fact of my being a deadhead on the road. The refractory iron horse was led back, and we went slowly forward again.

The conductor said he'd get us into Portland that night, certain, whereupon a gentleman from Bangor said, "he hoped so, tew, for he'd rather gin a quarter than not reach hum next day— I had, I snore!" he added, glancing around the car. "Darned if I hadn't."

Standing late at night in the great dismal depot at Portland, it occurred to me that when, many years ago, the Indians sold the land upon which that beautiful and brilliant city now stands, for a jug of indifferent rum, they considerably cheated the whites. But this was only the churlish crotchet of the moment. Portland is all right and abounds in inimitable clams; likewise pretty girls, who like to get fellows on a piece of twine and pull them around in a distracting manner. Portland has got over expecting the *Great Eastern*, its chief amusement now consisting of sliding down-hill and admiring the princely quarterly dividends (which are now declared three times a day) of the Grand

Trunk Railway, which thoroughfare is managed by British gentlemen with side-whiskers, who have vainly searched many weary years for their long lost H. But, as Lord Palmerston felicitously remarks, "What's the hods so long's we're 'appy?"

A city election was to occur next day, and, fearing that I might be elected alderman by one of those sublime uprisings of the honest masses which are sometimes witnessed when things assume a crisis shape, I hastily left by the early morning train. I go northward toward the White Mountains, which loom up in the distance like the ghosts of immense giants. A portion of the journey is performed by stage, and it pleases me to find an old friend and fellow-soldier in the gentleman who holds the reins over the spirited team. We both fought in the Madawaska war, carrying death and devastation among the foe wherever we appeared. At the memorable and bloody battle of Pipsywipsy we were both fatally wounded three times by falling out of the baggage-wagon; but the eagles of victory perched upon our banners, and in the language of my old friend, Dan Webster, "we ain't dead yet."

I am partial to sensations, and jumping from sunny and summery Madison Square to bleaky and breezy Maine is one of 'em, beyond peradventure. The snow is very deep. The people want it to go, but it's no go! The fences are completely buried, and in some instances drifts have surrounded houses like the walls of a fort. But it is quite cheerful in the section to which I allude when compared to some parts of the state, where I am informed it snows continually for fifteen months in the year.

CONTRIBUTIONS

This is the happy land of baked beans and pure religion. Here "I guess I can dew it!" Here men get rich on farms which at first sight look as if they could produce nothing but crops of rocks. Here land which an Illinois farmer wouldn't have on his premises at any rate is held at an elevated figure. Here when a man don't clearly understand you, he says, "Hay?" and when he is astonished, "Sho!" Here people talk through their noses to a great and sometimes alarming extent, nature having kindly provided some of them with noses like covered bridges, each nostril being large enough to let a double team of words go through. Here the people have just eccentricities enough to be interesting. Here they can invent, chop, swap, work, and (if necessary) fight. Here there is maple sugar, virtue, shrewdness, strong arms and big chests, pickerel, rosy cheeks and true hearts, ever-busy knitting-needles, cream, an undying love for Bunker Hill, honey, patriotism, stocking yarn, mountains, ponds, hoop-poles, churches, school-houses, pine logs, scenery that knocks Switzerland into a disordered chapeau, and air so pure that the New-Yorker is sorry he can't bottle some of it and carry it to the metropolis for daily use.

I must not forget to mention a rather singular circumstance that occurred in my voyage from Portland to Boston per steamboat. I went aboard, secured a state-room, and proceeded to fall into one of those sweet slumbers which ever reward the honest man and Son of Temperance. On awaking in the night, it occurred to me that I would go on deck and converse with the man at the helm in regard to nautical affairs, as I was an old sea-dog myself, having had perilous experience on the Oxford and Cumberland Canal in the capacity of assistant chambermaid. The man was not at the helm, but I discovered that the steamer was going bravely ahead, taking a large wharf and a considerable portion of Portland with her. I laughed one of my "silvery laughs," but didn't say anything to anybody about the matter, because it was such an excellent joke on Portland. I don't remember to have ever read of a more singular circumstance. It is true that certain unprincipled persons, who I have reason to believe are Secessionists at heart, stated that the boat remained tied at her wharf all night, and did not leave Portland in consequence of the storm; but I confidently call upon Longfellow, Holmes, Everett, and the rest of the boys in Boston, who met me at the wharf the next morning, to refute the calumny. Going from Portland to Boston in a steamboat with a large wharf and several flourishing warehouses attached is a rather large thing to do, I candidly confess, but I did it.

In the language of Mr. C. Melnotte, dost like the picter?   ALPHONSO THE BRAVE.

OIL VS. VINEGAR

OR

THE RANTANKEROUS LECTURER

(The Carpet Bag, June 19, 1852)

BY LIEUTENANT CHUB

MANY years ago when the temperance question was first being agitated, the good people of B——, Maine, were informed, by "posters," that Mr. B. Franklin Put-it-to-'em would, on —— evening, deliver, at the village school-house, a lecture on temperance.

At "early candle-light" on the evening appointed the "house" was crowded with villagers, among whom was 'Squire Thadeus Dobson, familiarly called "Uncle Thad."

Uncle Thad was a wealthy, jolly, toddy-drinking farmer, who took especial delight, like many in those days, in "poking sticks" at a temperance lecturer; and, it is hardly necessary to say, honored this meeting solely for the purpose of raising a "muss," or, in the modern classics, "having a time."

After the choir had favored the audience with that soul-stirring, never-to-be-sufficiently-appreciated hymn, "Drunkards, reform!" Mr. Put-it-to-'em arose and commenced his discourse. He sent distillers, sellers, and drinkers to the "old boy" with a rapidity that was truly remarkable. In short, he labored hard to convince his hearers that, to use the language of the estimable Mr. Stiggins, of Pickwick Club memory, "all drinks were wanities"·

"Yes!" roared the lecturer, in tones of thunder, hitting the desk a tremendous blow with his clenched fist, "every glass of liquor a man drinks is *a nail in his coffin!*"

"What's that? What's that? I say, are you sartin about that 'ar?" exclaimed Uncle Thad, in a very high key, jumping up in his seat.

"Yes! Oh yes, my friend! quite certain," returned Mr. Put-it-to-'em.

"Wall, if 'tis *so*, I've drank enough to make *mine* a

cast-iron one, and *seven or eight thicknesses at that!*"
bellowed Uncle Thad, amid the roars of the audience.
Mr. P., seeing that it would be useless to proceed
further, "left."

The next winter another lecturer visited B——, and,
being really a sincere, worthy man, succeeded in re-
claiming many of the old soakers, among whom was
Uncle Thad.

MORAL.—Strive to do good on the principles laid
down in the Bible; because if you don't, somehow or
other "folks don't take no interest."

A YANKEE "PASS"

(*The Carpet Bag, September 11, 1852*)

I HAVE met with many "rum" chaps during a brief
existence in this somewhat erratic world, but I'm
inclined to think Jonny Ray, of "down East" notoriety,
the "rummiest" of them all. In the expressive language of the young gentlemen who dwell in "Gotham's
Bowery," he is "a out-and-outer—a reg'lar trump!"
Far and wide the country o'er is Jonny renowned for
his wit, his cunning, and his joking disposition. He
is a blower, too; place Barnum, Bateman, Dow, and
Gleason alongside of him on *this*—they'd all, individually and collectively, sink into the most remote
insignificance.

During a recent visit to the "old folks at home," I,
of course, called on Jonny. He was glad to see me, and,
over a bottle of pop-beer, told the following anecdote:

CONTRIBUTIONS

In the early part of the season Sands & Quick's Menagerie and Circus combined exhibited at H——, where lives the renowned Jonny aforementioned. Now Jonny, like three or four men with whom I have the honor of being acquainted, is not always flush, and on this day hadn't the first cent. In the beautiful, impressive language of Capt. J. Rynders, he asked himself, "What the d—l is to be *did?*" He wanted to see the elephant; but how could he? With his hands in his pockets he paced the village tap-room for a few moments, "bursting," as Jillson, of *The Waverly*, would say, "into a *reverie.*" At last he somewhat astonished the inmates of the room by jumping up into the air with the exclamation, "I have it!" and immediately left for his cottage. In about ten minutes he returned, with his old hat filled with potatoes, and marched boldly up to the door of the circus tent.

"What'n thunder you goin' to dew with all o' them 'ar pertaters?" bellowed Tom Sykes, who was one of 'em.

"Oh," returned Jonny, in a very loud voice, "I'm goin' to gin 'em ter the old elephant! I've gin him *one* hatful already, and he likes 'em, you'd better b'lieve!"

"Y-e-s," replied Mr. Sykes, as he cocked his eyes in a manner which was not entirely meaningless, "I presume he duz!"

The doorkeeper, with a smile at Jonny's benevolence, stood one side, and Jonny went in, chuckling within himself at the idea of seeing the *whole* for a hatful of potatoes.

CHUB.

every-day affairs I ever saw. His mind was all wrapped with books, and he cared no more about what the world was up to than a pig cares about the Hottentots.

One morning his wife—who, by the way, differed vastly from her spouse in this respect—was reading aloud from the paper an account of a horrible murder. A man had, so the paper said, deliberately killed his whole family—consisting of some dozen members— with an ax! Mrs. R. laid down the paper with the exclamation, "What a wretch!"

"Yes," said her husband in a very quiet tone, looking up from his book, "he should be talked to!"

Old Bill Burnett, if he was a church member, was the meanest man about. One cold, stormy winter's night he asked a poor stroller who was passing his house to walk in and have a mug of cider. The poor fellow gladly accepted the invitation. After the cider had been drawn, warmed, and drank old Burnett told the man that a few cents would settle the bill! The wanderer paid the money and went on his way, leaving the old hunks to laugh at his shrewdness—or rather robbery!

Aunt Hetty Dillson, a very respectable young lady of forty, who used to live "solitary and alone" on a big farm her dad had left her on his exit from this world, prided herself on her modesty. Her neighbor, Mr. Carter, had a fine bull calf which she wished much to buy. For fifteen nights she lay awake, thinking how she could broach the subject to her neighbor without saying the "wulger" word *bull*. At last she hit it.

CONTRIBUTIONS

One day as Carter was passing he was accosted by Miss Dillson as follows:

"Mr. Carter, do you wish to dispose of your *gentleman bull calf?*"

Mr. Carter marveled at her great delicacy.

AN OLD-FASHIONED HUSKING

By Chub

(*The Carpet Bag, October 30, 1852*)

Reader, you have heard of Oxford County, that is to be found in the northern part of

> That famous fabled country,
>   'Way down East,

haven't you? Well, I first saw daylight there, and of course have a liking for everything thereabouts in general, huskings, doughnuts, and bouncing damsels in particular. The women, *i.e.*, the old uns—bless their "picters"—don't stick themselves up as our city dames do; no, no, sir!—not by a long chalk. They rejoice in making themselves useful, in bringing their sons and "darters" up in the way they should go, so that when they get old they may go it! They are indeed helpmates to their "old men," and always have an eye to what is going on. And the young women, what shall I say about 'em? Don't everybody know that they are everything they should be—that they are handsome, and make the best of wives, butter, and cheese? Of course everybody knows all this; if they don't, however, they are as bad off as the

[305]

man who never heard of the Stebbings! The men, too, old and young, are men that are men—the real noblemen of our land. They go round in their shirt-sleeves, smoke pipes, and a few of 'em, I regret to say, imbibe rum. In short, the men, women, and children are a hard-working, generous, honest, and jolly people. One of their peculiar characteristics is that of keeping up old times, going in for huskings, trainings, musters, etc. Without stopping to say whether I consider the latter characteristics correct or not, I will endeavor to describe an old-fashioned husking—such a one as can only be seen in these degenerate days, I think, in "Old Oxford."

When the farmer has gathered his corn, he invites his neighbors to come and help him husk it. With a wish to help their neighbor and eat some of his wife's good things, they come, old and young. The barn is usually brilliantly illuminated with a tin lantern, and the seats for the huskers to sit on are made of the softest plank. With a huge pile of corn before them they commence to husk, spin yarns, sing, etc. Soon the "jug" comes round, and after imbibing songs and fish stories become remarkably plenty. The old uns talk about "the times that tried men's souls," the men they had licked when in the logging swamp, good oxen, fat calves, politics, etc. Between the group of old ones usually sits an old gray-headed patriot—one who was with Washington at Valley Forge and with him at Monmouth. And as he tells his yarns for a hundredth time watch the earnest attention that the farmers give him. Now he relates some affecting incident that occurred while he was "out," and see! his auditors raise their hard hands of toil to wipe from their weather-beaten faces a tear. Now he tells about the "iron-gray" that Washington mounted to run the traitor, Arnold, down. His listeners are all attention. When the old man tells about that "infernal old scoundrel, King George," of the abuse which the English heaped upon the Continentalers, his auditors are justly indignant and cry: "Scoundrel!" "Shame!" "Knave!" etc. And so the evening passes by.

There is usually present a young man who has "followed the seas," and he entertains the company with a nautical song—perhaps "A wet sheet and a flowing sea" (did you ever hear that jolliest and cleverest of actors, Frank Whitman, sing this?).

Most likely there is a man present who from too frequent potations from the "jug" is a little "sprung." He sings an old but popular drinking-song in tones more loud than musical, in which he expresses in energetic terms his intention not to "fall as the leaves fall," but to be "mellow and die a clever fellow." The young and thoughtless laugh at his pranks, but the old uns look solemnly at each other, shake their heads and say, "Poor fellow," "Pity he will do so," etc.

It is now eleven o'clock—

> The golden corn's all husk'd,
> And the farmer's heart made glad,

and now comes the rush to the house, where the smiling dame and her daughters have a table prepared that "groans" with good things. Supper's over, lots of lasses are present, and now

> On with the dance, let joy be unconfined;
> No sleep till morn—

And so they go it until the crow of the morning cock warns them that it is time to quit. Then comes "going home with the girls," the parting kiss, and all that. So ends the husking.

Congressmen may boast of their levees; city exquisites of their soirées; fast young men of their "good times," but as for me, give me a real old-fashioned husking.

THE FUGITIVE SLAVE

By Chub

(The Carpet Bag, December 25, 1852)

THE milk of human kindness flows more freely in the rural districts than in the city. As the man in the play says—I forget which one—"The country's all heart; the city's all hollow!" City philanthropists, abolitionists, etc., *talk* loud, but when the time comes for them to act they don't take no interest or "have other fish to fry." Not so in the country. There the people not only talk, but act; hence their good nature is often imposed upon.

I am cognizant of a rich "sell" that came off in one of the back towns in Maine, which, though it shows the most lamentable depravity on the part of the perpetrator, is "too good to be lost."

The town to which I refer boasted quite a respectable abolition society, of which Deacon Isaac Freeman was president. He was a little, nervous, active, good-natured, and pious man—one whom everybody loved, although there were a few who thought him rather too

impulsive for the prosperity of the cause for which he
labored. Some idea of his zeal may be obtained when
I tell the reader that I once heard him in a public meeting—his hair dressed *à la* porcupine—suggest in tones
of thunder the propriety of our marching South, gun
in hand, and by force liberating our colored brethren
and sisters. Without stopping to say whether I think
this rather daring movement would result favorably to
the cause or not, I will proceed to inform you how
this society was once "taken in and done for."

One Saturday afternoon, a few months after the
fugitive slave bill had gone into effect, a colored woman
dashed into the village of Y——, and halted not until
she arrived at Deacon Freeman's door, upon which she
gave several loud raps.

"Hello!" said the deacon, as he opened the door,
"what's the matter?"

"Oh, massa," cried the woman, "save me, save me!
I'm a fugitive slave jest escaped from a cruel massa,
'way down in old Virginny."

"You *have?*" asked the deacon, striking an attitude.

"Yes, yes. I spec' they is after me now!" replied the
woman.

"Come in, come in," cried the deacon. "If any of
the bloodhounds come into my house for the purpose
of taking you back to whips, chains, and bondage,
they will find *me* in the way."

The reader will probably smile at this heroic expression of the deacon's when I tell him that he was a little
consumptive man, and weighed, with his cowhide boots
and greatcoat on, not more than one hundred and
twenty pounds.

The deacon's wife and daughters gathered round the woman, while he ran out into the village to inform his co-workers of her arrival. He soon attracted a crowd and, mounting the village hay-scales, addressed the people as follows:

"Gentlemen, in my house is a fugitive slave who had just escaped from a master who has whipped, bruised, and mangled her in the most horrible manner. She is on her way to Canada—the bloodhounds are after her. Shall we not help her?"

"Yes!" shouted the crowd, and twenty or thirty dollars were raised for her on the spot. The deacon harnessed his horse and carried her thirty miles on her way that night.

The succeeding fall the deacon and one of his neighbors, Mr. Glum, visited K——, shire town of the county. The court being in session, they dropped in. In the prisoner's box was a young mulatto man.

"What's that poor fellow been doing?" asked the deacon of a young man who sported a blue coat with brass buttons and a hat with a large weed upon it

"Poor fellow be d—d!" exclaimed the young man. "He's a mean, sneaking cuss—meaner than pizen. He's been through the state in woman's clothes, calling himself a fugitive slave girl. He went to Canada with a lot of counterfeit money and passed some of it, but he got cotched, and I'm glad of it."

"Let's be goin'," whispered the deacon to Glum. "Thunder and jews'-harps!" exclaimed the deacon, as soon as they got outdoors, "it's the same nigger we helped!"

"Well, of all the rum goes that have come under my

immediate observation, I'm rather inclined to think
this is the rummiest!" said Glum.

"Well, well," said the deacon, "let's have a drink
and go home. Keep dark, though!"

The deacon, as I before said, is pious and the leading
man of his church, yet if you should say "fugitive" to
him, I rather think he would forget himself and bless
you into heaps.

PAUL PRYISM

By Lieutenant Chub

(The Carpet Bag, February 5, 1853)

If Hudibras was right in the above remark, then
some I wot of will never have need of those optical
assistants vulgarly called spectacles. They see with
the greatest correctness, in their own sagacious minds,
the countless derelictions of duty in others. "Trifles
light as air are confirmations strong as proofs of holy
writ." Inflated and satisfied with their own acts,
they canvass the acts of others and pass them in
review. If they come not out of the ordeal of these
self-constituted judges unscathed, then comes the cry,
"Down with them!" What right, we ask, have these
meddlers, these self-made guardians of the public
morals, to pry into the business of others? Do they,
jure divino, pass in judgment on their fellows? No!
But on the contrary they transcend the laws of decency
and show conclusively their asinine propensities. To
these "vigilant watchmen on the outward towers" I
would say, "Physician, heal thine own infirmities!"

and let those of your neighbors alone. If you have business of your own, demanding your attention, do it. If you have not, go frankly, and like a good and true philanthropist, to those whose affairs you have taken into your hands, or whose conduct you think is wrong, and say, "You are wrong, sir (or madam, as the case may be); you are going to the devil at a two-forty lick! I feel an interest in your welfare, and wish to save you. Come, reform!"

Hamlet once, perhaps oftener, said, "Be thou as chaste as ice, as pure as snow, thou shalt not escape calumny."

I believe him. Did Hamlet now live I should go to him, take him by the hand, and say, "Hamlet, you're a brick; a truer thing was never said."

Paul Pryism and slander are one and the same thing. They go hand and hand together. They rage more—particularly the former—in the country than in the city, though I would willingly take an oath before any respectable justice of the peace that there is twenty-five—I'll be moderate—times as much of it as is needed in the last-named place.

"God made the country," and there, 'mid green fields and sparkling brooks, let us die. We love it dearly, and the dears that live in it, particularly those of the feminine gender. 'Tis natural we should; we were born there. But we do wish that slander and *pokeitiveness* (this latter word is my own) could be done away with, could be—to use a rare expression —"reformed altogether." Many and many a country village do I think of whose beautiful scenery makes them almost a paradise, and where one would say that the inhabitants could not but be happy, that is made a perfect purgatory by slanderers and meddlers.

But my prologue is much longer than my story, though no matter, if it is readable.

The village of T——, in a neighboring state, was cursed with as large a number of tattlers and Prys as any extant; and the most, if not all of them, were members of the church. Perhaps they didn't mean to "steal the livery of heaven to serve the devil in," but it amounted to precisely the same thing.

At the head of this respectable (?) body stood Mr. Zenas Poke. The first time I saw Warren as "Paul Pry" I at once came to the conclusion that he had sojourned in the village of T—— during "vacation," and had there made the acquaintance of Zenas, else, I argued, how could he so nicely "act him out," even to his every gait? Zenas knew everybody and what everybody did. No matter how trifling a misdeed a person might commit, he would make a mountain of it. In short, he was a second Paul Pry. He and his mates were taught a severe but just lesson, though, some years ago, the incidents of which I will relate.

In the year 18— there moved into the village a young, married doctor, who took the place of old Dr. Darius Dosem, deceased. The doctor was successful in his profession, paid his bills, became a member of the church, treated everybody well, minded his own business, and conducted himself like a good citizen. "Criticism was disarmed"; Poke and his followers could find nothing in the doctor's or his wife's conduct to condemn. Things were not destined to continue so long. An avalanche was coming—came, and amounted to— But the reader shall see what it amounted to, presently.

The doctor's wife went to Boston to see some friends. One evening shortly after Poke poked himself into the doctor's domicile. He had not been seated more than five minutes when a rosy-cheeked, bouncing damsel of "sweet sixteen" or thereabouts passed through the room.

"Why, who is that 'ar gal?" inquired Poke.

"Pretty, neighbor Poke, isn't she?" said the doctor, with a sly nod of his head.

"Yes, yes, but who is she?" again asked Poke, getting excited.

"Hush! Softly!" said the doctor, looking carefully around the room to see if there were no listeners, then softly whispering in Poke's ear, said, "Can you keep a secret?"

"Certainly, doctor, of course!" said Zenas, while wonder and astonishment were depicted on his face.

"Well," continued the doctor, "my wife being gone, I went over to C—— and got her. She's here sort of privately. Sly dog, ain't I?"

Zenas waited to hear no more. There was a "quilting" that evening at Deacon Blowhard's, and there he posted as fast as his legs could carry him.

"Doctor Mild is caugbt in his deviltry at last! He's got a bad woman at his house, and is keeping her sort of privately," bellowed Poke, bursting into the room.

"The wretch! I allers know'd he was no great shakes," said Aunt Susan Pitchfork.

"Monstrous depravity!" said Deacon Blowhard,

with a look that would have done credit to Aminadab Sleek.

"This affair must be looked into," said Parson Goody.

The next evening the doctor was to appear before the "Church." He came promptly. The meeting-house was crowded, and expectation was on tiptoe. Zenas Poke was called upon and testified to what we have before related.

"Is this true, doctor?" asked the parson.

"Yes," replied the doctor, "'tis true I have had a woman in my house to take care of it during my wife's absence, but I can see no harm in it, seeing that she is—"

"Who?" cried the congregation.

"My sister!" replied the doctor.

And so it was. It taught the tattlers of T—— a good lesson and they profited by it. The waggish doctor still lives there, and is yet a member of the church—"in good standing."

WALLACE THAXTER

(Boston Saturday Evening Gazette, June 18, 1864)

I SEEM to be standing in a graveyard, so many of my friends have fallen around me during the past few years.

I wish they had all been as good to the world as Wallace Thaxter was.

I need not go to the fresh-made grave of the dead dramatist and critic with an inky cloak upon my shoulders. There is grief enough in my heart over his far too early death without that.

No need, either, as we place the green turf over him, to say, God rest his soul! No need to say that for our dead friend, because his life was good and gentle.

When he died the stage lost one of the best friends it ever had. He stood by it faithfully for long years. He labored earnestly for its improvement. He worked to have it adhere to the good and beautiful. Fervently devoted to it, and with a scholar's admiration for the lofty efforts of genius that were showered upon it by the earlier dramatists, he could never consent to its being given up to baser uses. And his writings were all stainlessly beautiful.

I know that this is saying a great deal, but those who have for years read the dramatic column of the journal he loved so well know with what strict truth I speak. There were few as chastely elegant writers as he. There were few who understood how to soften and beautify our harsh language as well as he. And he was generous and just.

He had always a friendly word for the young actor. Many who have achieved eminence in the dramatic profession will gratefully remember the pleasant, cheering words he said for them at the commencement of their uncertain career. I say they will gratefully remember this; for while the people of the stage are sometimes accused of being ungrateful, I have found it, in an extensive acquaintance among them, quite otherwise with those who love and adorn their great art. And the kindly inquiries that have been made of me in all parts of the country about our late friend showed how sincere their regard was for him.

He was beloved by all who knew him personally.

I think he had no enemies.

I know how often we are told by noisy people that it is strictly necessary for a man of marked merit to have enemies, but sometimes the noisy people die and are forgotten, while the memory of the genuine and kind-hearted man, who in his life did good in a gentle and charming way, is always kept green in the hearts of his friends. And the friends of Wallace Thaxter can never forget him while they live in this world—oh, never!

I had hoped to have him with me in the country this summer, where the grass is so brightly green and the brooks run so beautifully clear, and he had promised to come. Only a few days ago I wrote him a cheerful note, reminding him of that promise. And I told him bright roses were laughing in the sunlight for him. The little note reached him while he was dying—while he was going where brighter roses grow, in the better land beyond the stars.

CHARLES F. BROWNE.

BIBLIOGRAPHY

CONTRIBUTIONS TO "THE CARPET BAG"

"The Surrender of Cornwallis." By Lieutenant Chub. *The Carpet Bag*, p. 5. Boston, April 17, 1852.

"Oil *vs*. Vinegar; or The Rantankerous Lecturer." By Lieutenant Chub. *The Carpet Bag*, p. 2. Boston, June 19, 1852.

"A Yankee Pass." *The Carpet Bag*, p. 6. Boston, September 11, 1852. (Signed "Chub.")

"Things from Chub's Knapsack." *The Carpet Bag*, p. 4. Boston, October 16, 1852.

"An Old-fashioned Husking." By Chub. *The Carpet Bag*, p. 4. Boston, October 30, 1852.

"Paul Pryism." By Lieutenant Chub. *The Carpet Bag*, p. 6. Boston, February 5, 1853.

"The Fugitive Slave." By Chub. *The Carpet Bag*, p. 6. Boston, December 25, 1853.

ARTEMUS WARD LETTERS IN THE CLEVELAND "PLAIN DEALER"

1. One of Mr. Ward's Business Letters, January 30, 1858.
2. Another Letter from Artemus Ward. (Wheeling, West Virginia.) February 8, 1858.
3. Letter from Artemus Ward. (Columbus, Ohio.) February 15, 1858.
4. Letter from Artemus Ward. (Tiffin, Ohio.) February 27, 1858.
5. Letter from Artemus Ward. (Toledo, Ohio.) March 9, 1858.
6. Our Ward Correspondence. (Sandusky, Ohio.) March 20, 1858.
7. Our Ward Correspondence. (The Celebrated Oberlin Letter— really the first high note struck.) March 30, 1858.
8. Letter from Artemus Ward. (Chicago, Illinois.) April 17, 1858.
9. Letter from Artemus Ward. (Baldwinsville, Indiana.) Has cut of "Artemus Ward" from an "autograph" by Ryder: a rude drawing by George Hoyt.) May 29, 1858.

10. Letter from Artemus Ward. (Dated Cincinnati: Appears in *His Book* as "Wax Figures *vs*. Shakespeare.") July 10, 1858.

11. The Atlantic Cable in Baldwinsville. September 6, 1858.

12. Letter from Artemus Ward. He visits Berlin Heights and Encounters the Free Lovers. October 11, 1858.

13. Artemus Ward Among the Spirits. December 13, 1858.

14. Our Local Heard From. (Exciting account of "The Capter of Mr. Broun in Baldwinsville.") February 2, 1859.

15. Letter from Artemus Ward. (Dated Baldwinsville, Indiana.) Contains much of the material preserved in "The Showman's Courtship.") February 14, 1859.

16. Artemus Ward Sees Piccolomini. April 26, 1859.

17. A Fourth of July oration delivered at Weathersfield, Connecticut. By Artemus Ward. July 16, 1859.

18. Joy in the House of Ward. November 12, 1859.

19. John Brown, Hero of Kansas and Harper's Ferry. February 2, 1860.

20. Artemus Ward Encounters the Octoroon. April 21, 1860

21. Patti. June 1, 1860.

22. Artemus Ward Sees the Prince of Wales. September 17, 1860.

"The Three Tigers of Cleveland Journalism." *Plain Dealer*, January 28, 1859.

CONTRIBUTIONS TO "VANITY FAIR"

"Artemus Ward Visits Brigham Young." Pp. 231–232, November 10, 1860.

"Artemus Ward on 'Forts.'" P. 243, November 17, 1860.

"Artemus Ward on His Visit to Abe Lincoln." Pp. 279–280, December 8, 1860.

"Artemus Ward Sees Forrest." P. 291, December 15, 1860.

"Artemus Ward on His Travels." P. 15, January 12, 1861. ("On the Wing" in *His Book*.)

"Artemus Ward on the Crisis." P. 37, January 26, 1861.

"Artemus Ward on the Shakers." Pp. 94–95, February 23, 1861.

"Cruise of the *Polly Ann*." By Artemus Ward. P. 141, March 23, 1861.

"East Side Theatricals." P. 136, March 23, 1861. (Signed "Alphonso the Brave.")

"Maine in March." P. 181, April 20, 1861. (Signed "Alphonso the Brave.")

BIBLIOGRAPHY

"Artemus Ward in the Southern Confederacy. The Show Is Confiscated." Pp. 229–230, May 11, 1861.

"Artemus Ward in the South. His Trials and Adventures." Pp. 251–252, May 25, 1861.

"Artemus Ward Among the Free Lovers." P. 253, June 1, 1861. (Revised from an earlier publication in the *Plain Dealer*, October 11, 1858.)

"Joy in the House of Ward." P. 263, June 8, 1861. (Revised from the *Plain Dealer* version of November 12, 1859.)

"Moses, the Sassy; or, The Disguised Duke." By Artemus Ward. P. 273, June 15, 1861.

"The War Fever in Baldwinsville." By Artemus Ward. P. 5, July 6, 1861.

"Artemus Ward's Weathersfield Oration." P. 15, July 13, 1861. (Revised from the *Plain Dealer* of July 16, 1859.)

"Marion: a French Romance." P. 24, July 13, 1861. (Not signed.)

"The Fair Inez; or, The Lone Lady of the Crimson Cliffs. A Tale of the Sea." Edited by Artemus Ward. Pp. 39–40, July 27; pp. 51–52, August 3; pp. 63–64, August 10; pp. 75–76, August 17; pp. 87–88, August 24, 1861.

"Artemus Ward Among the Spirits." Republished by request. P. 99, August 31, 1861.

"Artemus Ward Sees the Prince Napoleon." Pp. 135–136, September 21, 1861.

"Woshy-Boshy; or, The Prestidigitating Squaw of the Snake-heads." P. 199, November 2; p. 209, November 9; pp. 226–227, November 16; pp. 229–230, November 23, 1861.

"Artemus Ward in Washington." P. 199, April 26, 1862.

Cartoon: "Artemus Ward as a Popular Lecturer." First page, issue of May 24, "From a Portrait in Possession of *Vanity Fair*."

"The Draft in Baldwinsville." Pp. 136–137, September 20, 1862.

"The Showman at Home." Pp. 147–148, September 27, 1862.

"From A. Ward. Treating of the Noble Red Man—Domestic Affairs—A Serenade, Etc." P. 171, October 11, 1862.

"A. Ward in Canada." P. 207, November 1, 1862.

Artemus Ward; His Book. With many comic illustrations. 12mo, 264 pp. Engraved title. New York: Carleton, Publisher. (Late Rudd & Carleton). 1862.

Copyright by Charles F. Brown. Illustrations printed on yellow paper. Published May 17, 1862.

ARTEMUS WARD

"Wallace Thaxter." By Charles F. Browne. *Boston Saturday Evening Gazette,* June 18, 1864.

Artemus Ward; His Travels. Part I—Miscellaneous. Part II—Among the Mormons. With comic illustrations by Mullen. 12mo, 231 pp. Engraved title. New York: Carleton, Publisher, 413 Broadway. London: S. Low, Son & Co. 1865.

Published September 23, 1865.

Artemus Ward; His Book; or the Confessions and Experiences of a Showman. With an introduction by George Augustus Sala. Reprinted from the Original. 12mo, 96 pp. London: Ward, Lock & Tyler, 158 Fleet Street. MDCCCLXV.

Artemus Ward; His Travels. With an introduction by George Augustus Sala. Reprinted from the Original. 12mo, 121 pp. London: Ward, Lock & Tyler, 158 Fleet Street. MDCCCLXV.

Artemus Ward; His Book. With Notes and a Preface by the Editor of the Biglow Papers. 12mo, 167 pp. London: John Camden Hotten, Piccadilly. 1865.

Note: "At the Door of the Tent" before title.

Artemus Ward; His Book. Being the Confessions and Experiences of a Showman and Major Jack Downing. 32mo, 200–187–24 pp. London: Milner & Sowerby, Paternoster Row. N. D.

Artemus Ward; His Book. With Notes and a Preface by the Editor of the Biglow Papers. Comprising the whole of the Original Work, with Eight New Sketches. 12mo, 194 pp. London: John Camden Hotten, Piccadilly. 1865.

The cover title reads: "The only complete edition. Artemus Ward. His Book. With Notes and Introduction by the Editor of the Biglow Papers. Price one shilling." The cover is illustrated with a picture of a street musician playing several instruments at the same time, and across the picture is a slip marked with a red seal containing the letter "W" and reading, "The Author's Edition, with Extra Sketches," and a facsimile of the "A. Ward" signature.

Artemus Ward (His Travels) Among the Mormons. Part I—On the Rampage. Part II—Perlite Litteratoor. Edited by E. P. Hingston, the Companion and Agent of Artemus Ward whilst "On the Rampage." 12mo, xxx–192 pp. London: John Camden Hotten, Piccadilly. 1865.

Issued also under the same date without illustrations except frontispiece. Same size and number of pages.

Artemus Ward (His Travels) Among the Mormons. Part I— On the Rampage. Part II—Perlite Litteratoor. Edited by E. P. Hingston, the Companion and Agent of Artemus Ward whilst

BIBLIOGRAPHY

"On the Rampage." 12mo, xxx–192 pp. London: Ward, Lock & Co., Warwick House, Dorset Buildings, Salisbury Square, E. C. N. D.

Pictorial covers. Colored.

Author's Edition. *Artemus Ward; His Book.* With Notes and a Preface by the Editor of the Biglow Papers. Comprising the whole of the original work, with additional chapters and· extra sketches, now printed for the first time. 12mo, 210 pp. London: John Camden Hotten, Piccadilly. 1865.

The last sketch in the volume, "Mr. Ward Attends a Graffick," is spurious.

"Artemus Ward." *Chambers's Journal*, Vol. 42, p. 367. Edinburgh. 1865.

Artemus Ward Among the Fenians. With the Showman's Observations upon Life in Washington and Military Ardour in Baldwinsville. 16mo, 56 pp. London: John Camden Hotten, Piccadilly. N. D. (1866).

Warne's Christmas Annual. "The Five Alls." A Collection of Stories. With numerous illustrations. Edited by Tom Hood. 8vo, 96 pp. London: Frederick Warne & Co., Bedford Street, Covent Garden. New York: Scribner & Co. N. D. (1866).

"Pyrotechny." By Charles F. Browne (Artemus Ward). Pp. 34–35.

Artemus Ward. Grate Snaix. Only 25 cents. His Book. Comic illustrations by Mullen. Reprinted from the American Copyrighted Edition. 8vo, 70 pp. Montreal: Richard Worthington, Great Street. St. James Street. Printed by John Lovell. 1866. Pictorial cover.

"Yankee Humor." *The Quarterly Review*, Vol. 122, p. 224. London, 1866. Reproduced in *Littell's Living Age*. Boston, March 16, 1866.

"Artemus Ward in London." *Every Saturday*, Vol. 2, p. 765. London, 1866.

"Artemus Ward." *Every Saturday*, Vol. 3, p. 457. London, 1867.

Robert Heller, His Doings. 12mo, 64 pp. Glasgow: Printed by Hay Nisbet, 219 George Street. N. D.

Contains: "An Oad. Artemus Ward to Robert Heller. Commenced May First 1864; Finished 1866."

Attributed to Mr. Browne, but does not read as if it were his work. Heller was a famous "magician" and Dr. E. P. Hingston was at one time his manager. The little book contains a number of references to "Artemus."

ARTEMUS WARD

"Artemus Ward's Début." *The Queen*, London, November 17, 1866.

"Mr. Artemus Ward at the Egyptian Hall." *The Observer*, London, November 18, 1866.

"'Artemus Ward' at the Egyptian Gallery." *Reynolds's Newspaper*, November 18, 1866.

"Artemus Ward at the Egyptian Hall." *Lloyd's Weekly*, London, November 19, 1866.

"Artemus Ward." *The Spectator*. London, November 24, 1866.

"Artemus Ward's Lecture." *The Weekly Budget*, London, November 24, 1866

CONTRIBUTIONS TO LONDON "PUNCH." VOL. LI. JULY 7 TO DECEMBER 20, 1866

"Arrival in London." P. 95, September 1.
"Personal Recollections." P. 101, September 8.
"The Greenlion and Oliver Cromwell." P. 115, September 15.
"At the Tomb of Shakespeare." P. 135, September 29.
"Is Introduced at the Club." P. 145, October 6.
"The Tower of London." P. 155, October 13.
"Science and Natural History." P. 165, October 20.
"A Visit to the British Museum." P. 185, November 3.

"A Ward That Deserves Watching." *Punch*, p. 228, December 1. This last item is a very unusual tribute advising London to hear Artemus "speak his piece" at the Egyptian Hall. All the articles appeared under the same title: "Artemus Ward in London." I list them under the headings given when they took book form.

OBITUARY NOTICES

"Funeral of Artemus Ward (Mr. Charles F. Browne)." *The Observer*, London, March 10, 1867.

Weekly Budget, London, March 16, 1867.

The Atlas for India, London, March 16, 1867.

"Artemus Ward." Poem by James Rhoades, *The Spectator*, London, March 16, 1867. (Often incorrectly attributed to Algernon Charles Swinburne.)

"Humor and Faith." *The Spectator*, London, March 16, 1867.

Artemus Ward in London. Comprising the letters to *Punch* and other Humorous Papers. Small 4to, 195 pp. London: John Camden Hotten, Piccadilly. N. D.

BIBLIOGRAPHY

The cover title reads "Artemus Ward in London and the Letters to *Punch*, with other Humorous Papers," and is illustrated with an excellent portrait of the Author. Red lines under the title text.

Issued also in green cloth binding, without portrait. London. N. D.

Artemus Ward in London, and Other Papers. With comic illustrations by J. H. Howard. Frontispiece. 12mo, 229 pp. New York: G. W. Carleton & Co., Publishers. London: S. Low, Son & Co. 1867.

Published July 13, 1867.

Yankee Drolleries. The Most Celebrated Works of the Best American Humorists. Artemus Ward, His Book; Major Jack Downing, The Nasby Papers. Orpheus C. Kerr Papers. The Biglow Papers. With introduction by George Augustus Sala. 8vo, pp. 96–100–88–127–96. London: John Camden Hotten, Piccadilly. N. D.

"Artemus Ward; His Book," pp. 9–96.

More Yankee Drolleries. A Second Series of Celebrated Works by the Best American Humorists. Artemus Ward's Travels. Hans Breitmann. Professor at the Breakfast-Table. Biglow Papers, Part II. Josh Billings. With an Introduction by George Augustus Sala. 8vo, pp. 121–96–198–96–96. London: John Camden Hotten, Piccadilly. George Robertson, Melbourne. N. D.

A Third Supply of Yankee Drolleries. The most Recent Works of the Best American Humorists. Autocrat of the Breakfast-Table. Mark Twain. Artemus Ward. Luck of Roaring Camp. Innocents Abroad. With an Introduction by George Augustus Sala. 8vo, pp. 183–101–32–122–256. London: John Camden Hotten, Piccadilly. George Robertson, Melbourne. N. D.

"Artemus Ward Among the Fenians," pp. 5–32.

These three volumes were issued uniformly in series by Hotten with the pagination left as it appeared in the original books, as made up from the plates of his reprints of the several authors.

The Savage Club Papers. Edited by Andrew Halliday. Illustrated. 8vo, 341 pp. London: Tinsley Brothers, 18 Catherine St., Strand. 1867.

Contains first printing of Artemus Ward's "Converting the Nigger," p. 103.

Artemus Ward; His Book. With Comic Illustrations by Mullen. Reprinted from the American Copyright Edition. 8vo, 70 pp. Montreal: C. R. Chisholm, Railway and Steamboat News Agent. N. D.

ARTEMUS WARD

Artemus Ward; His Travels. Part I—Miscellaneous. Part II —Among the Mormons. With comic illustrations by Mullen. Reprinted from the American Copyright Edition. 8vo, 94 pp. Montreal (*sic*): C. R. Chisholm, Railway and Steamboat Agent. N. D.

Artemus Ward in London. 8vo. Montreal: C. R. Chisholm, Railway and Steamboat Agent. 1868.

The titles of the three above items are made up of the cuts from the engraved titles of the Carleton editions, with the type matter added. Very rare. But one copy of each has been noted as catalogued for sale in ten years of research. The matter is set in double-column measure.

Artemus Ward's Lecture (As delivered at the Egyptian Hall, London). Edited by his executors, T. W. Robertson & E. P. Hingston. With numerous illustrations from the Panorama. Square 12mo, 214 pp. London: John Camden Hotten, Piccadilly. New York: G. W. Carleton & Co., Broadway. 1869.

Frontispiece reproduces Geflowski's bust of the Humorist. Published June 26, 1869.

Sandwiches. By A. Ward. Illustrated. 4to, 36 pp. Pictorial covers. New York: G. W. Carleton & Co. 1869.

The Savage Club Papers. Second Series. Edited by Andrew Halliday. 12mo, 352 pp. Illustrated. London: Tinsley Brothers, 18 Catherine St., Strand. 1869.

"Artemus Ward Among the Shoshones." By Edward P. Hingston. Pp. 141–161.

The Genial Showman. Being Reminiscences of the Life of Artemus Ward and Pictures of a Showman's Career in the Western World. By Edward P. Hingston. In two volumes. 12mo, xii-363; 395 pp. London: John Camden Hotten, Piccadilly. N. D. (1870.)

Each volume has a frontispiece, drawn on wood by William Brunton, and hand colored. That in Vol. I depicts the "Genial Showman" at home; in Vol. II the parade of his Irish "Indians" on Broadway, New York, with Hingston and A. W. in the foreground.

"The Genial Showman." Review by Bret Harte. *Current Literature*, October, 1870.

MSS. now owned by Charles H. Taylor, Jr., of the Boston *Globe*.

The Genial Showman. Being Reminiscences of the Life of Artemus Ward and Pictures of a Showman's Career in the Western World. By Edward P. Hingston. New illustrated edition, complete in one volume. 12mo, x–519 pp. London: John Camden Hotten. N.D

This edition used Brunton's "Showman at Home," in colors, as frontispiece, and repeats the parade in the text. It is further embellished with replicas of the Panorama pictures and several excellent sketches made at the Chinese Theater in San Francisco, described as "found in Artemus Ward's portfolio"—evidently drawings made by some local artist for possible use in his proposed book.

The Complete Works of Charles F. Browne, better known as " Artemus Ward." With Portrait by Geflowski, the Sculptor, facsimile of Handwriting, etc. 8vo, xi–518 pp. London: John Camden Hotten, 74 and 75 Piccadilly. N.D

Includes "Artemus Ward as a Lecturer," by Dr. E. P. Hingston, together with many notes designed to "elucidate" for the English reader, and a considerable number of local sketches reproduced from the Cleveland *Plain Dealer.* Reissued frequently under the imprint of "Chatto & Windus." The pagination starts at p. 26.

The Genial Showman. Being Reminiscences of Artemus Ward and Pictures of a Showman's Career in the Western World. By Edward P. Hingston. Illustrations bound in before title-page. 8vo, 155 pp. New York: Harper & Brothers, Publishers. 1870.

Paper reprint of the London edition, with imprint of American News Company on cover. Title-page carries these quotations: "Sweet Speeches, Comedies, and Pleasing Shows," *Christopher Marlowe.* "'How 'bout my cabinet, Mister Ward?'" said Abe. "'Fill it up with Showmen, Sir.'" *Artemus Ward: Interview with President Lincoln.*

"Traveling with Artemus Ward." By Melville D. Landon (Eli Perkins). *The Galaxy,* pp. 442–445. New York, September, 1871.

"Les Humoristes Américains." II. Josh Billings, Artemus Ward, Hans Breitmann. Par Th. Bentzon. *Revue des Deux Mondes,* pp. 837; 862. Paris, August 15, 1872.

The first of Mme. Bentzon's articles, appearing in the *Revue* of July 15th, is devoted to Mark Twain, and includes that translation of "The Jumping Frog" which he later restored to English with such appalling results. The Artemus Ward article turns "Artemus Ward on the Shakers" into French with equally heartrending effect.

The Buyers' Manual and Business Guide; Being a Description of the Leading Business Houses, Manufactories, Inventions, Etc., of the Pacific Coast, together with Copious and Readable Selections, chiefly from California Writers. Compiled by J. Price and C. S. Haley. 8vo, viii–192 pp. San Francisco: Francis & Valentine,

Steam Book and Job Printing Establishment, No. 517 Clay Street, and 510 to 516 Commercial Street.   1872.

Contains "Mark Twain's First Interview with Artemus Ward."

Choice Bits from Mark Twain.   16mo, 192 pp.   London: Diprose & Bateman.   N. D.   (1872.)

"First Interview with Artemus Ward."

Public and Parlor Readings.   Prose and Poetry for the Use of Reading Clubs and for Public and Social Entertainments.   Humorous.   Edited by Lewis B. Monroe.   12mo.   Boston: Lee & Shepard.   1872.

Includes Mark Twain's "First Interview with Artemus Ward," credited to "S. J. Clemens."

Practical Jokes with Artemus Ward.   Including the Story of the Man Who Fought Cats.   By Mark Twain and Other Humorists. 16mo, xvi–176 pp.   London: John Camden Hotten, 74 Piccadilly.   All Rights Reserved.   N. D.   (1872.)

Letters to Punch.   Among the Witches and other Humorous Papers.   By Artemus Ward.   16mo, 195 pp.   London: John Camden Hotten, 74 & 75 Piccadilly.   N. D.   (1872.)

Pictorial covers.

Journalism in the United States, from 1690 to 1872.   By Frederic Hudson.   8vo, 789 pp.   New York: Harper & Brothers, Publishers, Franklin Square.   1873.

Artemus Ward, Chapter LXIV, pp. 688–696.

Artemus Ward: His Works.   Complete.   (Four volumes in one.)   With fifty Illustrations and a Biographical Sketch by Melville D. Landon ("Eli Perkins").   12mo, ix–347 pp.   New York: G. W. Carleton & Co., Publishers.   London: J. C. Hotten. MDCCCLXXVI.

Copyright 1875.

Mark Twain's Sketches, New and Old.   Now first published in complete form.   Sold only by subscription.   8vo, viii–320 pp. The American Publishing Company.   Hartford, Conn., and Chicago, Ill.   1875.

"First Interview with Artemus Ward," pp. 283–286.

"Artemus Ward at Cleveland."   By C. C. Ruthrauff.   Portrait, facsimile, and two drawings by George Hoyt.   *Scribner's Monthly,* pp. 785–791, New York, October, 1878.

Sketches by Mark Twain.   Now First Published in Complete Form.   12mo, viii–319 pp.   Toronto: Belfords, Clarke & Co. MDCCCLXXIX.

"First Interview with Artemus Ward," pp. 292–306.

BIBLIOGRAPHY

The History of Waterford, Oxford County, Maine. Comprising Historical address by Henry P. Warren; Record of Families, by Rev. William Warren, D.D.; Centennial Proceedings by Samuel Warren, Esq. Published by Direction of the Town. 8vo, 371 pp. Portland: Hoyt, Fogg & Donham. 1879.

"Charles F. Browne," p. 199. Brown Genealogy, p. 235; Farrar Genealogy, p. 246.

"Artemus Ward." By E. S. Nadal. *Scribner's Monthly*, pp. 144–159, New York, November, 1880.

The Genial Showman. Reminiscences of the Life of Artemus Ward and Pictures of a Showman's Career in the Western World. By Edward P. Hingston. A New Edition. Frontispiece. 12mo, viii–519 pp. London: Chatto & Windus, Piccadilly. 1881.

The Wanderer's Library.

"Artemus Ward; His Home and Family." By Don C. Seitz. Illustrated from photographs; drawings by Reginald Birch. *Scribner's Magazine*, pp. 46–53, New York, May, 1881.

Artemus Ward's Lecture on the Mormons. Edited with a Prefatory Note by Edward P. Hingston. With 32 illustrations. 16mo, 64 pp. London: Chatto & Windus, Piccadilly. 1882.

Paper covers, with portrait on first leaf. Printed at the Ballentyne Press.

Men and Events of Half a Century. By Frederick T. Wallace. 12mo, 363 pp. Cleveland: Evangelical Association. 1882.

Artemus Ward under "Humor and Its Uses," pp. 181–186.

"Artemus Ward." By H. R. Haweis. *Good Words*, Vol. 23, pp. 174 and 266. London. 1882.

Famous Funny Fellows. Brief Biographical Sketches of American Humorists. By Will M. Clemens. 12mo, 214 pp. Cleveland, Ohio: William W. Williams. 1882.

Artemus Ward, pp. 24–33.

Essays at Home and Elsewhere. By E. S. Nadal. 12mo, 281 pp. London: Macmillan & Co. 1882.

Artemus Ward, pp. 16–41.

American Humorists. By the Rev. H. R. Haweis, M.A. Author of *Music and Morals, Thoughts for the Times, Current Coin, Arrows in the Air,* etc. 8vo, 208 pp. and 1 p. of epilogue. London: Chatto & Windus, Piccadilly. 1883.

Artemus Ward, pp. 135–162.

Reminiscences of an Old Bohemian. Senex Loquæ—Old Age Is Garrulous. A New Edition. 8vo, 371 pp. London: Tinsley Brothers, 8 Catherine St., Strand. 1883.

ARTEMUS WARD

Written by Dr. G. L. M. Strauss. Artemus Ward, pp. 237–239.
Amerikanska Humorister (*Bilder och dikter af Artemus Ward, Bret Harte*, etc., etc.). 12mo, 220 pp. Stockholm: Selegman & Co. 1883.

Famous Funny Fellows; Brief Biographical Sketches of American Humorists. By Will M. Clemens. 12mo, 214 pp. New York: John W. Lovell Company, 1883. No. 291, Vol. 5, Lovell's Library. Artemus Ward, pp. 24–33.

"Artemas [*sic*] Ward." By H. R. Haweis. *The Elzevir Library*, a semi-weekly Magazine. 16mo, 26 pp. John B. Alden, Publisher. New York: March 2, 1883.

Bill Arp's Scrap Book; Humor and Philosophy. Letters "Pendente lite," Letters Historic, Domestic and Pictorial, with some true stories added. Illustrated by Moser.

> "If it pleases you, then I am happy,
> If it does not, it is all my fault;
> And you are much of a gentleman."

By Uncle Toby. 8vo, v–405 pp. Atlanta, Georgia: Jas. P. Harrison & Co., Publishers, Printers and Engravers, 1884.
"Bill Arp's Letter to Artemus Ward," pp. 56–63.

Fifty Years Among Authors, Books and Publishers. J. C. Derby.

> " . . . All of which I saw
> And part of which I was."

4to, 739 pp. New York: Copyright, 1884, by G. W. Carleton & Co., Publishers. London: S. Low, Son & Co. MDCCCLXXXIV. Artemus Ward, p. 242.

Phunny Phellows. Mark Twain, Josh Billings, Robert J. Burdette, Artemus Ward and Others. 12mo, iv-414 pp. Chicago: Rhodes & McClure. 1885.

Centennial History of Norway, Oxford County, Maine. 1786–1886. Including an account of the early Grants and Purchases, Sketches of the Grantees, Early Settlers, and Prominent Residents, etc., with Genealogical Registers and an Appendix. By William Berry Lapham.

> "The hills are ever dearest which our childish feet
> Have climbed the earliest, and the streams most sweet
> Are ever those at which our young lips drink—
> Stooped to their waters o'er the grassy brink."
> —*Whittier.*

BIBLIOGRAPHY

Imp. 8vo, xvi–659 pp. Portland, Maine: Brown, Thurston & Co., Publishers. 1886.

"Artemus Ward's Home." By Don C. Seitz. *The Sun*, New York, October 14, 1887.

Humorous Masterpieces from American Literature. Edited by Edward T. Mason. (Second Volume.) 12mo, iv–294 pp. New York and London: G. P. Putnam's Sons & The Knickerbocker Press, 1887.

Artemus Ward, pp. 153–167.

"Artemus Ward." By C. J. H. Northcroft. *Time*, Vol. 18, No. 452. London, 1888.

Reprinted in *Littell's Living Age*, Vol. 177, p. 301. Boston, 1888.

"Artemus Ward as Printer's Devil." By Don C. Seitz. *The Sun*, New York, September 15, 1889.

Half-Hours with Humorous Writers. Selected and arranged by Charles Morris. American. Two Vols. Cr. 8vo, 512; 511 pp. Philadelphia: J. B. Lippincott Company, 1889.

"Anecdote of Artemus Ward," by Mark Twain, Vol. 1, pp. 472–3; "Essay on Animals," Vol. 2, pp. 29–33; "A Mormon Romance," pp. 33–38.

"Personal Recollections of Artemus Ward." By George Hoyt. *The Weekly Graphic.* New York, Saturday, March 23, 1889.

"How Artemus Ward Became Lecturer." By J. W. Watson. In "Notes and Comments." *The North American Review*, pp. 521–522. New York, April, 1889.

Wise, Witty, Eloquent Kings of the Platform and Pulpit. By Melville D. Landon. Biographies, Reminiscences and Lectures of Artemus Ward, Mark Twain, Nasby, Josh Billings, Bill Nye, Sam Cox, Robert Burdette, Mrs. Partington, Danbury *News* Man, Fat Contributor, Eli Perkins, Bill Arp, George W. Peck, Doesticks, Bret Harte, Geo. W. Cable, and the Master Lectures of T. De Witt Talmage, Chauncey M. Depew, Wendell Phillips, Jos. Cook, Max O'Rell, Dwight L. Moody, Robert G. Ingersoll, Chas. H. Spurgeon, Eugene Field, Joseph Parker, Sam Jones, John B. Gough, Ben Butler, Horace Greeley, Robt. Collyer, and Personal Reminiscences and Anecdotes of Noted Americans. Profusely illustrated. 8vo, ix–570 pp. Chicago: F. C. Smedley & Co., Publishers, 1890.

Includes Bill Arp's "Letter to Artemus Ward."

"The Real Artemus Ward." By Enoch Knight. *Overland Monthly*, Vol. 18, p. 54. San Francisco: 1891.

Born 1834, Married 1835, "Artemus Ward's" Alleged Widow Claims His Estate. *The World*, New York, April 9, 1891.

Not Their "Artemus." *The World,* New York, April 10, 1891.

The Farm and Fireside: Sketches of Domestic Life in War and Peace. Written and Published for the Entertainment of the Good People at Home, and Dedicated especially to Mothers and Children. By Chas. H. Smith (Bill Arp). 8vo, vii–345 pp. Atlanta, Georgia: The Constitution Publishing Company. 1891.

"Bill Arp Addresses Artemus Ward," pp. 43–45.

Memoirs. By Charles Godfrey Leland (Hans Breitmann). In two volumes. 8vo, xiii–307; 306 pp. London: William Heinemann. 1893. (All rights reserved.)

Artemus Ward, pp. 19–21, Vol. **II**.

Memoirs. By Charles Godfrey Leland. (Hans Breitmann). 8vo, 439 pp. New York: D. Appleton & Company. 1893.

Artemus Ward and *Vanity Fair*, pp. 235–236.

The Library of Wit and Humor. Prose and Poetry. Selected from the Literature of all Time and all Nations. Edited with Biographies and Critical Notes by A. R. Spofford, Librarian of Congress, Washington, D. C., and Rufus E. Shapley, Author of *Solid for Mulhooly.* Illustrated with Fifty Choice Etchings engraved especially for this work. Volume V, viii–611 pp. Philadelphia: Gebbie & Co., Publishers. 1893.

Reproduces "Moses, the Sassy," "A Visit to Brigham Young," "A Mormon Romance," and "The Showman's Courtship," by Artemus Ward.

"Artemus Ward in Nevada." By Dan De Quille (William Wright). *California Illustrated Magazine*, pp. 403–406. San Francisco, August, 1893.

"Relics of Artemus Ward." By Don C. Seitz. Portrait of Charles F. Browne at twenty, and facsimile. *The Century Magazine*, pp. 132–135. New York, May, 1893.

Wit and Humor of the Age: Comprising Wit, Humor, Pathos, Ridicule, Satires, Dialects, Puns, Conundrums, Riddles, Charades, Jokes and Magic. By Mark Twain, Josh Billings, Robert J. Burdette, Alex. Sweet, Eli Perkins, With the Philosophy of Wit and Humor. By Melville D. Landon, A. M. Illustrated. 8vo, 776 pp. Chicago: Star Publishing Co. 1894.

Artemus Ward, pp. 46, 112, 124, 692. Portrait opp. p. 270.

"First Impressions of Literary New York." By William Dean Howells. *Harper's Magazine*, pp. 62–74. New York, July, 1895.

Artemus Ward, pp. 68 and 71.

"Some Reproductions of Artemus Ward. With Reminiscences

BIBLIOGRAPHY

of His Earlier Life in Cleveland, Ohio." *The Sun*, New York, March 22, 1896.

"Artemus Ward. Reminiscences of His Life in Cleveland." *The Sun*, New York, April 5, 1896.

The Complete Works of Artemus Ward (Charles F. Browne). A New Edition with portrait by Geflowski and a facsimile. Crown 8vo, 66–518 pp. London: Chatto & Windus. 1898.

The Complete Works of Artemus Ward (Charles Farrar Browne). With a Biographical Sketch by Melville D. Landon (Eli Perkins), and Many Humorous Illustrations. Revised. Edited. 12mo, x-449 pp. New York. G. W. Dillingham Company. 1898.

"Artemus Ward's Writings." By Joel Benton. *The New York Times Review of Books and Art.* New York, Saturday, October 1, 1898.

Review of above.

"Artemus Ward's Humor." *The Sun*, New York, September 17, 1899.

"The First Books of Some American Authors." By Luther S. Livingston. *The Bookman*, Vol. 8, p. 563, New York, 1899.

"Artemus Ward as a Journalist." *The Morning Telegraph*, New York, May 14, 1899.

Literary Friends and Acquaintance. A Personal Retrospect of American Authorship. By W. D. Howells. Illustrated. 8vo, viii–(1)–287–(1) pp. Harper & Brothers, Publishers, New York and London. 1900.

Portrait of Artemus Ward opp. p. 68. Reference p. 80.

Letters of Artemus Ward to Charles E. Wilson. 1858–1864. 12mo, 86 pp. Cleveland: The Rowfant Club. MCM.

"Maine in Literature." By William I. Cole. *The New England Magazine*, New Series, Vol. 22, p. 726. Boston, August, 1900.

"A Year of American Humor." *The Century Magazine*, Vol. LXIII. No. 1. New York, November, 1901.

"A Retrospect of American Humor," by W. P. Trent, pp. 45–64; "Recollections of Artemus Ward," by James F. Ryder, pp. 151–155.

New York: Old and New. Its Story, Streets, and Landmarks. By Rufus Rockwell Wilson, Author of "Washington: The Capital City," "Rambles in Colonial By-Ways," etc. With many illustrations from Prints and Photographs and with Decorations by Edward Stratton Holloway. Vol. II, 8vo, 390 pp. Philadelphia & London: J. B. Lippincott Company. 1902.

Artemus Ward, p. 141.

A Comic History of Cleveland; or, from Moses to Tom. 8vo, pp.

[383]

n.n. Published by The Students' Hospital Committee, Case-Reserve. 1902.

"Artemus Ward at Springfield, Massachusetts." By Charles J. Woodbury. *The Century Magazine*, pp. 636–637, New York, February, 1902.

Voigtlander and I in Pursuit of Shadow Catching. A Story of Fifty-two Years' Companionship with a Camera. By James F. Ryder. Frontispiece, Portrait and Illustrations. 8vo, 251 pp. Cleveland, Ohio. The Cleveland Printing and Publishing Co. The Imperial Press. 1902.

Interesting recollections of "Artemus Ward" in Chapter XXI, pp. 174–207. Two portraits and picture of birthplace, Waterford, Maine, with several letters in facsimile. Mr. Ryder was an intimate friend of the humorist.

My Own Story. With Recollections of Noted Persons. By John Townsend Trowbridge. Illustrated. *Ne cede Malis*—Heraldic motto. 8vo, vii–(2)–482 pp. Boston and New York: Houghton, Mifflin Company. The Riverside Press, Cambridge. 1903.

Artemus Ward, pp. 181–182.

Autobiography. Memories and Experiences of Moncure Daniel Conway. In two volumes. 8vo, xiv–451; x–482 pp. Boston and New York: Houghton, Mifflin & Company. The Riverside Press, Cambridge. 1904.

Artemus Ward's Funeral, p. 139, Vol. II.

"The Passing of the Egyptian Hall." *London Graphic*, December 14, 1904.

Portrait of "Artemus Ward."

"Artemus Ward. An Old Friend. Reminiscences of the Great American Humorist." *New York Times*, May 4, 1905.

The Breitmann Ballads. By Charles G. Leland. A New Edition. 12mo, 317 pp. London: Kegan Paul, Trench, Trubner & Co., Ltd., Dryden House, Gerrard Street, W. 1906

Artemus Ward, p. 251.

"To Artemus Ward in Elysium." By Harry Lyman Koopman. *Pine Tree Magazine*, Vol. 6, p. 241. 1906.

History of the United States from the Compromise of 1850 to the Final Restoration of Home Rule at the South in 1877. By James Ford Rhodes, LL.D., Litt.D. Member of the Massachusetts Historical Society. Vol. III. 1860–1862. 8vo, x–659 pp. New York: The Macmillan Company. London: Macmillan & Co., Ltd. 1906. All rights reserved.

Artemus Ward, pp. 109–110.

BIBLIOGRAPHY

Mark Twain's Library of Humor. Men and Things. Illustrated. 8vo, vii–304 pp. Harper & Brothers, Publishers, New York and London. MCMVI.

One of Mr. Ward's Business Letters, pp. 121–122.

Mark Twain's Library of Humor. A Little Nonsense. Illustrated. 8vo, vii–303 pp. Harper & Brothers, Publishers, New York and London. MCMVI.

"A Visit to Brigham Young," pp. 161–167.

A Pocket Book of the Early American Humorists. Selections from the best writings of Benjamin Franklin, Joseph C. Neal, Major Jack Downing, Mrs. Partington, Augustus B. Longstreet, John Phœnix, Orpheus C. Kerr, Artemus Ward, Bill Arp, and others. 8vo, 211 pp. Boston: Small, Maynard & Co. 1907.

"Mid-Century Humorists." Springfield (Mass.) *Republican*, September 9, 1907.

Pages from an Adventurous Life. By "Dick Donovan" (J. E. Preston Muddock). With thirty - one illustrations. Portrait Frontispiece. 8vo, 352 pp. London: T. Werner Laurie, Clifford's Inn. N. D. (1907.)

Artemus Ward references, pp. 93–100, 106, 160, 171–179.

"Charles F. Browne (Artemus Ward). The Tribute of a Friend and Fellow-Townsman." By Enoch Knight. *Putnam's Monthly*, pp. 599–600. New York, February, 1907.

"On the Death of Artemus Ward." Letter from James Rhoades, giving correct version of his poem by that title. *Putnam's Monthly*, p. 206. New York, May, 1907.

The Savage Club. A Medley of History, Anecdote, and Reminiscence. By Aaron Watson. With a Chapter by Mark Twain. 8vo, xii–327 pp. London: T. Fisher Unwin, Adelphi Terrace. 1907.

Artemus Ward: pp. 76, 119, 120, 121–124, 126, 239. Reproduces in colors the portrait drawn from life by Walter Dubisson, now in possession of the Savage Club, Adelphi Terrace, London.

American Wit and Humor. By One Hundred of America's Leading Humorists. Introduction by Joel Chandler Harris. Including World's Famous Cartoons and Caricatures. 4 vols., 12mo, 289, 290, 291, 340 pp. New York: The Review of Reviews Co. 1907.

Vol. I. Artemus Ward to Bret Harte.

With the Border Ruffians. Memories of the Far West. 1852–68. By R. H. Williams, sometime Lieutenant in the Kansas Rangers and afterward Captain in the Texas Rangers. Edited by E. W. Williams. With Portraits. 8vo, xviii–478 pp. New York: E. P. Dutton & Company. 1907.

ARTEMUS WARD

Artemus Ward, pp. 78–79; 452–453.

"Maine Stories of Artemus Ward." By Charles O. Stickney. Lewiston, Maine, *Journal Magazine*, April 4, 1908.

The Life of Thomas Bailey Aldrich. By Ferris Greenslet. Royal 8vo, xi–303 pp. Cambridge. Printed at the Riverside Press. MDCCCVIII.

Large paper edition of 500 copies. Artemus Ward, pp. 98–99. Letters between Mark Twain and Aldrich.

"Artemus Ward Relics." By Charles O. Stickney, Portland, Maine, *Telegram*, December 5, 1909.

Old Friends. Being Literary Recollections of Other Days. By William Winter. 8vo, 407 pp. Illustrated. New York: Moffat, Yard & Co. 1909.

"Artemus Ward," pp. 89, 284 to 291.

"Stories of Artemus Ward." Boston *Globe*, January 3, 4, 5, 6, 7, 1910.

"Artemus Ward. A Unique Portrait of the Undeniable Dean of American Humorists." *The Sun*, New York, December 10, 1911.

Mark Twain: A Biography. The Personal and Literary Life of Samuel Langhorne Clemens. By Albert Bigelow Paine. With Letters, Comments, and Incidental Writings hitherto unpublished; also new episodes, anecdotes, etc. Three volumes. Fully illustrated. 8vo, xiii–(4)–562; (vi–2)–563 to 1110; (vi–2)–1111 to 1718–(1) pp. Harper & Brothers, Publishers. New York and London. MCMXII.

Artemus Ward, Vol. I, pp. 238–243; 443–444.

Artemus Ward's Best Stories. Edited by Clifton Johnson, with an Introduction by W. D. Howells. Illustrated by Frank A. Nankivell. 8vo, 275 pp. Harper & Brothers, Publishers. New York and London. MCMXII.

Fifty Years in Theatrical Management. By M. B. Leavitt, with reproductions of over 500 photographs. 8vo, xii–735 pp. New York: Broadway Publishing Co. N. D. (1912.)

Artemus Ward, pp. 239–240.

Book of Old New York. By Henry Collins Brown. The rare Old Prints are from the Private collections of Mr. Robert Goelet, Mr. Percy R. Pyne, 2d, Mr. J. Pierpont Morgan, Mr. Robert W. De Forest, Mr. A. Van Horne Stuyvesant, Mr. Wm. F. Havemeyer, Mr. Simeon Ford, Mr. J. Clarence Davies, Mr. Robert E. Dowling, Mr. John N. Golding, Mr. John D. Crimmins, Mr. Henry Morganthau, and others. 4to, 392 pp. Privately Printed for the Subscribers, Fifteen East Fortieth Street, New York. 1913.

BIBLIOGRAPHY

Artemus Ward, p. 83.

Notes on the History of Waterford, Maine. Edited by Thomas Hovey Gage, Jr. 12mo, 85 pp. Worcester, Massachusetts. 1913.

Catalogue of the First and Other Editions of the Writings of "Mark Twain" (Samuel Langhorne Clemens) and of Lafcadio Hearn. The Property of the Tomlinson-Humes Company (in Bankruptcy) and of Mr. Merle Johnson. To be sold at unrestricted Public Sale on January Twentieth, 1914, under the management of the American Art Association, American Art Galleries, Madison Square South. 8vo, p.n.n. (New York, 1914.)

Contains Mark Twain's account of writing "The Jumping Frog." Suggested to him by Artemus Ward.

Highways and Byways of New England, including the States of Massachusetts, New Hampshire, Rhode Island, Connecticut, Vermont and Maine. Written and illustrated by Clifton Johnson. 12mo, xi–299 pp. New York: The Macmillan Company. London: Macmillan Co. December, 1915.

Humorous American Tales. Edited by Charles B. Neville, Editor of *Humorous Readings for Home and Hall, Humorous Readings from Charles Dickens,* etc., etc. Three series in one. 8vo, viii–314 pp. London: Simpkin, Marshall, Hamilton, Kent & Co. Glasgow: Thomas D. Morison. N. D.

Includes Artemus Ward, "Among the Shakers."

"Mark Twain. Some Chapters from an Extraordinary Life." By Albert Bigelow Paine. Fifth Paper. *Harper's Magazine,* pp. 583–597, March, 1912.

Describes the meeting of Twain and A. W. in Virginia City, Nevada.

Picture of the Artemus Ward Homestead. *Joe Chapple's News Letter.* Boston, May 26, 1912.

"Back to Maine." By Joe Mitchell Chapple. *The National Magazine,* pp. 127–149. Boston, October 1912.

Includes a visit to Waterford.

"Recollections of Artemus Ward." By Clifton Johnson. *The Overland Monthly,* New Series, pp. 28–33. San Francisco, January, 1916.

"When Artemus Ward Was Here." By Walter J. Thompson. San Francisco *Chronicle,* Sunday, September 17, 1916.

"Artemus Ward, Patriot." *The Spectator,* pp. 154–155. London, January 29, 1916.

Republished in *Littell's Living Age,* pp. 763–766, Boston, March 18, 1916.

[337]

ARTEMUS WARD

Mark Twain's Letters. Arranged with Comment. By Albert Bigelow Paine. Two Volumes. Illustrated. 8vo, (6)–855–(1). Harper & Brothers, Publishers. New York and London. N. D. (1917).

Artemus Ward, p. 7; letters, pp. 93 (portrait), 95, 183.

The New York of the Novelists. By Arthur Bartlett Maurice. With illustrations. 8vo, xxii–366 pp. New York: Dodd, Mead & Company. 1917.

Artemus Ward, p. 123.

"Doctor Holmes, the Friend and Neighbor." By M. A. De Wolfe Howe. *The Yale Review*, pp. 563–578. New Haven, April, 1918.

Artemus Ward, p. 565.

"Looking Backward." By Col. Henry Watterson. *The Saturday Evening Post*, pp. 18–19 and 45. Philadelphia, March 22, 1919. Recollections of Artemus Ward in London.

"Was Artemus Ward a Humorous [*sic*] only Professionally?" By Julius Chambers. *Brooklyn Daily Eagle*, March 26, 1919.

"Something About Artemus Ward." By C. E. Waterman. *The Oxford Democrat*, South Paris, Maine, April 8, 1919.

"Artemus Ward, Who Taught Americans to Laugh." By Albert Payson Terhune. *The Evening World*, New York, May 20, 1919.

LECTURES

"Children in the Wood."
"Sixty Minutes in Africa."
"The Ghosts."
"Artemus Ward Among the Mormons."

IMITATIONS

Artemus Ward on Wimmin's Rites 4 a Kollexshun Box. Every 1 mai pa, but nede not rede. 16mo, printed wrappers. Bath: T. B. Tabb. N. D.

Betsey Jane Ward (Better-half to Artemus) Hur Book of Goaks. With a Full Akkownt of the Coartship and Maridge to a 4 said Artemus, and Mister Ward's cutting-up with the Mormon Fare Secks. With Pikturs drawed by Mrs. B. Jane Ward. 12mo, 312 pp. New York: James O'Kane, Publisher, No. 126 Nassau St. 1866.

Written by William Comstock, described by Foley as "an obscure writer whose contributions figure in some of the periodicals of the 'fifties."